HOW TO
NEGOTIATE
ANYTHING
WITH
ANYONE
ANYWHERE

AROUND THE WORLD

FRANK L. ACUFF

amacom

American Management Association
New York • Atlanta • Boston • Chicago • Kansas City • San Francisco • Washington, D.C.
Brussels • Toronto • Mexico City

Library of Congress Cataloging-in-Publication Data

Acuff, Frank L.
    How to negotiate anything with anyone anywhere around the world /
Frank L. Acuff.
        p.   cm.
    Includes bibliographical references and index.
    ISBN 0-8144-5995-1 (hardcover)
    ISBN 0-8144-7873-5 (pbk.)
    1. Negotiation in business.   2. International business
enterprises—Management.   I. Title.
HD58.6.A27   1992
302.3—dc20   92-23751
                                                           CIP

Printing number

10   9   8   7   6   5   4   3   2   1

To
Yolanda, Kristin, Ryan, Joseph, and **Brendan,**
all tough negotiators

Contents

Preface   vii

Acknowledgments   ix

One: World-Class Negotiating   **1**

   1 The Global Negotiating Imperative   3
   2 Negotiating in Any Language:
     How Negotiations Work   20

Two: How Americans Negotiate   **39**

   3 Profile of the American Negotiator   41
   4 An American Report Card: Where
     Americans Go Wrong in Global
     Negotiations   50

Three: How Global Negotiations Work   **65**

   5 What Makes Global Negotiations
     Different?   67
   6 World-Class Negotiating Strategies   96
   7 The Six Most Difficult Problems
     Faced by Global Negotiators (and
     How to Deal With Them)   120

Four: Negotiating Around the World   **139**

8 Negotiating in Western Europe   143
*Negotiating Primers for Belgium 148;
France 150; Germany 154; Greece 158;
Italy 161; the Netherlands 165; Spain
168; Sweden 172; Switzerland 175; and
the United Kingdom 179*

9 Negotiating in Eastern Europe   183
*Negotiating Primers for Czechoslovakia
189; Hungary 191; Poland 194; and
Russia 197*

10 Negotiating in Latin America   201
*Negotiating Primers for Argentina 207;
Brazil 210; Colombia 214; Mexico 217;
and Venezuela 220*

11 Negotiating in North America   224
*Negotiating Primers for Canada 230;
and the United States 233*

12 Negotiating in the Middle East   238
*Negotiating Primers for Egypt 243;
Israel 246; Saudi Arabia 249; and the
United Arab Emirates 254*

13 Negotiating in the Pacific Rim   259
*Negotiating Primers for China 267;
Hong Kong 271; Indonesia 275; Japan
278; Malaysia 282; Philippines 285;
Singapore 289; South Korea 292;
Taiwan 295; and Thailand 300*

14 Negotiating in Other Important
Countries   303
*Negotiating Primers for Australia 304;
India 307; New Zealand 311; Nigeria
313; and Pakistan 317*

Index   323

Preface

This book is for the person in the trenches, who needs practical guidelines to get the very best deal possible with people and organizations which have very different backgrounds and experiences. This book is for the practitioner—for the person who faces an international negotiating challenge and who perhaps should have done his or her homework earlier, but didn't. I wrote this book largely from a "lessons-learned" perspective: these are the kinds of things I wish someone had told me before I entered into global negotiations.

If you will be interacting with people from different cultures in either business or travel, this book is for you. If you find that you are uncomfortable in dealing with people from different cultures and want to understand why, this book is for you. Or, if you are an experienced negotiator who is getting less-than-excellent results from your international negotiations, this book is for you. This book is for anyone who works or travels abroad, and for those who must deal here in the United States with people who have recently come from other countries. It is for managers, sales representatives, marketers, traders, diplomats, military personnel, attorneys, entrepreneurs and other professionals whose success will depend on their ability to influence others.

Objectives

This book has four main objectives:

1. To help you to avoid the typical mistakes and pitfalls of international negotiating
2. To enable you to build on your current negotiating strengths
3. To help you to understand the process of international negotiations
4. To lead you to strengthen your cultural awareness and skills

This book will help protect you from making an agreement you should reject, and it will help you make the most of your assets.

In years past it was typical to court our negotiating counterparts here at home. We now must ask, "Your place or mine?" Regardless of our personal knowledge of international business, many negotiating parties have in fact moved overseas. We can either sit outside and wonder what's going on inside the dance hall, or we can join the party. This book will help you not only to show up, but to dance every dance.

Overall Approach

We will first examine how others see Americans as negotiators and where Americans often go wrong in global negotiations. Next, we will briefly review negotiations in any language, an overview of the negotiations process as a whole, regardless of culture. Global negotiations will then be examined: what to look for in other cultures; how these cultural factors affect negotiations; problems faced by global negotiators; how to deal with your boss; and how to be prepared for the phases of international adjustment. The term TOS refers to The Other Side in the negotiation.

This book is divided into four parts. Part One explores the extraordinary place occupied by global negotiations and examines key aspects of the negotiating process. Part Two profiles American negotiators and assesses their abilities on the global landscape. Part Three addresses the unique aspects of global negotiations and explores practical strategies to help you on your global journey. Part Three also examines the most difficult negotiating problems that you are likely to experience internationally and offers solutions that you can use on the job.

Part Four takes you on an intercultural journey to forty-one countries, including the United States and the largest trading partners of the United States, as well as countries that have large potential markets. Specific guidelines, called Negotiating Primers, are given for virtually anywhere in the world you are likely to do business. A profile of typical negotiators and specific negotiating strategies will be discussed for six regions of the world: Western Europe, Eastern Europe, Latin America, North America, the Middle East, and the Pacific Rim. Negotiating guidelines are also provided for five additional countries: Australia, India, New Zealand, Nigeria, and Pakistan. These countries are important for many global negotiators even though they don't fit neatly into the geographical, political, and cultural boundaries of the six regions noted above. For each of these regions, you will learn such critical factors as pace of the negotiation, negotiating style, emphasis on personal relationships, decision-making, and contractual and administrative factors. You will strengthen your negotiating skills for these regions, learning the do's and don'ts of global negotiating that will most affect you on a day-to-day basis.

Let's get busy on putting you on the international map!

Acknowledgments

Distilling the many extraordinary aspects of global negotiating into an understandable and practical form is indeed challenging and, thankfully, stimulating and fun. This undertaking could not have happened, however, without the help of many people. It is impossible to acknowledge appropriately all the many individuals whose experiences, insights, and support influenced the development and writing of this book. But there are specific people to whom I especially owe a great deal of thanks. While these individuals share in the quality of the book, any errors or limitations are mine alone. My thanks to: Kristin Acuff; Robin Allen and Anchie Vicenzio of the American Management Association; Mike Apple and Daniel Ledet of McDermott International; Salvador Avila of Exxon Company, U.S.A.; Adelaide Bannon; Miriam Ben-Yoseph; Susan Cherion of the Billy Graham Evangelistic Association; Marek Ciesielzyk of the University of Illinois; Edward Cline; Robert Coshland of Tribol; Moira E. Crean of MasterCard International, Inc.; John Delaney of the U.S. Office of Personnel Management; Ken Ellis and Alex Neyin of Chevron U.S.A.; Ron Hansek of McDonald's Corporation; Robert Hentzen of Baxter Healthcare Corporation; Isa Laurinsilta of Genencor; Mohammad Shoaib Khan; Susan Koscis of American Management Association International; Foster Lin of the Far East Trade Service; Mamdough Mahfouz of Agiba Petroleum; Lee Meader; Isobel Morgan; Maggie Neal of the Kellogg School of Northwestern University; Ken Nelson of Yokohama Academy USA; Lawrence Rubly of the Keller Graduate

School of Management; Bill Usner of Pennzoil; Tom Wilson; Walter Winkler of Arco International Oil and Gas; and Beryl York.

The contributions of Andrea Pedolsky, AMACOM acquisitions editor, were enormous. Her many perceptive questions and comments always moved the book toward relevance and clarity.

I especially want to thank Elizabeth Greene, who joyfully and expertly added value to the manuscript draft. And finally, and certainly far from least, my thanks go to Yolanda, my wife, whose support was constant and far-ranging over the course of writing this book.

The research and writing of others was helpful in preparation of the country-by-country Negotiating Primers and other aspects of the book. The following resources were particularly helpful: Nancy J. Adler, *International Dimensions of Organizational Behavior* (Boston: Kent Publishing, 1986); Herb Cohen, *You Can Negotiate Anything* (Toronto: Bantam Books, 1980); Lennie Copeland and Lewis Griggs, *Going International* (New York: Random House, 1985); W. James Cossé, *Negotiating to Win* (New York: American Management Association, 1990); Lynne Hall, *Latecomer's Guide to the New Europe: Doing Business in Central Europe* (New York: American Management Association, 1992); Donald W. Hendon and Rebecca Angeles Hendon, *World-Class Negotiating: Dealmaking in the Global Marketplace* (New York: John Wiley & Sons, 1990); Marlene L. Rossman, *International Business of the '90s: A Guide to Success in the Global Market* (New York: Praeger, 1990); Grant P. Skabelund, ed., *Culturegrams for the '90s* (Provo, Utah: David M. Kennedy Center for International Studies, Brigham Young University, 1991); *The World Bank Atlas 1991* (Washington, D.C.: World Bank, 1991), John W. Wright, ed. *The Universal Almanac 1992* (Kansas City, Mo.: Andrews & McMeel, 1991).

Part One

World-Class Negotiating

Let's get started on our journey! Chapter 1, "The Global Negotiating Imperative," explores the vital role that global negotiating increasingly is playing among nations, and what that means for us, the individuals who must breathe life into global initiatives. Chapter 2, "Negotiating in Any Language—How Negotiations Work," reviews the common ingredients of effective negotiations, regardless of the culture involved. This basis is important to the ensuing discussion of the international aspects of negotiations and to the negotiations process as a whole.

Chapter 1

The Global Negotiating Imperative

Every firm over $2 million in revenues should take first steps to examine international-market–creation opportunities in the next twelve months. Every firm over $25 million should be alarmed if it is not doing 25 percent of its business overseas, including in Japan.

Tom Peters, *Thriving on Chaos*

- The Emergence of a Global Economy
- The Increase of Foreign Investment in the United States
- The Multitude of International Business Arrangements
- Why International Negotiating Skills Are Critical for Your Success

At no time in history has there been so great a need for international negotiating skills—that is, for each negotiator to influence the other in positive, constructive ways. If we are to be effective as organizations and as individuals within these organizations, we must learn to think globally. And more importantly, we must be *effective* globally. Specifically, there are three key reasons why becoming a world-class negotiator is so vital today: (1) the emergence of a global economy, (2) the increase of foreign investment in the United States, and (3) the multitude of international business arrangements. Let's examine each of these.

The Emergence of a Global Economy

If you need convincing as to your involvement in a global economy, think about how your day began. You may have glanced at
your Bulova watch and turned on your RCA TV while you were
showering and getting ready for work. You may have brushed
your teeth with Close-Up toothpaste, blow-dried your hair with a
Conair dryer, had some Sanka coffee, munched on a Keebler
breakfast roll, or fed your dog some Alpo as you rushed out the
door to your Honda, sporting Firestone tires and filled with Shell
gasoline.[1] In all these cases, you were using consumer products
made by non-U.S. companies.

Label from a bottle of Tropicana apple juice: "Contains
concentrate from Austria, Italy, Hungary, and Argentina."

For many years, the United States prospered even though it
relied primarily on its huge internal market. It did not focus on
selling or sourcing overseas. But today, for both U.S. organizations and their leaders, effectiveness at home means effectiveness
on a global basis. The playing field has expanded from being located primarily in the United States to the world. The days of producing and selling products and services mainly on U.S. turf are
gone forever. It is hard to imagine many organizational scenarios
that won't include an international aspect over the next few years.

The increase in globalization can be seen in the explosive
growth in both the size and number of U.S. and foreign multinational concerns since the early 1960s. According to the United
Nations Centre on Transnational Corporations, although most of
the multinational corporations (MNCs) have annual sales of less
than $1 billion, the fifty-six largest have sales ranging from $19
billion to $125 billion. It also estimates that the 600 largest multi-
national companies account for between one-fifth and one-fourth
of the value added in the production of all the goods in the
world's market economies.[2]

Exhibit 1-1 points to the enormous financial power of MNCs (indicated in italics). Only twenty-one nations have GNPs (gross national products) greater than the total annual sales of General Motors, the world's largest multinational company. Even the twenty-fifth largest MNC on the list, Nestlé, has sales greater than the GNP of many countries.

The United States continues to be a key part of the global economy, with by far the most companies on *Fortune*'s 1991 list of the world's largest industrial corporations: 164 for the United States, compared with 111 for Japan, forty-three for Britain, and thirty each for France and Germany.

The United States does not, however, do as well in the global economy when it comes to banking. Exhibit 1-2 shows the world-wide impact of non-U.S. banks. Of the world's fifteen largest banks, none is a U.S. bank. Of the world's fifty largest banks, twenty-four are from the European Community and twenty-one are Japanese. You would have to go to the twenty-sixth largest bank to find a U.S. enterprise—Citibank.[3] What does this mean to you? It means that you should familiarize yourself with the names listed in Exhibit 1-2 and other large international banks, since you may be doing business with them.

It won't be unusual for you to work for an organization that does business in many different countries. The U.S. Postal Service is perhaps the best example of a multinational enterprise, with facilities in virtually every foreign country. At this moment you may be concerned about successfully negotiating with a counter-part in one particular country. Over time, however, the individuals with whom you are likely to negotiate may come from many places. Exhibit 1-3 reflects the countries where U.S. companies conduct most of their foreign trade.

While every part of the world is represented in the list of major U.S. trading partners, most U.S. trade is centered in four areas: (1) the Pacific Rim, (2) the European Community (EC), (3) Canada, and (4) Latin America. Exhibit 1-4 illustrates the importance of these regions. Of these top twenty-five trading partners, 97 percent of the exports and 94 percent of the imports come from these four regions. Further, the Pacific Rim has taken the lead over all other areas of the world as a U.S. trading partner.

Globalization has also been spurred by the radical political,

Exhibit 1-1. Ranking of multinational companies and nations according to GNP or total sales.

Rankings	Nation or Company	GNP or Total Sales for 1990 ($ billions)
21.	Finland	$129.8
22.	General Motors (U.S.)	125.1
23.	Denmark	113.5
24.	Royal Dutch Shell Group (Netherlands)	107.2
25.	Exxon (U.S.)	105.9
26.	Indonesia	101.2
27.	Ford Motor (U.S.)	98.3
28.	Norway	98.1
29.	Turkey	91.7
30.	South Africa	90.4
31.	Thailand	79.0
32.	Argentina	76.5
33.	Yugoslavia	72.9
34.	IBM (U.S.)	69.0
35.	Hong Kong	66.7
36.	Toyota Motor (Japan)	64.5
37.	Poland	64.5
38.	IRI (Italy)	64.1
39.	Greece	60.2
40.	British Petroleum (U.K.)	59.5
41.	Mobil (U.S.)	58.8
42.	General Electric (U.S.)	58.4
43.	Daimler-Benz (Germany)	54.3
44.	Algeria	51.6
45.	Israel	50.9
46.	Hitachi (Japan)	50.7
47.	Portugal	50.7
48.	Venezuela	50.6
49.	Czechoslovakia	49.2
50.	Fiat (Sweden)	47.8
51.	Samsung (South Korea)	45.0
52.	Philip Morris (U.S.)	44.3
53.	Philippines	44.0
54.	Volkswagen (Germany)	43.7

55.	*Matsushita Electric Industrial* (Japan)	43.5
56.	New Zealand	43.2
57.	Pakistan	42.6
58.	*ENI* (Italy)	41.8
59.	Malaysia	41.5
60.	*Texaco* (U.S.)	41.2
61.	Colombia	40.8
62.	*Nissan Motor* (Japan)	40.2
63.	*Unilever* (U.K./Netherlands)	40.0
64.	*Du Pont* (U.S.)	39.8
65.	*Chevron* (U.S.)	39.3
66.	*Siemens* (Germany)	39.2
67.	Romania	38.0
68.	*Nestle* (Switzerland)	33.6
69.	Singapore	33.5

Note: Does not include nations that do not report GNPs to the World Bank (e.g., some Eastern European countries).

Source: "The World's 50 Biggest Industrial Corporations," *Fortune*, July 29, 1991, and *The World Bank Atlas 1991* (Washington, D.C.: World Bank, 1991).

social, and economic changes taking place in many parts of the world, illustrated by the realization of the European Community (EC) and the reorganization of Eastern Europe. These and other new alliances bring business negotiating challenges and opportunities to those who dare to make an impact with this new world order.

"We're All Connected"
A Typical Day's Business Headlines Overseas

"Singapore Strengthens Economic Ties with U.S."
"Firm's Profit Cut Over U.S. Link"
"Thailand, U.S. Move to End Copyright Row"
"(The Hong Kong) Index Falls on Fears of U.S. Curbs"
"U.S. Recovery Some Time Off Say CEO's"

Exhibit 1-2. The world's fifteen largest banks, ranked by assets.

Rank/Company	Country	Assets ($ billions)
1. Dai-Ichi Kangyo Bank	Japan	$428.2
2. Sumitomo Bank	Japan	409.2
3. Mitsui Taiyo Kobe Bank	Japan	408.8
4. Sanwa Bank	Japan	402.7
5. Fuji Bank	Japan	400.0
6. Mitsubishi Bank	Japan	391.5
7. Credit Agricole Mutuel	France	305.2
8. Banque Nationale de Paris	France	291.9
9. Industrial Bank of Japan	Japan	290.1
10. Credit Lyonnais	France	287.3
11. Deutsche Bank	Germany	266.3
12. Barclays Bank	U.K.	259.0
13. Tokai Bank	Japan	249.8
14. Norinchukin Bank	Japan	249.7
15. Mitsubishi Trust & Banking Corporation	Japan	237.7

Source: "The Top 500 Banks in the World," *The American Banker*, July 26, 1991, pp. 16A-24A.

'Mobil Set to Drill for Oil Where Other Companies Fear to Tread"
"Beijing Displeased by U.S. Trade Inquiry"
"Aquino Sets Up Panel to Negotiate Pullout" (from Subic Bay)

The Standard, Hong Kong (Oct. 12, 1991)

The Increase of Foreign Investment in the United States

The second reason why becoming a world-class negotiator is so vital bears on the increased foreign investment in the United States. There is such a large amount of foreign investment in the United States that international business negotiating may simply

Exhibit 1-3. Major trading partners of the United States.

1991		*1991*	
Exports to	*Amount ($ billions)*	*Imports from*	*Amount ($ billions)*
1. Canada	$85.1	1. Japan	$95.0
2. Japan	48.1	2. Canada	93.7
3. Mexico	33.3	3. Mexico	31.9
4. United Kingdom	22.1	4. Germany	27.0
5. Germany	21.3	5. Taiwan	24.2
6. South Korea	15.5	6. China	20.3
		7. United Kingdom	19.1
7. France	15.4		
8. Netherlands	13.5	8. South Korea	17.7
9. Taiwan	13.2	9. France	13.8
10. Belgium/ Luxembourg	10.6	10. Italy	12.3
11. Singapore	8.8	11. Saudi Arabia	12.2
12. Italy	8.6	12. Singapore	10.2
13. Australia	8.4	13. Hong Kong	9.7
14. Hong Kong	8.1	14. Venezuela	8.8
15. Saudi Arabia	6.6	15. Brazil	7.2
16. China	6.3	16. Thailand	6.5
17. Brazil	6.2	17. Malaysia	6.3
18. Switzerland	5.6	18. Nigeria	5.7
19. Spain	5.5	19. Switzerland	5.7
20. Venezuela	4.7	20. Netherlands	5.1
21. Malaysia	3.9	21. Sweden	4.7
22. Israel	3.9	22. Australia	4.3
		23. Belgium/ Luxembourg	4.1
23. Thailand	3.8		
24. Russia	3.6	24. Philippines	3.7
25. Sweden	3.3	25. Israel	3.6

Note: Export data consist of domestic and foreign merchandise, f.a.s.; import data consist of general imports and customs. Russia formerly reported as USSR.

Source: U.S. Department of Commerce, International Trade Administration.

Exhibit 1-4. Major U.S. trading partners by regions of the world.

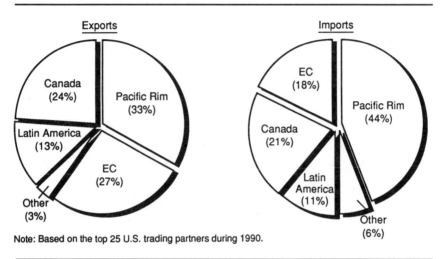

Note: Based on the top 25 U.S. trading partners during 1990.

mean going to another city here at home—for example, negotiating with representatives from a Japanese-owned company in Ohio or with Latin Americans working in Miami.

Foreign investment in the United States is largely the result of the massive U.S. market and of U.S. political stability. A weak U.S. dollar also stimulates interest in U.S. markets, making U.S. products, services, and real estate even more attractive as investments. Foreign investment in the United States has soared in recent years, from a total of about $13 billion in 1970, to $83 billion in 1980, to more than $403 billion in 1990.[4] Exhibit 1-5 lists the countries that are the major investors in the United States: Japan, the Netherlands, Switzerland, Germany, Canada, and the United Kingdom. Together, these six countries accounted for over 75 percent of the foreign direct investment in the United States in 1990. The Japanese have greatly expanded their U.S. investments in recent years, employing about 400,000 people in their U.S.-based companies in 1990.[5] The biggest investors in the United States remain the Dutch and the British, due to their past U.S. investments.[6]

Exhibit 1-5. Foreign direct investment in the United States in 1990.

All Countries:	$403.7 billion
Japan	$108.1
Netherlands	83.5
Switzerland	64.3
Germany	27.8
Canada	27.7
United Kingdom	17.5

Source: U.S. Department of Commerce, Bureau of Economic Analysis.

The Multitude of International Business Arrangements

The third reason why becoming a world-class negotiator is so vital relates to the multitude of business arrangements that are occurring internationally. This means that the specific type of international business negotiation with which you may become involved may take many different forms. In addition to direct foreign investments, multinational corporations are increasing participation in the following six types of arrangements.

1. *Joint ventures:* Cooperative arrangements between two or more organizations that share in the ownership of a business enterprise or undertaking. A joint venture can take many forms but is usually a corporate entity set up between an MNC and local owners in a host country. For example, Goodyear Tire and Rubber is involved in a 51 percent–owned tire manufacturing joint venture with Pernos, a Malaysian government holding company and conglomerate.[7] U.S. MNCs have historically sought majority ownership in their joint ventures, but they have been more likely to accept minority ownership since the 1960s. Western European MNCs have generally been more willing to enter into 50–50 or minority-owned joint ventures in developing countries than have U.S. firms. Japanese MNCs have shown a preference for joint ventures in developing Asian and Latin American countries where labor and resources are abundant.[8]

2. *Licensing agreements:* Rights one company gives to another to use such assets as trade marks, patents, copyrights, or know-how for a fee. Joint ventures often include a licensing agreement between the MNC and the joint venture. In exchange for the significant manufacturing and product technology provided by the MNC, the MNC seeks a licensing agreement with the local partner in order to gain a return on these assets. The transfer of these resources becomes an essential ingredient for establishing a joint venture manufacturing operation. For example, a U.S. MNC has entered into a 50 percent–owned joint venture with a national company in Peru to manufacture chemicals, rayon, acetate, and other fibers. Along with the joint venture agreement, the U.S. MNC negotiated a licensing agreement in which the local partner pays a royalty as a percent of the process and product technology, and another as a percent of profits earned.[9]

3. *Turnkey projects:* Contracts for the construction of an operating facility that is transferred to the owner once it is finished and ready for operations. Under this arrangement, the contractor is responsible for delivering the materials, equipment, work force, and managerial personnel to accomplish the entire project. Bechtel Corporation, for example, negotiates turnkey projects in many parts of the world to build oil refineries and gasoline processing plants.

4. *Subcontracts:* Arrangements in which a company pays another company to perform part of the production process in manufacturing a product. For example, McDermott International negotiates subcontract labor agreements with suppliers in the Philippines, Thailand, and Lebanon to perform craft duties in its Middle East construction projects.

5. *Management contracts:* Arrangements through which one company provides another company with management know-how to perform managerial tasks for a fee, usually ranging from 2 to 5 percent of sales. For example, the Hospital Corporation of America manages hospitals in which they have no ownership. Management contracts are also often part of joint venture agreements, especially where the MNC provides substantial input from its management and engages in training the local partner's managers. For example, a U.S. MNC entered into a management con-

tract with a 51 percent–owned joint venture in Thailand that produces appliances. The MNC provides production, technical, and marketing management for five years for a fixed fee.[10]

6. *Financial arrangements:* Various types of financing, such as debt-financing or local guarantees, or financing by international commercial banks, Eurodollar banks, or regional and international financial organizations. The patterns of financing can be quite complex, involving the establishment or expansion of a joint venture. For example, a U.S. MNC that formed a joint venture to manufacture industrial chemicals in Brazil assisted the local company in negotiating a Eurodollar five-year loan through a commercial bank in New York. At the same time, the Inter-American Bank negotiated a ten-year loan for the operation guaranteed by the government of Brazil.[11]

While these forms of international business are not new, there is now more participation from MNCs from many countries than ever before. You don't have to be an expert in all these different business arrangements, but you should know what options are available to you as an international negotiator, know the obstacles that you may face, and seek technical help as required by the situation at hand. If, for example, you feel that a successful new joint venture is possible only if you can discover a way to help your local partner in financing, involve the financial experts who can offer you advice.

A Light Goes On in Budapest

In one of the most closely watched deals between an American company and the rapidly privatizing Eastern Europe, GE has invested more than $200 million in the once-moribund light-bulb concern—the largest gamble yet by any American company in Hungary. "A GE deal is of major significance to the business community that has an eye on that part of the world," says Richard Hammer, director of international tax policy for Price Waterhouse. "It's showing that these things can be done, and done profitably. It's the carrot that companies see, and it's making them focus on the possibilities for their own ventures."[12]

Why International Negotiating Skills Are Critical for Your Success

The increase in globalization and in foreign investment in the United States, as well as the burgeoning mixture of business arrangements, are all reasons enough for you to become a world-class negotiator. Indeed, these are powerful trends that affect our organizations and whole nations. But on a more personal level, you may ask, "Does intercultural savvy really matter in international negotiations?" You bet it does! Your international negotiating counterpart often judges your company by your expertise and polish more than by the company's size or reputation. Whatever the definition of "polish," which differs from country to country, you must shine in the eyes of your international counterparts.

Americans, however, have sometimes been slow at getting the message about globalization. In 1987, for example, Japan increased its imports of manufactured goods by 22 percent, while other Asians increased their sales of such goods to Japan almost 60 percent. Overall European sales grew by 27 percent during this period. U.S. sales of manufactured goods grew by an astonishingly low 0.12 percent, however.[13] Part of the problem may lie with trade barriers in Japan, Taiwan, or other parts of the world, but the biggest problem is a U.S. barrier: Americans' own attitudes about where and how to do business.

This relative lack of international focus starts at the top echelon of corporate America. Exhibit 1-6 summarizes a study of 1,500 senior executives from twenty countries and points to a wide gap in how U.S. top executives view internationalization as compared with their foreign counterparts. U.S. executives placed substantially less emphasis on all the categories—international outlook, experience outside one's home country, and training in a foreign language—than did non-U.S. executives.

As the famous philosopher Pogo said, "We have met the en-

Exhibit 1-6. The gap in international emphasis in the United States.

Responses to the question, "Which of these attributes are very important for the CEO of tomorrow?"

	Responses by:	
	U.S. Executives	*Foreign Executives*
Emphasis on international outlook	62%	82%
Experience outside home country	35%	70%
Training in a foreign language	19%	64%

Source: Lester B. Korn, "How the Next CEO Will Be Different," *Fortune*, May 22, 1989.

emy, and he is us." Americans can solve this problem first by making quality products and providing superior services, and then by getting out there in the world and negotiating!

The increase in globalization and in foreign investment in the United States may have another impact. They increase the chances that over the next few years you may be dealing with *many* different cultures in your working and personal life, whether this is overseas or in the United States with someone from a different culture living here or merely visiting.

Here's a quick quiz to check your current international negotiating savvy. Be completely candid in your answers. The results aren't going in your personnel file.

A QUICK QUIZ

1. You have been in Osaka, Japan, for four days to begin negotiations on a manufacturing joint venture. Though your hosts have been gracious, you haven't discussed one iota of business in your three meetings. Pressures are mounting back in the home office, and you have only a couple more days that you can stay in Japan. You should:

    a. Be observant of the local business norms and ride out the delay.

    b. Be assertive and at the next meeting politely ask your coun-

terparts when you will be able to discuss the business aspects of the joint venture.
c. Ask your local agent in Japan to intervene to help you get unstuck.

Your Options and Your Best Bet

a. Your Japanese hosts may think you're a lovely person, but this isn't going to help your relationship with your boss back home.
b. The worst choice. This may address the business needs, but it jeopardizes the all-so-important relationship aspects of Japanese deal making.
c. Your best bet. An agent can discreetly inquire as to the timetable and appropriately prompt your Japanese counterpart to address business issues.

2. You are in Moscow to draw up a contract for your company's computer software. Which of these can you expect to be a tough negotiating point in the opening session?

a. Price.
b. Performance standards.
c. Delivery.

Your Options and Your Best Bet

a. Price is not likely to be a major issue for high-tech goods. The Russians are in great need of these from the West.
b. You got it. Russian managers are looking to you to fill technical gaps and are usually under a tough production quota. Bring along a technical expert if you can't field the questions yourself.
c. Not likely a problem. With the Russian inability to deliver the goods, almost any delivery date on your part will be an improvement.

3. You are ready to sign an agreement, when your German counterpart tells you that he will buy your communications equipment only if you cut your price another 8 percent. You should:

a. Say yes.
b. Say no.
c. Agree, but only if payment terms are accelerated.

Your Options and Your Best Bet

a. Avoid this if you can. You are setting a precedent that your counterpart is likely to remember.
b. Your best bet. Germans are tough bargainers. Say no or keep something in reserve that you can give away as a closing concession.
c. If you have to make the concession, get something in return.

4. An Indonesian government official has let it be known to you that that sale of construction equipment in Jakarta is probably very likely if you could help his son get into a U.S. college, and if you could find it in your heart to begin construction on a swimming pool for his family. Your best bet is to:

a. Politely advise the person that you'd like to help him, but unfortunately these requests are really outside your areas of responsibility. Then stress how good the deal will be for all parties concerned.
b. Immediately get busy making contacts at U.S. colleges, lining up the construction equipment, and getting the deal signed.
c. Help with the college request, but check with your company's legal staff on the construction equipment request.

Your Options and Your Best Bet

a. A lame response. This Indonesian official could care less about your job description and will see you as someone who is not serious about doing business there.
b. Being cooperative is one thing, but putting your firm and yourself in legal jeopardy is something else. The U.S. government may not be nice to you if the swimming pool construction is viewed as a bribe of a foreign official.
c. Your best option. You can find a guide to U.S. colleges and universities, send for a couple of course catalogs, and supply a couple of contacts, which will show respect and good faith on your part. This will be especially helpful if your legal staff strongly advises you against agreeing to the swimming pool request.

5. You are in your Saudi counterpart's elaborate office for your first meeting to negotiate specialty steel tubing supplies. He asks you about your trip to Saudi Arabia. You should respond and then politely inquire about your counterpart's:

a. Knowledge of local culture.
b. Wife and family.
c. View on current Middle East politics.
d. The timing of product delivery.

Your Options and Your Best Bet

a. Always a safe topic.
b. The family issue may be all right—the wife definitely not. Discussion of one's wife is a bad idea in Saudi Arabia.
c. The subject of politics is a loser—anywhere. This has to do with values and is a landmine of potential problems.
d. Saudis may not be very concerned about this, even in your fifth meeting. Chances are they've been without your product for centuries, and another couple of months is not a heart-breaker.

6. You have a heavy international travel schedule. In which of these cities do you want to be sure to be punctual for your negotiating meetings?

a. Cairo.
b. Mexico City.
c. Manila.
d. London.

Answer:

All of them. Okay, this was a trick question. Punctuality on your part is important, even if it isn't reciprocated on the part of the other party. It shows respect and helps build the relationship.

Is international negotiating always going to be easy? As you can see from this quiz, of course not. Is it "doable"? Absolutely. You don't need years of living in many cultures to be a world-class negotiator! But you *do* need an awareness of the key factors that affect successful international negotiations and skill in using these factors to your benefit.

This doesn't mean you must be an expert with regard to every country where you do business. We all make mistakes. But for every behavior to which you are attuned, for every nuance you notice, for every strategy you can successfully employ, you are that much further along the road to mastering the skills that will help you get what you want internationally.

Let's now review the negotiating process as a whole in order to gain a foundation for improving your skills as a world-class negotiator!

Notes

1. Adapted from Donald A. Ball and Wendell H. McCulloch, Jr., *International Business: Introduction and Essentials.* 4th ed. (Homewood, Il.: BPI/Irwin, 1990), p. 7.
2. *Transnational Corporations in World Development* (New York: United Nations Centre on Transnational Corporations, 1988), p. 16; "Fortune Global 500," *Fortune* (July 29, 1991): 245–246.
3. John W. Wright, ed., *The Universal Almanac 1992* (Kansas City, Mo.: Andrews & McMeel, 1991), p. 328.
4. Bureau of Economic Analysis, U.S. Department of Commerce, 1990.
5. Stratford P. Sherman, "Japan's Influence on American Life," *Fortune* (June 17, 1991): 115–118.
6. Ball and McCulloch, *International Business,* p. 39.
7. "Arrangements Between Joint Venture Partners in Developing Countries," No. 2, UNTC Advisory Series (New York: United Nations, 1987): 9.
8. Ibid., pp. 1–5.
9. Ibid., p. 33.
10. Ibid., p. 35.
11. Ibid., pp. 35–36.
12. Emily Listfield, "A Light Goes On in Budapest," *American Way* (October 1991): 28–32.
13. Victor Hoa Li, "The World's Biggest Boom," *World Monitor* (December 1991): 28.

Chapter 2

Negotiating in Any Language: How Negotiations Work

Have more than thou showest, speak less than thou knowest.

Shakespeare, *King Lear*

- Negotiating Defined
- The Importance of Win-Win
- The Stages of Negotiation
- Planning Your Negotiation
- What it Takes to Close a Deal

The subject of negotiations is both timely and timeless. It is *timely* because almost everything about our society in general, and our workplace in particular, is increasingly complicated. Today there is more litigation, more cultural diversity, more regulation, more technology, and—in line with the focus of this book—more globalization among businesses. The subject is *timeless* because life is a series of endless negotiations.

Moses, for example, was more than an Old Testament prophet. He was an ace negotiator. He had been up on the mountain all day negotiating the Ten Commandments with the Supreme Other Side. His buddies asked, "Hey Mo, how'd it go?" "It was rough up there today," Moses answered, quite exhausted.

"The good news is I got Him down to ten. The bad news is adultery's still in there!"

Certain fundamentals of negotiations apply whether you are negotiating in Tulsa or Bombay. It is important to understand these fundamentals: They are the foundation on which you will later build your international negotiating strengths. These fundamentals include understanding the concept of negotiation, appreciating the importance of the win-win approach, understanding the stages of negotiation, being able to plan your negotiation, and knowing what it takes to close a deal.

In many ways, the negotiating skills we seek to master are those you practiced as a child but forgot as you became older and more sophisticated. Anyone with a six-year-old is reminded of this on a daily basis. Children are excellent negotiators because:

- They are persistent.
- They don't know the meaning of the word *no*. They know that when we say no, we often mean maybe.
- They are never embarrassed.
- They often read *us* better than we read *them*.

Let's begin relearning these skills by defining our subject.

Negotiating Defined

Negotiating is the process of communicating back and forth for the purpose of reaching a joint agreement about differing needs or ideas. Negotiating has to do with persuasion rather than the use of crude power. What's more, negotiating has to do with the other side feeling good about the outcome of the negotiation. As such, negotiating is a collection of behaviors that involves communications, sales, marketing, psychology, sociology, assertiveness, and conflict resolution. Above all, it has to do with the clear understanding of our own motivations and those of the other side as we try to persuade them to do what we want them to do. A negotiator may be a buyer or seller, a customer or supplier, a boss or employee, a business partner, a diplomat, or a civil servant. On a more personal level, a negotiator may be your spouse, friend, parent, or child. In all these cases, your negotiating skill strongly influences your ability to get ahead in both your organizational life and in your other interpersonal relationships.

Some negotiations involve business counterparts outside your organization, while some involve those within your organization, such as the boss, top management, attorneys, accountants, and other technocrats. With both internal and external situations, the main objective of a negotiation is to help you get what you want.

Since the focus of this book is international business negotiations, we refer to our counterpart from a foreign culture as TOS (The Other Side). TOS can be a negotiating counterpart in a foreign country (or host country) where the negotiation is taking place or a negotiator visiting the United States to do business with you.

What Can You Negotiate About?

Though the details of business negotiations can be quite complex, there are really only six subjects about which you can negotiate. Everything else is a variation on these themes:

1. Price
2. Terms
3. Delivery
4. Quality
5. Service
6. Training

The Importance of Win-Win

Almost any book about negotiating written since 1980 includes great tributes to the virtues of win-win negotiations. This means that both you and TOS win in the negotiation. After having conducted seminars on negotiating with thousands of participants around the world, I can tell you that virtually every individual is quick to agree publicly with the idea of win-win negotiations. Yet in real-life—particularly in the United States—negotiations are often conducted with an "I win, you lose" type of behavior. Intellectually, we know that the cool, even-handed, win-win approach is appropriate, but this is sometimes difficult to remember when the heat is on.

You might ask, "What's so bad about win-lose negotiations as long as I make sure that I'm not the loser? I mean, I'm under a lot of pressure, so if the other person bleeds a little, this is not one of my life's great problems. It's nothing personal, but I'm not in the charity business." So we put our foot right on the other person's neck and proceed with the negotiation.

The problem with win-lose negotiations is this. The loser usually behaves quite predictably and tries to get even. The loser's thinking goes something like this: "I'm going to get you. It may not be today. It may not be tomorrow, but I *will* get you. You will bleed and not even know it." Losers usually wind up pouring much of their energy into all kinds of dysfunctional behavior, aimed at getting out of the losing position. Sometimes the result is even lose-lose. The air traffic controllers' strike early in President Reagan's first term is an example of a win-lose negotiation that ended up lose-lose. The workers lost their jobs, the union went out of existence, and the public was denied trained air traffic controllers. Given the outcry from some members of the public, it is a matter of debate as to whether President Reagan was a winner or a loser in this situation.

You can see much evidence of win-lose problems on the geopolitical level. The conflicts that have been sustained for decades, or sometimes even centuries, are really unresolved conflicts from previous win-lose situations. The Middle East antagonisms are a good example—a series of situations where the various parties have sought to "win" only at the expense of TOS.

Win-win negotiation is critical, not for you to be a wonderful, kind human being, but because it is the practical thing to do. It will help you get more of what you want. And how is this achieved? In two key ways:

1. *Meet the needs of TOS (The Other Side).* Switch to the frequency that others can tune in to, which is known as WIIFT ("What's In It For Them"). The idea here is that we can get much of what we want if we help others get what they want.*
2. *Focus on interests and not positions.*[1] Positions are almost always unresolvable, but finding out interests helps you access the real needs of TOS.

It's like two people fighting over an orange. "I want the orange." says one. "No, I want the orange," says the other, and a win-lose confrontation ensues. With enough patience and empathy, you might find out that one person wants the fruit of the orange to eat, while the other person wants the peel to make marmalade.

It is sometimes difficult to establish a win-win framework in a domestic business negotiation, even when one has honorable intentions. Your counterpart may doubt your sincerity, or the condition under which you are negotiating may not lend itself to a feeling of collaboration and mutual trust. Achieving a win-win outcome can be especially difficult, however, in global business negotiations. The different cultural backgrounds of negotiators may cause them to bring different expectations to the bargaining sessions, create stereotypes of TOS, and develop a climate of suspicion or distrust.

Thousands of such examples abound in international business negotiations. Achieving win-win negotiations, and tuning in to WIIFT, takes an enormous amount of empathy, understanding, listening, patience—and skill. A California-based distributor of computer software relates the frustration she felt during her first trip to the Pacific Rim. "I left California for ten days to accomplish some fairly routine business in Japan and more complicated business in Singapore. I knew that business takes longer in Japan than in the United States, but I had no idea it would take several days to really get down to business in Tokyo. The tone of the negotiation was very bad because I really felt they were dragging their feet." The situation changed in Singapore. "I was equally sur-

*Zig Ziglar, the well-known sales and motivation writer and lecturer, stresses this point to his audiences.

prised to find that in Singapore I was in and out of there in no time. Things got off to a bad start because I felt I should make small talk—I'd been doing it for five days in Japan—and I think the Singaporeans felt *I* was being evasive and not really wanting to move ahead on the deal. I finally convinced them that we had the same objectives. I had scheduled five days there, but I needed only a morning. The Singaporean buyers wanted to talk business as much as I did. After a nice lunch with them, I headed for the airport, mission accomplished."

WIIFT for the Japanese negotiators in this case was patience on the U.S. negotiator's part, patience that indicated interest and respect for the long-term relationship. WIIFT for the Singaporeans was different. They were looking for the U.S. negotiator to demonstrate interest by moving along crisply in the business deal.

The Stages of Negotiation

In both domestic and international negotiations, there are six stages through which negotiations proceed: (1) orientation and fact-finding, (2) resistance, (3) reformulation of strategies, (4) hard bargaining and decision making, (5) agreement, and (6) follow-up. Knowledge of these stages helps you understand the overall shape of the negotiating process and gives you a bearing as you proceed through each negotiation. Here is a summary of the six stages:

1. *Orientation and Fact-Finding.* This first stage is critical for what is to come in the negotiations. The saying "information is power" is never more true than in the early stages of the negotiation process. The more information you can obtain here, the bigger the dividends will be in the negotiation's later stages. Unfortunately, many U.S. negotiators pay little attention to this critical stage of the negotiation. Orientation and fact-finding should begin even before one sits down with TOS. Orientation may mean learning about the organization of TOS, the history of similar negotiations with TOS, or the individual styles of your counterparts. Does the organization have a good reputation? Are there any re-

cent management shake-ups? How much power do you think your negotiating counterpart has within his or her organization? How are negotiating issues to be addressed: individually, or as a group? How important will a written contract be? Are these people generally easy to do business with? And why is this the case or not the case?

There is a misconception in the American culture that "what you don't know can't hurt you." In business negotiating, what you don't know can kill you.

---

2. *Resistance.* This can be a painful, if predictable, part of any negotiation. Indeed, TOS is usually not devoted to showing you a good time. Don't be upset by the resistance you encounter in the negotiation. In fact, if you encounter no resistance, this could be a signal that there is little genuine interest in meaningful negotiations. As long as there is resistance, there is interest, and knowing the source of the resistance allows you to work on overcoming TOS's objections. To break through this resistance, we must again tune in to the frequency that TOS can understand: WIIFT—What's In It For Them. This means finding ways to meet the needs of TOS. Here are typical reasons why you may encounter resistance from TOS:

- *Logic:* "Your price is too high." "We need it sooner."
- *Emotion:* "I really don't like doing business with these people." "This guy is obnoxious."
- *Change:* People are usually more comfortable with predictable, familiar situations than the changes you want them to adopt, such as a different product line or price.
- *Testing your limits:* "How far is this person willing to go?" "Is this really her bottom line?"
- *Organizational constraint:* A budget, policy, or boss overrules TOS's decision.

- *Personal rule:* No concessions will be made at the first meeting.

3. *Reformulation of Strategies.* You develop negotiating strategies when you plan the negotiation. As you gain new data, it is important to reassess earlier strategies. What is the motivation of the parties to do this deal? What strategies worked? What didn't work? This is the time to put your creativity and ingenuity to work.

4. *Hard Bargaining and Decision Making.* Concentrate on the real needs of both sides, not just on the formal positions being taken at the negotiating table. Here you concentrate on the determination of real objectives. What are TOS's main objections? How can they be overcome? What are the key issues involved? Determining WIIFT becomes critical. Here is the time to invent options for mutual gain that will result in a win-win outcome.[2]

5. *Agreement.* Here you work out the details of the negotiation and ensure understanding. The negotiators ratify the agreement with their respective sides. In your case, ratification may be by your boss, attorneys, or financial management.

6. *Follow-up.* This stage is often forgotten by US negotiators. We work hard to sign the contract, then its *adios, au revoir, syanora, arrivederci*—I'm outta here. But by effective follow-up, you set the stage for the *next* negotiation. Use this follow-up as an opportunity for relationship building. Be sure to remind TOS that they made a good decision in negotiating the agreed-upon deal.

Exhibit 2-1 outlines the stages of negotiation and the activities within each of these stages. Note that there are both task (or content) issues and relationship (or process) issues in each stage. The content issues have to do with logic or facts, while the process issues have more to do with emotions and feelings. For example, the task aspects of Stage 1, Orientation and Fact-Finding, are to introduce the parties to the negotiation and to define the negotiating issues. The relationship aspects to Stage 1, however, include setting the climate for the negotiations and building rapport with TOS. It is important to address both task and relationship issues in order to have a successful negotiation.

Exhibit 2-1. Issues in the stages of negotiations.

Task (or Content) Issues	*Relationship (or Process) Issues*

1. Orientation and Fact-Finding

• Introductions	• Rituals
• Opening statements	• Setting the climate
• Overview of the situation	• Building rapport
• Defining issues	• Defining roles
• Prioritizing	• Assumptions about the negotiators as individuals
	• "Could I ask you a few more questions?"

2. Resistance

• Position taking	• Protecting turf
• Logical points of view	• WIIFM (What's in It for Me)
	• Debating/arguing
	• Speech making
	• Psychological warfare
	• "Trust me. This is good for you."
	• "Be reasonable."

3. Reformulation of Strategies

• Introduction of new data	• Problem solving
• Redefinition of issues	• "Maybe we should try another approach."
• Reassessment of original strategies	

4. Hard Bargaining and Decision Making

• Determination of real objectives	• WIIFT (What's In It For Them)
• Probing alternatives	• Collaboration
• Creating options for mutual gain	• Mutual problem solving
	• "What will it take to close this deal?"

5. Agreement

- Finding areas of agreement
- Ensuring understanding
- Drafting and reviewing the agreement
- Ratification

- Recapping
- Little ambiguity
- "Done deal."
- "It's good doing business with you."

6. Follow-Up

- Checking the implementation of the negotiated agreement

- Setting the stage for future negotiations
- "You made a good deal."

Planning Your Negotiation

Intellectually, U.S. negotiators know that proper planning is important. Practically, however, many American negotiators would rather take a beating than write a business plan of any kind. This resistance stems from three negative fantasy scripts: (1) "Someone might actually hold me responsible for this plan"; (2) "Once I write it down, I can't change it"; and (3) "I know what I want to say, but I just can't say it." None of these fantasies need be true. With regard to No. 3, psychologists tell us that when we have this script, we in fact *don't* know what it is we are trying to say, and trying to write it down can make this painfully clear. Planning your negotiation means doing your homework. Without this vital preparation, you will concede the power that comes from making informed business decisions.

Planning your negotiation is a straightforward, four-step process that must be applied to both your side and TOS. For both sides, you must: (1) identify all the issues; (2) prioritize the issues; (3) establish a settlement range; and (4) develop strategies and tactics. Let's look at each of these steps in detail.

1. Be sure to *identify all the issues* you can think of for both your side and TOS. Brainstorm the issues with your colleagues—

aiming for quantity, not quality—to compile your lists. Be post-judicial, not prejudicial, in this process, thereby allowing a free flow of ideas from you and your negotiating team or other relevant players. The idea is to get a long list of every issue that *could* arise during the negotiations, for both your side and TOS.

2. *Prioritize the issues* for both sides in the negotiation. This will, of course, be an estimate as to the priorities of TOS. Don't worry about perfection. The key point is to start thinking in terms of TOS's needs.

3. *Establish a settlement range,* defining the areas within which agreement is possible:

- *Maximum supportable position.* The agreement that you want under ideal conditions, and to which some degree of logic can be attached.
- *What I'm really asking.* The agreement you really want.
- *Least acceptable agreement.* The agreement that can be accepted if the going gets really rough. Your bottom line.
- *Deal breaker.* The condition under which an agreement cannot be reached. This can be one dollar less than the least acceptable agreement.

Settlement range is discussed further in the next section.

4. *Develop strategies and tactics* that help you achieve your goals and that meet the needs of TOS. Strategies determine the overall approach your side plans to take, while tactics are the actions you will take to carry out your strategy.[3] Strategies may include which of your priorities you choose to emphasize and the overall emphasis you give to each of the subjects being negotiated.

Tactics are sometimes viewed as having to do with being manipulative, playing games, or having a hidden agenda. That is not the intent here. Rather, tactics are meant to be the "how to" part of achieving the overall negotiating strategies. Tactics may include whether or not to make the first offer, how much to offer, when to make concessions, and the speed at which you plan to make concessions. Many strategies and tactics are discussed in this book—not for you to be manipulative, but rather for you to avoid being a victim and to be aware of manipulations. In order for a negotiating subterfuge or "game" to be successful, TOS needs a victim—some poor slob who doesn't know any better. For example, TOS may ask for your airline ticket when you first get to Yokohama in order to help you with further flight arrangements. This may be an act of courtesy on the part of TOS, but it also provides TOS with valuable information on pacing the negotiations. They know you will be there for eight days, piling up large expenses, and if they can be patient, you will probably be willing to agree to almost anything come the eighth day if little progress has been made. (There are many American negotiators who have found that little content was discussed until the ride back to the airport.) In this case, be alert to TOS's game and avoid being a victim by trying not to be specific about return travel plans and being aware that TOS's patience is putting you at a disadvantage.

We have been unabashed at saying that if anybody comes at us with abusive or manipulative tactics, we will beat the living hell out of them.

John Bryan, Chairman, Sara Lee Coporation[4]

Let's return to the issue of the settlement range, since you will be operating within it throughout the negotiation.

The Zone of "Doability" Within the Settlement Range

Is the negotiation doable? That is, is a successful conclusion of the negotiation possible given your settlement range and that estimated for TOS? The answer is yes if the settlement ranges overlap. In terms of the planning steps just discussed, the zone of "doability" is the area of agreement that is possible when the least acceptable amount is less or equal for the seller compared to the buyer—in other words, if the seller will accept an amount less or equal to that which the buyer is willing to pay. For example, if a seller will accept $20,000 for a concrete block machine, and the buyer is willing to pay $21,000, then the deal is doable. Exhibit 2-2 illustrates negotiations that are doable and not doable. In Situation A, there is a range of doability of $2,000 (between $38,000 and $40,000). In Situation B, this range is $22,000 (between $38,000 and $60,000). Anything beyond the least acceptable amounts is not doable because that would be a deal breaker. Situation B should be particularly doable because the buyer is really asking even more ($50,000) than the seller is really asking ($40,000) for this product or service. Neither Situation C nor D is doable because the seller is asking more than the buyer is willing to pay (unless, of course, one of the parties can be convinced to change his or her settlement range).

Remember, establish your settlement range and then esti-

Exhibit 2-2. Doable and not doable negotiations.

	Doable			
	Situation A		Situation B	
	Yours (Seller)	Theirs (Buyer)	Yours (Seller)	Theirs (Buyer)
Maximum supportable	$50K	$25K	$50K	$40K
Really asking	$40K	$35K	$40K	$50K
Least acceptable	$38K	$40K	$38K	$60K
Deal breaker	$37K	$41K	$37K	$61K

☐ Zone of Do-Ability

	Not Doable			
	Situation C		Situation D	
	Yours (Seller)	Theirs (Buyer)	Yours (Seller)	Theirs (Buyer)
Maximum supportable	$50K	$25K	$50K	$10K
Really asking	$40K	$30K	$40K	$20K
Least acceptable	$38K	$35K	$38K	$30K
Deal breaker	$37K	$36K	$37K	$40K

mate the settlement range for TOS. Will you guess wrong some-times? Of course. The key point here is not one of precision but of empathy and understanding. It is critical to get in the mind-set of thinking about the needs of TOS, of what they may be after. You can always readjust your estimate of TOS's settlement range with new information from the negotiation.

There are two important rules for effective use of the settlement range. First, prepare your settlement range before the negotiation. Second, have a logical reason for moving from your "maximum supportable" position to your "really asking" position and so on through the range. Let's look at these two rules.

Preparing the Settlement Range Prior to the Negotiation

You must decide your settlement range before the negotiation takes place. This is important for one key reason: to help prevent you from making concessions you might not have wanted to make had not the pressures of the moment been so great during the negotiation process. This is particularly true in international negotiations. For example, let's say you have been in Jakarta for three weeks and have a perpetual stomachache; the work is piling up on your desk back at the office; and your boss wants to know the holdup on the deal. Meanwhile, you're a week late in negotiating another agreement, your travel expenses are beginning to look like the national debt, your friends at home have found a permanent replacement for you on your softball team, and your significant other hasn't exactly shown the greatest compassion in the world for your plight. It would be very tempting at this point to make a deal simply to get on with your organizational and personal life. Developing a settlement range helps keep you focused when these type of pressures mount.

Establishing Credible Reasons for Movement Within the Settlement Range

Skilled negotiators offer reasons as to why they are moving within the settlement range. Otherwise, the negotiators are simply bantering out respective positions, with no credibility attached to their positions. Does this sound familiar?

Seller: My best selling price is $100 per unit.
Buyer: I'll offer you $60.
Seller: Well, perhaps I could accept $90.
Buyer: Maybe I can pay $65.
Seller: $85.
Buyer: $75.
Seller: Let's split it down the middle.
Buyer: Okay, $80 it is.

Reasons to move within the settlement range must pass the credibility "smell test"—that is, in order to be effective, the reason you give for movement within the range can't smell like garbage to your counterpart. Here are possible reasons you can give TOS for moving within your settlement range. As a seller, you might say, "I am willing to lower my price . . .

. . . because of our long-term relationship."
. . . as a volume discount."
. . . as part of a package deal."
. . . because we look forward to your future business."
. . . because we have a special sale going on right now."
. . . because we are trying to move our inventory."
. . . if you can pay cash."
. . . in order to get your account."
. . . to get the process moving."
. . . because this is a discontinued model."
. . . because I recognize your budget limitations."
. . . if you can help us test this product."
. . . if you will give us a testimonial."

Exhibit 2-3 presents a typical negotiating planner for selling a new piece of equipment to a prestigious client who is currently experiencing some business reversals. From a price viewpoint, the negotiation shown in the exhibit is anticipated to be doable, because the estimated settlement ranges are expected to overlap between $75,000 and $80,000 in the "least acceptable" portion of the range.

A key challenge in negotiations is to learn the actual needs versus the positions, or posturing, of TOS. This can be best done by working hard from the beginning of the negotiation, in the

Exhibit 2-3. Negotiating planner for selling equipment.

	Yours	Theirs
Identifying the Issues	Price Delivery Terms Training Long-term relationship	Price Delivery Terms Training Quality
Prioritizing the Issues	Long-term relationship Price Terms Training Delivery	Price Terms Delivery Quality

Establishing the Settlement Range

	Yours	Theirs
Maximum supportable	$100K	$60K
Really asking	$80K	$75K
Least acceptable	$75K	$80K
Deal breaker	$73K	$82K

Developing Strategies and Tactics

Yours	Theirs
• Arrange plant tour • Have president stop by to shake hands with TOS • Maintain "really asking" price • Suggest TOS have discussions with other satisfied customers • Help with financing	• Be persistent re: maximum supportable price • Demand help for financing • Insist on early delivery • Ask for detailed data on quality

orientation and fact-finding stage, to start determining the real needs of TOS.

What It Takes to Close a Deal

There are both logical and emotional aspects to each stage of the negotiation. With these points in mind, there are three things you must do in order to close a deal successfully: (1) satisfy the logical needs of TOS; (2) satisfy the emotional needs of TOS; and (3) convince TOS that you are at your bottom line.

1. *Satisfy logical needs.* The logical, hard-data world is a very potent one, predictable and certain. Most U.S. negotiators tend to focus on logical issues, thinking, "If I can show TOS the force of my logic, then I will prevail in the negotiation by the very force of this reasoning." It is true that we must convince TOS that 2 + 2 = 4 in order to conclude the negotiation. For example, TOS may like you personally, but unless the equipment you are selling does what you say it will do, you are unlikely to consummate the negotiation. However, while logic is a key part of the playing field, it is by no means the only part.

2. *Satisfy emotional needs.* While we almost always pay attention to the logical needs of TOS, we often neglect the emotional needs. "If 2 + 2 = 4, then what do emotions have to do with it?" you may ask. Everything. In fact, emotions are often more important in negotiations than logic. If TOS's emotional needs aren't met, this can block TOS's willingness to deal fully with the facts you have gathered. Think of your own reaction when negotiating with someone you really detest, compared with negotiating with someone you trust and respect. You may *say,* "It doesn't really matter, because business is business." But if you're like most people, you will behave very differently in these two cases. You can bet that there is a much better chance of successfully concluding a deal in the second situation.

Consumers routinely defy logic in their purchase decisions. For example, in the purchase of luxury cars, the incremental cost of producing a Cadillac is not much more than that of a Buick or an Oldsmobile. So why do consumers love to pay big bucks for a Cadillac? Because of prestige and status. Not very logical, but certain key needs are being met.

3. *Convince TOS that you are at your bottom line.* The final step in successfully closing a deal is to convince TOS that this is as far as you are willing to go. This has a lot to do with the emotional climate and trust that you have developed with TOS. If you have established a positive climate of believability, then you will have a much better chance of convincing TOS that this is as far as you can or will go with your offer.

Which of these three actions are the most important to concluding a negotiation? The answer lies in a remark made by Andrew Carnegie: "Which is the most important leg of a three-legged stool?" They are all important: Each of the three factors is critical in closing a deal.

Remember, though, that it is not always necessary to close a deal and reach agreement with TOS. If you have to exceed your deal breaker in order to conclude the negotiation, you may decide it is better *not* to make the deal. Ask these questions often: "Is this deal a must?" and "What is the cost of walking out?" Keep in mind that sometimes the best deal is no deal.

In this chapter, we have examined key elements of the negotiating process that can be applied to negotiations: (1) the win-win approach; (2) knowing the stages of negotiation; (3) planning your negotiation; and (4) closing the deal. Though we will explore the differences among cultures throughout the balance of this book, these fundamentals of negotiating apply anywhere in the world. The specific styles and methods of the negotiators involved differ significantly, however, from culture to culture. Let's begin our intercultural journey in the United States by learning how Americans negotiate.

Notes

1. Roger Fisher and William Ury, *Getting to Yes: Negotiating Agreement Without Giving In* (New York: Penguin, 1983), pp. 40–55.
2. Fisher and Ury, *Getting to Yes,* pp. 56–80.
3. Donald W. Hendon and Rebecca Angeles Hendon, *World-Class Negotiating: Dealmaking in the Global Marketplace* (New York: John Wiley & Sons, 1990), p. 125.
4. John Bryan, *Vis à Vis* (1989).

Part Two

How Americans Negotiate

How we are perceived as negotiators has partly to do with the individual involved and partly with the stereotypes that accompany every culture. The stereotypes we all hold about others are very powerful, with instant images coming to mind. Certainly this is true when Americans think of people from other countries. The comedian George Carlin makes this point when he tells audiences that if there's a heaven, there are German mechanics, Swiss hotels, French chefs, Italian lovers, and British police. And if there's a hell, he adds, there are Italian mechanics, French hotels, British chefs, Swiss lovers, and German police. Like all stereotypes, there usually isn't much basis for this in fact, yet these stereotypes remain powerful because they affect our perceptions—and our perceptions affect our behavior.

Perceptions of Americans by TOS impact negotiations as much as an American's perceptions of others. To negotiate effectively with people from other cultures, you need insight into your own negotiating style. With this personal insight you will be able to adjust your behavior and negotiating strategies according to the particular country in which you are conducting business. Chapter 3 helps you do that. It examines the key traits of American negotiators and focuses on how these traits are perceived by our foreign counterparts. You will see how these perceptions impact on the negotiating process. And

Chapter 4, "An American Report Card: Where Americans Go Wrong in Global Negotiations," explores those areas where Americans are most likely to get tripped up on the international landscape and evaluates the overall effectiveness of typical American negotiators.

Chapter 3
Profile of the American Negotiator

Oh God, give me patience. And please hurry up.

Anonymous

- How Foreign Counterparts See Americans
- Seven Key Traits of American Negotiators

I became acquainted firsthand with how Americans are stereotyped when I moved to Singapore. A local employee asked me where I had grown up in the United States. I responded, "Chicago." (It's actually Peoria, Illinois, but who in Singapore would have heard of Peoria?) The immediate response was a very rapid "Eh-eh-eh-eh-eh."

"I'm sorry," I said, not understanding.

"Eh-eh-eh-eh-eh," he repeated. "Al Capone."

I was to hear many renditions of machine-gun fire during my tenure in Singapore and soon learned that *The Untouchables* was a popular television show there. I was stereotyped through no fault of my own—save geography and television.

How Foreign Counterparts See Americans

I wish I could tell you that U.S. negotiators have wonderful reputations around the world. Unfortunately, that is often not the case. This is the result partly of the individual negotiators involved and partly of the overall perception of Americans. Americans evoke strong stereotypes in the minds and the hearts of people in foreign lands. And yet few American negotiators are aware of how they are viewed by their foreign counterparts. Knowing whether this view is positive or negative is crucial to the success of any business relationship—new or ongoing. That is why I want to stress how important it is for you to become culturally literate, not only in your perception of other nationalities but in how other nationalities perceive Americans. Only in this way can you tune in to the sensitivities, negotiating landmines, and opportunities unique to each of the cultures where we do business.

Exhibit 3-1 summarizes a study of fourteen characteristics most often and least often generally associated with Americans by the general populations of five different nations. There are common threads among the perceptions. "Intelligent" and "energetic" ranked high on the list of a number of countries as characteristics most often associated with Americans, and none see Americans as lazy. There are also differences among the perceptions. The Japanese, for example, rarely associate being "industrious" with Americans, while this is a perception found among

Exhibit 3-1. Characteristics most and least often associated with Americans by populations of five nations.

France	Japan	Great Britain	Brazil	Mexico
Most Often				
Industrious	Nationalistic	Friendly	Intelligent	Industrious
Energetic	Friendly	Self-indulgent	Inventive	Intelligent
Inventive	Decisive	Energetic	Energetic	Inventive
Decisive	Rude	Industrious	Industrious	Decisive
Friendly	Self-indulgent	Nationalistic	Greedy	Greedy
Least Often				
Lazy	Industrious	Lazy	Lazy	Lazy
Rude	Lazy	Sophisticated	Self-indulgent	Honest
Honest	Honest	Sexy	Sexy	Rude
Sophisticated	Sexy	Decisive	Sophisticated	Sexy

Source: Adapted from "What the World Thinks of America," *Newsweek*, July 11, 1983, pp. 44–52.

the French, British, Brazilians, and Mexicans. The British, Japanese, and French see Americans as "friendly," while this trait doesn't make the list of the Brazilians or Mexicans.

What can you infer from this list? That it is important to overcome the negative perceptions and use the positive perceptions to your advantage. If, for example, Americans are generally perceived as nationalistic by the Japanese, you should downplay the use of pro–United States comments in your conversation so as not to form an unnecessary barrier. On the other hand, since the French and Mexicans perceive Americans as industrious, there will tend to be more credibility when you talk to them about delivery times and service.

You should also be aware of another perception and its potential impact: that American negotiators are wealthy. TOS may see American negotiators as having "deep pockets"—that is, as having plenty of money to spread around. And so TOS may conclude, "Since you have so much money, equity should dictate that you make most of the concessions in our negotiations." To counter this thinking, it is important to personalize the negotiation. Emphasize to TOS that it is just you, Juan, and me, Phyllis—two individuals—trying to work out something beneficial for both parties. Minimize the number of times you invoke the name of your organization, particularly if it is a large multinational. No one cares about taking advantage of a large organization such as AT&T, IBM, Exxon, or the U.S. government. If you do mention the name of such an organization throughout your discussions, TOS will reason, "If one of us is going to get hurt in this deal, it should be this rich, billion-dollar organization, not me." Let TOS know that regardless of the size of your organization, you as an individual are held accountable for your conduct and performance.

Let's examine seven specific traits of U.S. negotiators and how they affect the negotiating process.

Seven Key Traits of American Negotiators

Seven key traits form a profile of American negotiators. There are two factors to remember in considering them. First, these traits should be viewed in a cultural context. As you saw in Exhibit 3-1, the Brazilians don't see Americans as self-indulgent, but the British do. In other words, these traits are relative. Second, the degree to which these traits apply varies according to the individual American negotiator involved. A negotiator from New York City may be more impatient than one from Tupelo, Mississippi. All in all, however, these traits serve as a useful guideline in understanding how the American negotiator compares to negotiators from other cultures, how TOS perceives us, and how these traits impact on the negotiating process.

1. American Negotiators Prize Direct and Open Communications

"Tell it like it is," "What's the bottom line?" and "Let's net it out" typify the directness that is prized by American negotiators. It is acceptable to ask one's U.S. counterpart, "Tell me what you really think about this proposal."

Perception by TOS: Americans are pushy. They look you in the eye for long periods, then very bluntly ask you, "Tell me what you really think about this proposal." This is embarrassing and rude.

Potential impact on negotiations: Americans may easily offend their foreign counterparts with such directness. It is not typical in many cultures, especially in Latin and Asian countries. While you may consider this approach as the way to determine the bargaining position of TOS and to try to get on with the business at hand, TOS could see such behavior as abrupt and unpleasant. In addition, directness may result in your missing some of the subtleties being communicated by your foreign counterpart. For example, it is unlikely in Mexico or Japan that TOS is going to answer "yes" or "no" to any question. You have to discern answers to questions through the context of what is being said rather than from the more obvious, direct cues that U.S. negotiators use.

This is really the craziest thing. I was in Japan for a week, and I swear to God that I didn't know if they liked the damned proposal or not. They just seemed to sit there with more or less blank looks on their faces. As it turned out, I had to make another trip just to find out if we were on the right track. We weren't.

Manufacturer's representative from Los Angeles

---

2. American Negotiators Are Impatient

American negotiators usually operate on a faster time clock than others. "Get it done yesterday" is a phrase used in many U.S. organizations. The adage "Lead, follow, or get out of the way" often seems to be how American negotiators go about their business.

Perception by TOS: The American negotiator wants to hurry through the negotiation.

Potential impact on negotiations: You may be faced with the practical problem of generating enough interest from TOS to negotiate the deal as expeditiously as you would like. More important, you may make unnecessary concessions, which often happens when faced with a TOS who is *very* patient. The success of your negotiation might be more assured if you take that extra hour to pursue a point, listen to TOS, or simply not make a concession until the next meeting. Hurrying the negotiation can be an advantage in one case, however. When TOS needs you more than you need him or her, you can often use a deadline to get what you want. For example, if TOS is desperate for replacement parts for machinery being used in a major project, declaring that you must be on an airplane by Tuesday at 8:00 A.M. can be very effective.

3. American Negotiators Prefer to Negotiate Alone Rather Than in Teams

Americans often take a "Lone Ranger" approach to negotiations, preferring to go it alone or to include very few people at the negotiating table. The thinking seems to be, "Come on boss, give it to me. I've got broad shoulders. I'll take care of it."

Perception by TOS: American negotiators do not take the negotiations seriously and are not properly prepared with the appropriate expertise and support personnel to conduct meaningful business.

Potential impact on negotiations: It can be quite overwhelming if only you and perhaps one other person are facing a large negotiating team, as is often the case in Japan and other Asian countries. When this happens TOS can wear you down. There is also usually a faster erosion of your negotiating position than if it were only one-on-one—a kind of "power in numbers" effect. Having foreknowledge of TOS's reliance on teams would be critical in this case, as would an understanding of how to manage your own team appropriately.

It seems we do not really know our American business friends very well. They do not seem very interested in us or how our company really operates. These things could really help them. The Americans mainly like to talk about their contracts. They want to get the transaction done right away and go home. Can you tell me why they always come alone to talk to our team?

Managing director of a Japanese company

---

4. *American Negotiators Emphasize the Short-Term*

American negotiators tend to think in terms of the immediate deal rather than of developing a business relationship that will bear long-term benefits. This short-term perspective is strongly influenced by U.S. pay systems. You are probably compensated according to quarterly or yearly performance measurements. (If you are the CEO or chairperson of the board, this vista may extend, at most, to five or so years.) But your foreign counterpart may be compensated according to results over a period of years and years.

Perception by TOS: American negotiators are out simply to "make a fast buck" for their companies.

Potential impact on negotiations: TOS may be reluctant to enter into a significant business arrangement that does not suit their long-term interests. TOS in many countries are increasingly looking for long-term supplier-buyer relationships and other business arrangements that have reliability, quality, and predictability built into the deal. The *keiretsu* in Japan is such an example. These are industrial groups consisting of a coalition of stakeholders such as employers, suppliers, financial backers, and the Japanese government itself. This arrangement assures that substantial business deals are made only after an exhaustive examination is made of their counterpart's long-term capabilities.[1]

5. American Negotiators Have Limited Experience With Other Cultures

There has traditionally been neither a desire nor perceived practical necessity for the U.S. negotiator to learn about other cultures. Both the assumed advantages of living in the United States and national pride contribute to a preoccupation with "the American way." Too, the vast U.S. market has been one where we expect "Mohammed to come to the mountain"—that is, for TOS to come to the United States to do business or for TOS to speak our language. Finally, unlike most Europeans who speak more than one language, including English, most Americans know no foreign language.

Perception by TOS: Americans are culturally myopic and arrogant about their nationality. They usually refuse to learn a foreign language, understand local customs, or accept my country's approaches to business or personal life.

Potential impact on negotiations: Cultural illiteracy is perhaps the major source of problems in international negotiations. The perception of superiority can be a major obstacle to building a climate of trust and friendship. U.S. negotiators who try to cut corners on host country regulations (e.g., routinely demanding that paperwork be waived or speeded up) may run the risk of irritating or embarrassing TOS with key peers and others who are important to them.

6. American Negotiators Emphasize Content Over the Relationships Involved in the Negotiation

American negotiators focus on the mechanics of the deal more than on the process and emotions. Logical, practical concerns predominate. Though U.S. negotiators may be polite and good-natured, we pay little heed to building a relationship. Rather, we tend to think—and often say—after a few pleasantries, "Now, let's get down to business."

Perception by TOS: This American negotiator is not really interested in building a relationship with us. He is too concerned with logic and facts. I do not know enough about either this person as an individual or the detailed inner workings of his organization to entrust my company's business dealings to him.

Potential impact on negotiations: The personal relationship between negotiators is highly valued in many cultures. In Japan, for example, any significant business arrangement is preceded by a great deal of relationship building. If you are unwilling to participate in relationship building, questions may arise in the mind of TOS, none of which help further the negotiating process: What is the American negotiator trying to hide? Can I trust this person? Is she really interested in doing business with us over a period of time? Doesn't she like us? In addition, if TOS feels too much emphasis is being placed on logic and content, the thinking from TOS may go something like this: "Americans seem to live to work, not work to live. There are other things in life that are more important than all this serious business about business. She should slow down—get to know me, my city, and my country."

7. American Negotiators Are Legalistic

It is typical for Americans to be very precise in written contracts. Long, detailed documents are often the norm. The litigious nature of U.S. society is certainly the major contributor to this tendency.

Perception by TOS: Americans are so distrustful of themselves and those with whom they do business that they are preoccupied with legal documents.

Potential impact on negotiations: TOS may see insistence on legal documents as an affront to friendship and trust. The presence of a detailed contract is almost always a sticky point with Middle Eastern and Latin American negotiators. Therefore, you should be sensitive to different cultural perceptions of written contracts, and modify your approach while protecting your own interests.

The key question to ask yourself about your negotiating style is: "Is it effective?" These seven traits of American negotiators may serve you well when dealing with other Americans. But they may cause trouble on the international horizon when you are dealing with those from other cultures.

Note

1. W. Carl Kester, *Japanese Takeovers: The Global Conquest for Corporate Control* (Cambridge, Mass.: Harvard Business Press, 1990).

Chapter 4

An American Report Card: Where Americans Go Wrong in Global Negotiations

One of the greatest stumbling blocks to understanding other peoples within or without a particular culture is the tendency to judge others' behavior by our own standards.

James Downs, *Cultures in Crisis*

- A Myth Cherished by Ineffective American International Negotiators
- An American Negotiator's Report Card
- The Seven SINs

It is the very areas in which American negotiators excel at home that they falter in international arenas. American negotiators are task-oriented. They can move mountains. They take responsibility and push things through to their conclusion like few others in the world. They get things done. That's the good news. The bad news is that this approach gives heartburn to almost everyone else in the world. Also, American negotiators are viewed as so concerned with the technical parts of the negotiation that they forget about all-important relationships with people. Their insen-

sitivity to cultural differences and failure to adapt to the negotiating process of the host country environment can lead to serious
international negotiating problems.

You took a global negotiating quiz in Chapter 1. How did you
do? Chances are that if you were candid with yourself, you have
several areas in which to improve. Compare your results with the
areas summarized below, describing where American negotiators
most often go wrong.

A Myth Cherished by Ineffective American International Negotiators

A myth is prevalent among ineffective American international negotiators—the belief that "there's no good reason why I should
have to do so much of the adapting in my approach to negotiations. Let *them* do the adapting." This is a myth because in the
international world of give-and-take, there is no universally accepted standard by which to judge one's approach to negotiations. While reluctance to adapt to another culture's behaviors is
understandable, such an approach will not contribute to your success as an international negotiator.

"Now don't get me wrong," you might say. "I don't have
anything against them, but why can't *they* do more of the changing? My approach may not be perfect, but I don't think I should
be ashamed of the way Americans do business. I don't see any
other nationality that's got the negotiating process all figured out.
What's so wrong with the way we do things?" If you have ever
experienced these sentiments, then you are like many U.S. negotiators doing business overseas.

There are two reasons why this approach is dysfunctional
abroad. First, it is not a question of apologizing for the U.S. approach to negotiations, nor is it a question of what is "right or
wrong" from a moral yardstick. The key question is whether your
current approach will help you get what you want out of your
current negotiation. For example, you may feel that it is important
to be honest and open in your communication. Internationally,
this directness might mean that you tell TOS during the negotiation, "Chin, I really have to tell you that I have a big problem with

your proposal, and I want to tell you why." This approach would probably be appropriate and forthright in many U.S. negotiating sessions. In Asia and Latin America, however, such directness would be considered abrupt and brusque. Adapting a more indirect approach would reap you more benefits. For example, you might say, "Chin, we have a concern about your proposal that we would appreciate discussing with you when you feel it is appropriate." Or, you might consider having a third party bring up the concern.

Effective interaction means giving of yourself—trying to see the world of others and to respect their life ways. It means not forcing your ways on them. Yet at the same time, it means being true to yourself and your ways. To be really effective, interaction must be a two-way street or, of course, it is not interaction at all. That is, all interacting individuals should be doing so from the basis of awareness, understanding, and knowledge.

                                                    Clarence C. Chaffee[1]

A second fallacy to this approach is that U.S. negotiators are not the ones who are doing all the adapting. For example, it is much more likely that foreign counterparts are learning English than it is that we are learning their language. This adaptation takes place in the formal education process in some cultures. Ken Nelson, director of Yokohama Academy USA* and a former Fulbright scholar, stresses the dedication of the Japanese students at the Baltimore facility: "My experience has been that the Japanese students are very focused in learning about U.S. customs and business practices. They want to know how to sell us things."

*Yokohama Academy USA is a branch of the Yokohama Academy, a non-profit educational corporation founded in 1958 in Yokohama, Japan. The USA branch helps Japanese students learn American customs, business conduct, and English.

This is just one example that points to the concessions made by our negotiating counterparts to U.S. ways of doing business.

You might reasonably ask why adapting your negotiating behavior is so important since other international organizations are stressing cross-cultural familiarity. But is that enough? Nancy J. Adler, a Canadian scholar, has asked the question, "Is the world gradually creating one way of doing business or is it really a set of distinct economic markets defined by equally distinct national boundaries, each with its own unique approaches to business?" She concludes that while organizational structures are becoming quite similar, the behavior of people within those organizations is maintaining its cultural uniqueness. This means that organizations in the United States and France might look the same from the outside, but Americans and the French behave differently within these organizations.[2]

There is no one best way. The point is to determine what will work best to serve your negotiating objectives, and to discover which approaches will help you be effective in getting what you want internationally. Adapting your behavior is usually painful, for you must unlearn some of your preconceptions and explore new approaches. And such flexibility requires adapting to change on your part and accommodating to intercultural differences.[3] One U.S. negotiator who spends much of his year in Europe makes this observation: "More than anything else, success in an international environment requires open-mindedness and flexibility. I have to work on this even though I've been doing business here for seven years."

An American Negotiator's Report Card

How do American negotiators stack up in their global negotiating skills? Let's look at their report card, as shown in Exhibit 4-1. It itemizes the criteria that will make you a world-class negotiator. This assessment is based on discussions with hundreds of Americans who negotiate internationally as well as with our international counterparts abroad. Our challenge as individuals is to improve the grades on the report card. In these times of intense competition, nothing short of straight *As* is good enough.

Exhibit 4-1. The American negotiator's report card.

Global Business Negotiating Performance

Skill	Comments	Grade
Planning the negotiation	Most American negotiators would rather take a beating than do any kind of business plan, but our logical orientation helps us along.	B −
Win-win approach	Competitiveness is hard to overcome.	D
Cultural IQ	Often well-traveled but not well-versed as to how our counterparts really think and behave.	D
Adapting the negotiating process to the host country environment	Old habits are hard to change, especially when they work so well in the massive U.S. market.	D
Patience	Are you kidding? "Time is money."	D
Listening skill	Among the greatest interrupters in the world.	D
Using language that is simple and accessible	The English language is complicated enough and we complicate it even more with jargon, slang, and acronyms.	C
High aspirations	Often a strong point.	B +
Personal integrity	American negotiators have a reputation for sticking to their word.	A −
Building solid relationships	No global warming on our part. "Sounds really good, but I've got 'real' business to do," is a typical approach.	D
	Overall Grade	C −

U.S. negotiators, like anyone else, have their strengths and weaknesses. Personal integrity, for example, is an area where American negotiators often excel. Liwen Tsao, the president of a Taiwanese trading firm, notes, "I like doing business with Americans because once you have negotiated a deal, you can count on it." Graham Wedlake, a British solicitor living in London, agrees: "I have found that Americans stand by their word." And a Mexican marketing manager for a consumer products company recalls his first negotiation with Americans: "I got the feeling that these people would follow through. This turned out to be correct." American negotiators also often have high aspirations, asking for what they really want in the negotiation. And while often less than thorough in planning the negotiation, American negotiators do better than most others in this regard.

There are American negotiating strong points. Let's turn to the areas where improvement is needed.

The Seven SINs

There are many challenges in keeping a firm footing on the international negotiating terrain. There are, however, seven main areas where U.S. negotiators tend to stumble. These are what I call the seven SINs (Slips in International Negotiating) of international negotiating. These SINs are areas where American negotiators tend to score a *C* or below in terms of key international negotiating skills.

    SIN 1: Falling into the win-lose trap
    SIN 2: Ignoring cultural gaps
    SIN 3: Failing to recognize the host country's negotiating obstacles
    SIN 4: Being in too much of a hurry
    SIN 5: Not listening for communication barriers
    SIN 6: Wearing blinders with respect to relationships and emotions
    SIN 7: Using language that is too hard to understand

These SINs decrease your organization's effectiveness and create barriers for your own career growth. In negotiating terms,

these SINs hinder you from getting what you want out of
the deal.

SIN 1: Falling Into the Win-Lose Trap

Our general approach to resolving negotiating issues tends to be
a little like Hulk Hogan's approach to wrestling: The last one
standing wins. American negotiators tend to be very competitive,
and individual achievement is prized in the American culture.
The U.S. businessperson's achievement may be seen in charts on
office walls and in various forms of individually based pay incen-
tives. The American style of quick wit and "getting in the last
word" are other subtle forms of a competitive, win-lose style.
Though such behavior may be natural to U.S. negotiators, it might
be overbearing and disagreeable to TOS.

Our global counterparts also complain that American negotiators tend to pass over areas of agreement and emphasize disagreement.[4] For example, American negotiators often interpret periods of silence from the Japanese as rejection and begin dealing
with a disagreement that may not exist.[5]

Some parties to a dispute seem to follow the rule, *When
you're strong on the law, argue the law; when you're strong
on the facts, argue the facts; and when you're not strong on
either one, just argue.*

Martin Wagner, U.S. labor arbitrator

SIN 2: Ignoring Cultural Gaps

Not knowing the nuances of behavior in different cultures—and
not recognizing that they exist at all—can raise serious problems
for international negotiators. One research study identifies nine-
teen mistakes that global negotiators tend to make. Almost all of
them have to do with cultural differences such as insufficient
knowledge of the host country and of the use of time there and

insufficient attention to saving face.[6] Similarly, it seems that most Americans would rather take a beating than learn a foreign language, which makes Americans seem disrespectful of other cultures.

Middle East Business Practices 101: When Compliments Are Costly

The Labour Minister for the United Arab Emirates was in my office to help negotiate an end to a work stoppage by the local Dubai construction workers. The meeting went well until we finished our discussions. While walking with His Highness to the door of my office, I mentioned that he had a beautiful briefcase (mine was in a general state of disrepair). As I reached the door I noticed that he was no longer walking with me. I turned around to see His Highness emptying the contents of his briefcase on my desk.

"Did you lose something?" I tried to ask helpfully.

"No, no," he replied. "I want you to have," he added, as he presented his briefcase to me. "This is for you. You are my friend."

After profusely apologizing, I convinced him that I really couldn't accept the briefcase.

The lesson learned? In that part of the world, don't go around complimenting people on their possessions. You just might end up with them.

American cultural insensitivity covers many behaviors and can be seen in numerous day-to-day negotiating situations. For example, Ace Dealmaker comes back after a week in Japan, and the boss asks, "So how'd it go over there, Ace?"

"Oh, pretty well overall."

"Good. Did you get a contract?"

"Well, no. We're still working on it."

"Well, what did you think of the people?"

"Oh, they were very nice." He closes the door and whispers, "But I'll tell you one thing."

"What's that?" asks the boss.

"They're sneaky little devils, aren't they?"

"What?!"

"Look," Ace explains. "I was over there for a whole week, and not once did Sato ever look me in the eye."

That's right, Ace. Your Japanese counterpart didn't and he's probably not going to—at least not to the degree that most Americans would be comfortable with—because the Japanese culture does not prize direct eye contact. In fact, it is considered a sign of disrespect to maintain eye contact for sustained periods—say nine or ten seconds—and few cultures have the practice of "looking people in the eye" as Americans do. In this case, cultural sensitivity to differences in eye contact would have greatly helped this American negotiator.

SIN 3: Failing to Recognize the Host Country's Negotiating Obstacles

There are many aspects of the negotiating process that must be adapted from your home-country style to that of the host country. These aspects include the pace of the negotiation, the formality of your presentation, how you deal with differences, your method of making concessions, your handling of special interests, and your attunement to the host country's business etiquette and practices.

Almost every aspect of the international negotiating process differs from that of the United States. The degree of difference depends on the specific host country. The use of contracts is a good example. U.S. negotiators are accustomed to detailed contracts, while negotiators from many host countries (e.g., those in Latin America and the Middle East) find such specificity repugnant and embarrassing. Middle Easterners may not accept even a broad contract. The Germans, Swiss, and Japanese, on the other hand, tend to be comfortable with detailed written agreements.

SIN 4: Being in Too Much of a Hurry

Americans are obsessed with time. U.S. corporate classrooms are crammed with employees taking time management courses. Our technological society is closely calibrated. In my hometown of Peoria, Illinois, the shift change at Caterpillar Tractor Company is at 3:17 P.M. Not 3:16 . . . not 3:18! Yet as strange as it may seem, thirty minutes past the appointed meeting time is "prompt" in many parts of the world.

Just-in-Time Management

I was in the small Central American country of Belize to address a management conference. I was scheduled to speak at 9:00 A.M., so I was ready to go about 8:00 A.M., waiting for my hosts in the hotel lobby. They weren't there. 8:15—no one. 8:30—nobody. 8:45—nope. I checked with the front desk to make sure I had set my watch to the correct time zone. 9:00—9:15—still no one. Now I'm getting out my letter of invitation, thinking, "Could this be my worst nightmare? Could I be in the wrong country on the wrong date? At about 9:20 my hosts showed up, and we drove to the hotel where the conference was being held. After a short discussion about my flight, the weather, and related items, I said, "It's about 9:30. Wasn't I on the agenda for 9:00 A.M.?"

No response.

"I'm just curious, but if it's about 9:35, aren't we late for the conference?" I persisted.

"Oh no, Mr. Acuff" one of my hosts said jovially. "Nothing here in Belize starts at the time on the agenda. We'll be quite early. The conference won't start for another hour or so."

"Thank you," I said, relieved. My life was good again.

The discrepancy persists when it comes to actually conducting the negotiations. The human part of Americans seems to be overtaken by an automatic "time" alarm, and we tend to proceed like Sherman's March to the Sea, wanting to press onward relentlessly until we've cut the deal. American negotiators want to get down to business and conclude the negotiations as quickly as possible. This impatience can seriously limit your negotiating power, since as a result American negotiators are often the first to make concessions.

SIN 5: Not Listening for Communication Barriers

Listening is hard work. How many people in your whole professional or personal life really listen to you? If you are like most U.S. negotiators, you won't have to use all the fingers on one hand. American negotiators are among the greatest interrupters in the world. We become uneasy if there is silence of even four or five seconds in a business discussion. If, for example, non–native English speakers are negotiating with us in English, we're right in there, interjecting our point of view, if they pause to understand our meaning fully, or to formulate their thoughts.

Isobel Morgan, an Australian who has been involved with many international negotiations, has identified another key listening problem related to impatience. "American negotiators seem in such a hurry that they miss the nuances in the behavior of other people," she notes. "It has been my experience that they often don't listen at all levels—to take the time to really understand the effect their proposals or behavior are having on other people." This can severely limit our effectiveness in some cultures, such as Japan, China, or Saudi Arabia, where negotiators don't tend to communicate in direct, open patterns.

SIN 6: Wearing Blinders With Respect to Relationships and Emotions

I find that American negotiators are often quite puzzled as to why their international negotiating experiences don't go well, or they blame TOS for being difficult to deal with. Usually there is a preoccupation with the mechanics of the particular negotiation in question: "If I had just quoted a lower price," "I bet we should have promised delivery earlier," or whatever. In international business negotiations, however, the real problem is as often with the relationship as it is with logic.

When it comes to building relationships, American negotiators often seem a little like Steve McQueen when he said to Natalie Wood in the movie *Love With the Proper Stranger,* "You know, we're both very much in love: You're in love with you, and I'm in love with me." Yet by many standards, Americans are a warm, friendly people. At least we're not so bad once you get to know us. The trouble is, our foreign counterparts may never really get to know us because we emphasize the logical aspects of the negotiation and downplay the personal side. The typical U.S. negotiator sees facts, figures, opening offers, and concessions as the playing field. Getting to know the other party is only ancillary. To much of the world, however, the relationship *is* the playing field.

American negotiators sometimes feel that TOS is being nosy about their personal lives. TOS, however, may simply see their questions as a means to obtain more data about the individuals and thereby reduce uncertainty. The Japanese, for example, tend to put great emphasis on the relationship because as a culture they tend to avoid risk. Learning more about you provides the data that will make you more predictable, and thus reduce their risk.[7]

I know I shouldn't feel this way, but I find negotiating in Mexico a little annoying sometimes when they press me about my personal situation. I love my family and I certainly don't have anything to hide, but I don't feel that this should be an area of emphasis in a negotiation. I'm a friendly person, but it seems like I know more about their family members than I know about my own. I'm trying to get comfortable with this, but I'm not there yet.

International sales representative, automotive parts distributor, Ohio

---

SIN 7: Using Language That Is Too Hard to Understand

The English language is hard to learn, largely because of the rules associated with the parts of speech and the many exceptions to these rules. U.S. negotiators tend to complicate matters by using a wide assortment of slang expressions. As a result, "learning the language" for use with U.S. negotiators means more than learning English words. It means learning the considerable number of clichés and amount of jargon used by Americans. What international counterpart, for example, would have any idea about the meaning of the following phrases, all based on sports analogies, unless the person happened to be knowledgeable about the particular sport involved?

Phrases	*Typical Meanings*	*Sport*
"What's your game plan?"	"What's your approach to this negotiation?"	American football, basketball, etc.
"We're not going to throw in the towel."	"We're not going to give up."	Boxing, American football, etc.
"They're trying an end run."	"They are going around normal organizational channels."	American football
"You threw us a curve."	"We didn't do well in this situation."	Baseball
"You're batting a thousand."	"You've had all your demands met."	Baseball
"Have we covered all the bases?"	"Have we considered all the options?"	Baseball
"That's the way the ball bounces."	"It was unpredictable but it is over now and there is no use to worrying about it."	American football, basketball, etc.

This reliance on slang makes it very difficult for TOS to grasp our meaning, even if TOS speaks English. By using simple, straightforward language, we can help ourselves by helping others understand us.

Teenage What?

The session had been interesting, with a good exchange of ideas. About thirty top Russian managers were learning about "How to Negotiate With Americans." Each of the participants was wired so that we could communicate with each other through an interpreter. I would say a few words and wait four or five seconds for the translation from English to Russian to be completed, listening through my earphones to the translator's crisp, confident tone.

All this was working fine until we began discussing Americans' need for achievement and how this affected the competitive approach of many American negotiators. One of the participants asked about what heroes represented this achievement orientation, and whether this achievement orientation impacted American children. I made a few observations about various American heroes and then made my big mistake. I noted that, yes, American children have their achievement-oriented heroes too, and I mentioned the Teenage Mutant Ninja Turtles as an example. Suddenly there was silence from the translator. I looked to the back of the room where he was sitting in a booth. The participants looked around nervously at him. He had a blank look on his face. Finally, after about fifteen seconds, some tentative, awkward sounds came forth.

Then I realized how impossible a job I had given him. What would his translation possibly be . . . something like, "Turtles in their teenage years . . . who have physical deformities . . . and practice Far Eastern martial arts"?

We have examined the American negotiator's report card and some of the places where Americans tend to stumble on the global negotiating landscape. Chapters 5 and 6 examine ways to help us sprint to the front of the crowd.

Notes

1. Clarence C. Chaffee, *Problems in Effective Cross-Cultural Communication* (Columbus, Ohio: Battelle Memorial Institute, 1971).
2. Nancy J. Adler, *International Dimensions of Organizational Behavior*, 2nd ed. (Boston: Kent Publishing, 1990), pp. 45–46.
3. William B. Gudykunst and Young Yun Kim, *Communicating with Strangers: An Approach to Intercultural Communication* (New York: Random House, 1984), p. 235.
4. Cynthia Barnum and Natasha Wolniansky, "Why Americans Fail at Overseas Negotiations," *Management Review* (October 1989): 55.
5. Adler, *International Dimensions*, p. 182.
6. J. Fayerweather and A. Kapoor, *Strategy and Negotiation for the International Corporation* (Cambridge, Mass.: Ballinger, 1976).
7. Gudykunst and Kim, *Communicating With Strangers*, pp. 179–183.

Part Three

How Global Negotiations Work

There are forces that tend to minimize differences among international business negotiators. These forces include a common purpose (such as profit) and gradually, common references (as both parties learn to work with each other). Generally, however, there are wide differences between what constitutes effective negotiating strategies in the United States versus those in other cultures.

It is difficult enough to be persuasive and get what we want when we know the players, understand the game, and have a home field advantage. But when we lose the familiar guideposts of how to deal with others and of how to do business, we experience not only culture shock, but—from a negotiating viewpoint—a "we-got-schlocked" shock. In fact, we may bleed and not even know it.

Chapter 5, "What Makes Global Negotiations Different?" examines the key factors that make international negotiations different from domestic negotiations. Specifically, cultural differences and their effects on international negotiations are applied to a negotiating model used for the individual countries examined. Chapter 6, "World-Class Negotiating Strategies," explores the ten specific negotiating strategies that work anywhere in the world.

There are unique problems associated with international negotiating. In Chapter 7, "The Six Most Difficult Problems Faced by International Negotiators," we identify these problems and suggest specific actions for their resolution.

Chapter 5

What Makes Global Negotiations Different?

Human beings draw close to one another by their common nature, but habits and customs keep them apart.

Confucian saying

- Cultural Factors That Affect Global Business Negotiations
- How Negotiations Differ From Region to Region
- Gender Issues in Global Business Negotiations

There are numerous "macro-factors" that influence your international business negotiations, such as the politics and economic climate of the region involved. There are also organizational aspects that impact TOS, such as upsizings or downsizings or the organizational clout of your negotiating counterpart. Attention to these factors helps you assess the overall business and organizational climate in which the negotiation is taking place. More important than any other key influences, however, are cultural factors. In this chapter we first examine the cultural factors that affect international negotiations and then explore how these factors influence the pace, style, strategies, and other aspects of the international negotiation process. We also explore the part played by gender issues in international negotiating.

Cultural Factors That Affect Global Business Negotiations

There are four cultural factors that most affect negotiations among cultures: (1) use of time; (2) individualism versus collectivism; (3) role orderliness and conformity; and (4) patterns of communication. Let's examine each of these factors and how they affect negotiations.

Use of Time

Cultures differ in their use of time. The Americans, Swiss, Germans, and Australians are usually fast-paced and exact in their approach to time. Their professional and personal lives tend to be closely calibrated. A negotiating session that is scheduled for 9:30 A.M. on Tuesday is expected to start at 9:30 A.M. on Tuesday.

U.S. negotiators, especially, are noted for time-consciousness. ("Will we be able to complete the project by March 1? Yes, but would it help you make a decision in our favor if we were to guarantee completion by February 1?") Much of this time emphasis is related to the technological roots of American society. The demands of machinery, the interrelationships of information software and hardware, and other issues all make time a critical factor. Can you imagine the New York Stock Exchange opening every business day "sometime between 9:00 and 10:00 A.M."? Or the second shift of a factory starting at "three-ish"?

To those in many other cultures, Americans seem obsessed with time—prisoners of clocks and time constraints. In Latin America starting a negotiating session a half hour after the appointed time may be considered and even expected. A manager from a U.S.–based organization found this to be the case when negotiating a contract to buy television time. She notes, "I had an appointment with the minister of communications in Argentina for an interview. Because of his position, we were told that we'd better be there a little earlier. We wanted to make sure we were not putting ourselves in a position of wasting his time. Nevertheless, we waited for two hours and he never showed up." A Middle East project delayed for two months may be more usual than unusual. The thinking may be, "Our country has done without this new equipment for many centuries, and it will be okay if we don't have it for another two months."

Postmortem: Is This Meeting Dead?

Follow-up telephone conversation between a U.S. manager and his counterpart from the United Arab Emirates about a scheduled negotiating meeting that didn't take place:

"Rashid, this is Joe Dokes. I was just following up on our meeting. I believe we were supposed to meet this morning at 10:00 A.M. at the Intercontinental Hotel. Did I get the wrong hotel?"

"Oh no, Mr. Dokes, you were at the right hotel. I'm sorry. We can meet tomorrow morning at the hotel *ansh-'Allah.*"

Note: The *ansh'Allah* means "Allah willing." As this and other American negotiators sometimes find in the Middle East, Allah doesn't always will that the meeting take place!

Individualism vs. Collectivism

Individualism refers to the "I" consciousness found in some cultures as contrasted with the "we" (or group) consciousness found in others. A classic study done by Dutch researcher Geert Hofstede found a wide difference among countries, summarized in Exhibit 5-1. With 100 the highest on the scale, U.S. managers score 91, making them the most individualistic of all surveyed countries. This includes other Western countries such as Australia (90), Great Britain (89), and Canada (77). Most Pacific Rim cultures score much lower on the scale, indicating the collective, group consciousness: Japan (46), Hong King (25), Singapore (20), and Taiwan (17). This is also true to a lesser extent in Latin American

Exhibit 5-1. Individualism versus collectivism in selected countries.

Score	Managers' Country of Origin
91	United States
90	Australia
89	Great Britain
77	Canada
75	Denmark
74	Italy
74	Belgium
71	Sweden
70	Switzerland
70	France
55	Israel
53	Spain
48	India
46	Japan
46	Argentina
38	Brazil
32	Mexico
25	Hong Kong
20	Singapore
17	Taiwan
16	Venezuela

Source: S. G. Redding, "Results-Orientations and the Orient: Individualism as a Cultural Determinant of Western Managerial Techniques," *International HRD Annual,* vol. 1 (February 1985).

countries, where scores range from 46 (Argentina) to 16 (Venezuela).[1]

Americans want an individual winner to emerge. This can be seen in the way we structure the prize system of athletic contests. If, for example, the first prize in a golf or tennis tournament this weekend is $150,000, how much the second prize? Well, the right answer isn't $149,900. The second prize is usually half the first prize—about $75,000.

The emphasis on the group helps explain why the Japanese are so slow making negotiating decisions. It takes time to ensure that there is "buy-in" from all members of the team. The group emphasis also influences whom you are trying to convince at the negotiating table. U.S. negotiators bargaining with other Americans usually look for the top person who represents TOS. They don't want to waste precious time on anyone who isn't a key decision maker. In "we"-oriented cultures, however, it is the group, not an individual, that you must convince. This is why you may feel like you have become best friends with *sushi* before you ever even meet the senior Japanese negotiator, let alone convince him of your point of view. This group emphasis also explains why the Japanese pack the negotiating table with fourteen people while you have only three—and that includes your driver.

Role Orderliness and Conformity

Some cultures, such as those in the Pacific Rim, are characterized by a high need for role orderliness and conformity. Often more emphasis is put on the form or structure of behavior than on content. *How* things are done is of paramount importance. Other cultures, typified by the United States, have a low need in this regard and are much more at ease with ambiguity.

This factor helps explain why the Japanese emphasize the relationship with one's counterpart. Getting to know the other person helps to bring orderliness and predictability to the negotiating process. Similarly, the Japanese pay great attention to ritual, such as presenting business cards. Little is left to guesswork. On the other hand, negotiators from the United States, Germany, and Switzerland tend to put more emphasis on the content of the negotiations than on the procedures for achieving the end results. This is evident in the legal and administrative aspects of the negotiation process, where detailed contracts to legitimize the content are common. Too, U.S. negotiators generally have a much more informal negotiating style, with relatively little rigid status distinction when dealing with others. You, for example, are probably comfortable using first names when addressing business associates. And if you are like most American negotiators, you may find it difficult to adapt to the flowery language, complex methods of address, and ritualistic manners that reflect the hierarchical social structure in many other cultures.[2]

Patterns of Communication

In one way, the communications process is very simple. A sender is trying to get a message through to a receiver. The model shown in Exhibit 5-2 represents this basic concept. The responsibility of the sender is to send a clear message. The responsibility of the receiver is to listen. Notice that this simple process becomes more complicated as the sender encodes the message sent, and the receiver decodes the message received. For example, as the seller of a new machine, you might say to TOS: "I'd like to review with you the detailed calibrations of our new X-15 model. You'll be pleased to know that output has been increased by 16.23 percent, and conformance to standards is now 99.74 percent at close-tolerance machining. Here's a schematic of the X-15." The message you might have encoded in this example is the importance your company attaches to productivity and quality. But no matter how noble your intentions, if the TOS receiver is from Brazil or Egypt, such emphasis on logic and detail is likely to be decoded as somewhat inappropriate. (Emphasis on concepts, grace, and beauty would have been a better starting point in these cultures.)

Such different perceptions between the sender and the receiver result in communications "noise." Sometimes this noise is so great that little, if any, of the communications gets through. Such noise is common in international negotiating and requires much awareness and effort on the parts of both the sender and the receiver to ensure clear communication. This noise can come

Exhibit 5-2. Sending a message to a receiver.

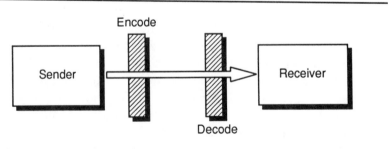

from both verbal and nonverbal communication. Let's first consider verbal communication.

Verbal Communication: "Would Somebody Please Talk to Me in Terms That Even I Can Understand?"

Communication patterns can be understood in terms of "high-context" or "low-context" cultures. Some countries, such as those in the Pacific Rim, are considered high-context cultures, where the meaning of the message is embedded in the context of the communication. Individuals from these cultures tend to put more responsibility on the receiver than on the sender. It is the receiver's responsibility to determine the full intent of the message from the context in which the message was sent. In other words, the sender provides most of the pieces of the puzzle, but it is the responsibility of the receiver to provide the missing links.[3]

Other countries, such as the United States, Canada, and most of Western Europe, are considered to be low-context cultures. That is, the meaning of the message is in what is explicitly stated, not in the context of what is stated. In the United States, there is generally an equal responsibility for both the sender and the receiver. The sender is to speak in a way that can be understood, and the receiver is to listen.

These differences in communication patterns influence the international negotiation process. U.S. negotiators, in particular, prize direct and open communication. ("Just lay it on the line." "Let's net it out." "What's the bottom line?") Individuals from high-context cultures may perceive this approach to be insensitive and aggressive. Tom Wilson, a British management consultant, notes, "American negotiators sometimes appear to delight in their bluntness—which doesn't work very well with the British." Americans, on the other hand, may consider the indirect communication of those from high-context societies difficult to follow and even deceptive, thinking, "This person must be shifty since he won't give me a 'yes' or 'no' answer."

An important part of verbal communication is literally speaking the same language. You might wonder if you really have to learn a foreign language to talk to these people. The short answer to this question is of course "yes." Communication is enhanced when both parties are working to share a common language. The degree to which this is necessary, however, depends on the individuals with whom you are negotiating, their language, their culture, and the amount of business you are doing with them. A one-week trip to Hong Kong to finalize a deal at Citibank would not merit a great effort on your part to learn Chinese. It would be impractical and would not be expected by TOS. On the other hand, protracted joint venture negotiations in Paris would probably justify your learning French. The French expect it, they're unlikely to go out of their way to speak English, it would help build amicable relationships, and it would certainly help you understand the content and context of discussions. Keep in mind that in many countries the chief spokesperson for TOS may in fact speak excellent English, but others on the negotiating team may not. International consultants Lennie Copeland and Lewis Griggs point out that there is more of a need than ever to learn a "medley of languages" in today's international marketplace.[4]

Nonverbal Communication: The Unspoken Language

Nonverbal communication, or body language, is important for two reasons: (1) to help determine the meaning of what TOS is saying; and (2) to help you get your own message across. Body language varies widely among cultures. Facial behaviors, hand gestures, eye contact, touching, and other "nonverbals" are culturally driven. Greetings and handshakes come in different forms. For example, U.S., German, and Russian negotiators have very firm handshakes compared with most others. This can cause some practical perceptual problems: TOS may view Americans as too abrupt and, literally and figuratively, heavy-handed, while Americans may view those with less firm handshakes as unassertive. This perception has caused difficulty for many American negotiators who later learn that their foreign counterparts are indeed quite assertive, and maybe even aggressive when it comes to negotiating an agreement. "I thought the Chinese might be somewhat of a piece of cake because their handshakes seemed so wimpy," recalls a California importer of his first trip to Beijing. "I soon found out that they were quietly effective, and the weak handshakes had nothing to do with the firmness of their positions."

Americans generally like a lot of physical space in their organizational lives. Many American clichés point to this: "Give me some space," "Get out of my face," "Back off." This translates into a typical distance of about three feet when addressing others in business situations. Very little touching takes place. When it does occur, it is usually somewhat conspicuous and a source of sensitivity. Handshakes last only a second or so. If two passengers remain after a crowded elevator has emptied, they immediately take dancelike steps to their respective corners. In many cultures, the social and business distance is much closer than it is in the United States. It is customary in parts of Latin America and the Middle East for business associates to embrace each other, to kiss each other lightly on the cheek, and to put only one foot or so between them in a business discussion. Indeed, a distance of about a foot between business associates is customary in many cultures.

Nonverbal communication is critical in decoding rites, gestures, forms of politeness, the concept of "face," silence, and pauses. Decoding, like all ways of finding the real meaning, often proves difficult because it is done through our filters of domestic norms and habits. What constitutes extreme versus appropriate nonverbal behavior is a matter of cultural interpretation. For example, the Latins touch more than Americans or Canadians, who in turn touch more than the Swedes or British. The language of gestures varies widely too. While Americans, Canadians, and most Europeans understand the "thumbs up" gesture to mean "all right," Greeks and Southern Italians decode this gesture in a way Americans would normally reserve for the middle finger.

Observe one caution with nonverbal communication: Look for *clusters of behavior* rather than only one action. If, for example, you ask TOS, "Is this your best price?" and TOS folds his arms, this doesn't necessarily mean he's being defensive or lying. Maybe the room is cold, or he simply is comfortable sitting that way. If, however, he suddenly folds his arms, moves in his seat, clears his throat, and starts blinking rapidly, then probe this situation further.

Exhibit 5-3 compares verbal and nonverbal communication

Exhibit 5-3. A multicultural comparison of negotiating communication patterns.

Behavior	Japanese	Americans	Brazilians
Verbal Communication			
Conversational overlaps (number per 10 minutes)	12.6	10.3	28.6
Nonverbal Communication			
Silent periods (number of periods greater than 10 seconds, per 30 minutes)	5.5	3.5	0
Facial gazing/direct eye contact (minutes per 10-minute period)	1.3	3.3	5.3
Touching (not including handshaking, per 30 minutes)	0	0	4.7

Source: Based on John Graham, "The Influence of Culture on Business Negotiations," *Journal of International Business Studies,* vol. XVI, no. 1 (Spring 1985).

patterns among American, Japanese, and Brazilian negotiators. In verbal communication, American negotiators tend to have about the same number of conversational overlaps (interruptions) as the Japanese, but far fewer than Brazilians. Nonverbally, American negotiators tend to be silent less than the Japanese, but more than Brazilians, and they sustain eye contact more than the Japanese, but less than Brazilians. The Brazilian negotiators do far more touching than their American or Japanese counterparts.

International negotiators must continually ask what kind of verbal and nonverbal images their foreign counterparts grasp, and what kind of words and actions convey these images. "Holy cow" might be an appropriate exclamation in Chicago, but not in India, where a literal translation would be likely—and, of course, offensive, in a culture where cows are sacred to many.[5] A hearty

pat on the back to Bubba in Houston might indicate ⌐
but it would be perceived as overbearing pushiness to ⌐uresh in
New Delhi.

How Negotiations Differ From Region to Region

We have just examined four factors that differ among cultures. As
illustrated in Exhibit 5-4, these cultural factors impact the six aspects of the international negotiating process: (1) pace of the negotiations; (2) negotiating strategies; (3) emphasis on personal relationships; (4) emotional aspects; (5) decision making; and (6)
contractual and administrative factors.

Let's now review each of these six factors. They lay the foundation for how you will specifically approach negotiations in various parts of the world.

Pace

The negotiating process is shorter in the United States than in
most other cultures. Exhibit 5-5 illustrates the different negotiating paces at work. American negotiators typically invest little time
in orientation and fact-finding as compared with their international counterparts. American negotiators want to get down to
business, while their international counterparts may take additional time to build relationships or to reduce the ambiguity
associated with this stranger (i.e., you, the U.S. negotiator).
American negotiators tend to spend more of their time than TOS
in the resistance stage: debating, posturing, and taking positions.
Reformulation of strategies, hard bargaining and decision making, and agreement are often truncated by U.S. negotiators as a
result of factors such as organizational time pressures and a desire
to "get on with it." Agreement can languish, particularly in
group-oriented cultures where the decision making process is often slower than in the United States. Follow-up is not considered
an integral part of the bargaining process, if at all, by many U.S.
negotiators. This is more likely to be the case with TOS, particularly where strong personal and supplier relationships have been
established.

Exhibit 5-4. Cultural factors and the international negotiating process.

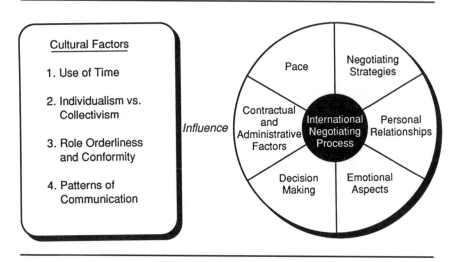

The international negotiating time frame illustrated in Exhibit 5-5 is especially representative of negotiators from the Pacific Rim and Latin America. As with all guidelines, however, there are important exceptions. Australian, Swiss, British, and Singaporean negotiators, for example, practice rapid-paced negotiations much like those in the United States.

Negotiating Strategies

The negotiating strategies you employ—which have to do with your overall approach to the negotiation and include such issues as opening offers, the formality of your approach, how you deal with differences, and concession making—also differ from region to region.

The opening offer tends to be very close to the final settlement in some countries, such as Australia and Sweden, where haggling back and forth is not part of everyday business. Your opening offer in Sydney need not normally be as high (as a seller) or low (as a buyer) as in some other locations. In other countries,

Exhibit 5-5. A comparison between time frames for American negotiators engaged in typical domestic and international negotiations.

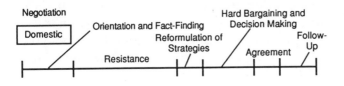

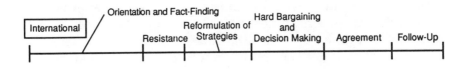

such as Russia, Egypt, and China, the opening offer tends to be far away from the final settlement. It would be wise to leave yourself a lot of room to negotiate in Cairo, where haggling is a way of life.

Another difference in strategy lies with the degree of formality in your negotiating approach. Specific, well-organized, data-oriented presentations are expected in Germany, the United Kingdom, Switzerland, and Japan. It would probably be a good idea to use color slides rather than transparencies in a formal presentation in these countries. An emphasis on broad concepts would be much more effective in other countries, such as those in Latin America or the Middle East.

Cultures also vary in the way they deal with differences. On one end of the spectrum is the expressive, demonstrative approach that one encounters in the Middle East. Beryl York, a New York–based management consultant who deals regularly with Egyptian companies, notes, "A disagreement with Middle Easterners can be quite an event. The individual might almost scream, wave his arms, sigh loudly in amazement at your intransigence— you name it. This is really nothing to take personally, however.

Overstatement and emotion are their normal forms of expression when they want to make a point." On the other hand, in other cultures one finds an understated, unexpressive approach to dealing with differences. Just getting TOS to tell you "no" directly would take a Herculean effort in Pacific Rim cultures where surface harmony is of paramount importance. In this latter case, don't let the placid approach to dealing with differences fool you: TOS may be every bit as tough or resilient as another negotiator with a more direct style.

Concessions are a necessary part in the give and take of negotiations, regardless of culture. International negotiating researchers Donald and Rebecca Hendon studied concession patterns across cultures and found that concession patterns varied widely. An American negotiator, for example, concedes in a pattern much different from a Taiwanese, Singaporean, Thai, or Indian negotiator. Let's see how you would go about making concessions. Given the facts and these concession patterns, which one is most appealing to you?

Facts: The following table lists seven concession patterns. Assume that your boss has told you that you can give away $100 during your next negotiation session. The other side doesn't know how much you have to give away, or even if you have anything at all to give away. Assume that the negotiating session lasts one hour. Four times during that hour you have an opportunity to give away all or part of the $100 to the other side. Please ignore how much you get from TOS in return when you are doing this exercise.

Directions: Circle the way you like best of giving away $100 worth of concessions.

Number	Time Periods			
	1	2	3	4
1	$25	$25	$25	$25
2	50	50	0	0
3	0	0	0	100
4	100	0	0	0
5	10	20	30	40
6	40	30	20	10
7	50	30	25	−5

If you were like most U.S. negotiators, you chose number 3, saving your concession until the end.

Hendon and Hendon found that three distinct concession patterns emerged among countries. The first is a "hard-nosed" pattern (Number 3), chosen by negotiators from the United States, South Africa, and Brazil, where negotiators concede grudgingly. The second pattern, one of "de-escalation" (Number 6), was chosen by negotiators from Australia, New Zealand, Taiwan, and Thailand. These negotiators are generous at first, then taper off, perhaps sending the message that "the well is getting drier and drier." The third pattern was one of "escalation" (Number 5), preferred by negotiators from Indonesia, the Philippines, India, and Kenya. These negotiators tend to begin with a low amount and increase it at each negotiating session.[6]

Meeting the needs of one's opponent is critical to any successful negotiation, yet not all domestic or international negotiators look for win-win solutions to the negotiation. Some negotiators use negotiating "games," or unfair tactics, where a hidden agenda or subterfuge is at work in order to "win" at your expense. Exhibit 5-6 summarizes typical negotiating games and appropriate responses to counteract them. The recommended responses are generally excellent methods for addressing the stated tactics. If you suspect that your negotiating counterpart has dubious intentions, for example, certainly it makes sense to ask for details and to double-check his or her facts and positions, regardless of the culture involved.

Dealing with negotiating games is more complex internationally than it is domestically. The same behavior can have varied meanings in different cultures. In the case of dubious intentions mentioned above, *how* one goes about asking for details could be critical. In New York, you might say, "Fred, let's review your numbers again. I'm having trouble making them add up to mine." Such directness would almost surely create new obstacles in Osaka or Jakarta, where "loss of face" would be a big issue.

Effective international negotiators must also be careful not to misread behavior from TOS. In Rio de Janeiro, TOS may be forthcoming with few details as to their proposed financial responsibility in a joint venture. This might be perceived as a dubious

(text continues on page 84)

Exhibit 5-6. Negotiating games TOS might use.

Tactic	Example (Ex) and Recommended Response (R)
Deliberate Deception	Lies of commission or omission by TOS.
Phony facts	R: Unless you have good reason to trust someone, don't.
Ambiguous authority	R: "All right. We'll treat it as a joint draft to which neither side is committed."
Dubious intentions	R: Ask for details and double-check TOS's facts and positions.
Psychological Warfare	Tactics designed to make you feel uncomfortable so that you will have a subconscious desire to end the negotiation as soon as possible.
Stressful situation	Ex: No place to talk; room too hot or cold. R: Acknowledge it and address the situation.
Personal attacks	Ex: Opponent comments on your clothes or appearance ("You look a little tired from your trip"), your status (by making you wait or interrupting you), or your intelligence (making you repeat things), or makes too much or too little eye contact. R: Acknowledging it usually ends it (e.g., "John, I'd like to finish my sentence.")
Pressure Tactics	Bargaining tactics designed to structure a situation so that only one side can effectively make concessions.
Refusal to negotiate	Ex: TOS says he's ending the negotiation.

	R:	Ask why he refuses to negotiate. Suggest alternatives (e.g., negotiate through third parties, negotiate in private).
Extreme demands	Ex:	TOS has such a high demand that you feel pressured into a concession to appear reasonable.
	R:	Ask why they feel their demand (e.g., price) is reasonable. Bring the tactic to their attention.
Escalating demands	Ex:	Making one concession and then adding new demands or reopening old demands.
	R:	Call the tactic to their attention and then take a break while you consider which issues you are willing to continue to negotiate.
Hardheaded partner	Ex:	"I would agree, but my partner (e.g., boss) won't."
	R:	Get it in writing and/or negotiate directly with the hardheaded partner.
Calculated delay	Ex:	Waiting for the eleventh hour.
	R:	Make the delaying tactic explicit and negotiate about it. Also create objective deadlines (such as starting to negotiate with another company).
Take it or leave it	Ex:	This is brinksmanship—a "my way or no way" approach.
	R:	Ignore it. Or, explicitly recognize it, let them know what they have to lose if no agreement is reached, and look for a face-saving way for them to back off from using this tactic.

Source: Adapted from Roger Fisher, William Ury, and Bruce Patton, *Getting to Yes: Negotiating Agreement Without Giving In* (New York: Penguin, 1991), and Nancy J. Adler, *International Dimensions of Organizational Behavior,* 2nd ed. (Boston: Kent Publishing, 1990).

intention by a Cleveland-based negotiator, who wonders, "Why are these people so secretive? What are they trying to hide?" To the Brazilian negotiators, a detailed level of financial involvement might seem less important that other issues. No attempt at a cover-up is intended. Understanding the different patterns of communication is important in determining which behaviors are intended games and which are unintended expressions of a culture's normal behavior patterns.

There are six ways for you to counteract negotiating games or unfair tactics:

1. Don't use them yourself.
2. Recognize them when TOS uses them.
3. Explicitly point them out and negotiate about their use (i.e., establish the "rules of the game").
4. Know the cost of walking out if the other party refuses to negotiate fairly.
5. Recognize that tactics that may appear unfair to you may be acceptable to people from another culture.
6. Recognize that tactics that may appear fair to you may be unacceptable to people from another culture.[7]

A tactic perceived is no longer a tactic.

> Herb Cohen, author
> of *You Can Negotiate Anything*

Emphasis on Personal Relationships

A key aspect of building any relationship is trust, and international negotiating is no exception. In fact, in order to be a world-class negotiator, you must build trust with TOS. This is not an easy task. The lack of trust and credibility is greater in international business negotiations, largely because of stereotypes, biases, and uncertainty about TOS. Think of how you would feel in this situation. You've been in Taipei for negotiations on your new joint venture. Your first meeting has been in progress for two hours and seems to be proceeding quite well—if slowly—in English. Your Taiwanese counterparts have been friendly, but pretty much expressionless. Then suddenly, the five members of the Taiwanese bargaining team begin talking to each other in animated Chinese, with jovial, approving expressions on their faces. This goes on for five minutes. You might begin thinking, "What are they talking about? What's the big secret? I don't want to be paranoid, but I wonder if I'm about to get hosed and don't even know it." This might be a normal reaction, yet expressing these feelings to TOS would almost surely damage the relationship. The Taiwanese team may be merely engaging in a dialogue among themselves to understand your position better. Patience on your part is probably justified.

Building a good relationship is critical even if you are dealing with negotiators from cultures that are relatively standoffish, such as those from Switzerland, Germany, or Great Britain. The best way to build a relationship with a German negotiator is to respect the emotional distance and get down to business before too long. As for Great Britain, a British management consultant notes, "My idea of a good negotiating relationship is one where the other party is friendly, doesn't get extremely personal, and knows his business." With these people, you are still building relationships—but relationships that are geared to their cultures.

Emotional Aspects

Emotional aspects deal with sensitivity, the degree of emotions, and loyalty. Sensitivity, too, is culturally defined. In the United States, it is normally associated with the female gender. Empathy for others' feelings, for example, is more often attributed to women, while displays of emotion such as crying are often considered unmanly. In Latin America such behavior is viewed as more appropriate for men than it is in the United States. In other cultures, such as the Swiss and German, emotions are more subdued than among American males.

Loyalty differs among cultures according to allegiance to organizations as a whole and to whom that allegiance is given within the organization. The loyalty factor influences where you as a negotiator want to base your appeals: to the individual or to the whole company group. American negotiators complain that little loyalty exists in the United States from either organizations or their employees. Loyalty is often to oneself first, then to the organization. In other cultures, such as in Japan, Brazil, and Mexico, there is strong loyalty to organizations. This organizational loyalty may be directed to owners (such as in Brazil) or to the group as a whole (as in Japan). Bob Coshland, an international manager for a California company that sells high-performance lubricants, sees this concept at work in Pacific Rim negotiations: "When I'm in South Korea, I try to remember to emphasize how the sale will be really good for Hyundai as a whole. They are proud of their company and this means a lot to them. Try this approach in Boston or Minneapolis and I don't think you'd get very far."

Decision Making

The way negotiators make decisions also differs from culture to culture. As a result, before you begin a negotiation it is important for you to determine the way your negotiating counterpart makes decisions. We evaluate decisions in terms of their overall objective (good of the group versus the individual), the overall method (spontaneous versus planned), the emphasis on the group or team, the emphasis on face-saving, and the emphasis of special interest groups that influence decisions. Exhibit 5-7 compares two different approaches to a typical five-step decision-making model. In Variation A, typified by U.S. negotiators, change is accepted, facts are gathered for future-oriented alternatives, and individuals make fast decisions. In Variation B, the status quo is a more acceptable frame of reference, ideas are gathered in relation to a historical base, and decisions are slowly implemented at the group level. Indonesian and Malaysian negotiators tend to make decisions more in line with Variation B than A.

Knowing how your counterpart makes decisions is vital to help gauge the approach you should take to persuade TOS. Cornering an individual Indonesian negotiator to convince him to make a quick decision by showing him detailed data would al-

Exhibit 5-7. Cultural differences in decision making.

Five Steps in Decision Making	Cultural Variations	
	A	*B*
1. Problem Recognition	*Problem solving* Situation should be changed	*Situation accepting* Some situations should be accepted, not changed
2. Information Search	*Gather facts*	*Gather ideas and possibilities*
3. Construction of Alternatives	*New, future-oriented alternatives*	*Focus includes past, present, and future alternatives*
4. Choice	*Individuals make decisions* Decisions made quickly Decision rule: Is it true or false?	*Groups make decisions* Decisions made slowly Decision rule: Is it good or bad?
5. Implementation	*Fast* Managed from the top Responsibility of one person	*Slow* Involves participation at all levels Responsibility of the group

Source: Adapted from Nancy J. Adler, *International Dimensions of Organizational Behavior,* 2nd ed. (Boston: Kent Publishing, 1990).

most surely lead to disarray in the negotiation. A German or Swiss negotiator, on the other hand, might thank you for the interest you have shown in carefully detailing your data, and the attention you are giving to the time constraints involved.

Special interest groups play a routine part of decision making in many cultures. In Latin America, for example, the influence from special interest groups such as government agencies is expected and condoned. Michael Kane, a New Orleans–based management consultant who works extensively in Latin America, puts it this way: "There is a system of reciprocity at work in much of Latin America. It is seen as proper and ethical for government parties to exercise influence on behalf of their party members. Special access to government ministries, for example, is likely only for a businessperson who is aligned with the party in power." Ted Cline, an engineering and construction executive who deals regularly with Saudi Arabian firms, sees a similar situation there: "Unless you do your homework, negotiations can be quite complicated because you're not always sure whom you're dealing with. Somebody's brother-in-law at one of the government ministries can really help or hurt a deal. Be aware that you are dealing with factions that may help or hurt your cause."

A Discussion of Japanese Decision Making

Japanese manager: Why do Americans make decisions so quickly? I cannot. Proper decisions take time. I want to know everything my boss knows about a negotiation or project, and I want my boss to know everything I know.

Acuff: What about people on your work team?

Japanese manager: I want everybody to be informed.

Acuff: Is this process slow?

Japanese manager: Oh yes. Very slow, but very effective. Everybody knows what to do.

Source: Discussion between the author and a Japanese manager on a two and one-half year assignment to the United States.

Contractual and Administrative Factors

Finally, negotiations differ from region to region according to contractual and administrative factors. These differences express themselves in the need for an agent, degree of contract specificity, degree of bureaucracy, and need for an agenda at meetings.

The need for agents or local representatives differs from country to country. Agents in Japan can be helpful in such areas as making introductions to key people, providing translations, and resolving sensitive areas of the negotiation.[8] Some areas, such as Canada or the United Kingdom, where information on local business is more readily available, justify only a more limited role of an agent. Here are ten specific ways you may want to use an agent or local representative:

1. To introduce you to key people
2. For information on local negotiation practices
3. To translate the dialogue during the negotiation
4. As a go-between during sensitive areas of the negotiation
5. For special knowledge about products or services in the host country
6. To assist in developing market strategies
7. For government, customer, and public relations.
8. To resolve problems with import regulations or permits
9. To assist in arranging financing
10. For collections

A technical dimension of international business negotiations lies with contractual considerations. There are significant differences in various "families" of law: Roman-based law, case-based law, socialist law, and Islamic law. You needn't be an expert in all these different legal approaches. It is important, however, that you are aware that key differences do exist between U.S. case-based law and other legal systems. Regardless of the legal approach involved, international agreements are more likely to be committed to paper than are domestic agreements. This is due to differences in expectations and language—even after an agreement has been reached—and to a low degree of trust between the parties. Furthermore, you will be required to write contracts in the local languages of countries such as Germany, Belgium, Spain, India, and Pakistan.[9]

Misters Lo and Mo

Many feel that having a contract with the Chinese is a joke because, when you get right down to it, the Chinese do not view the contract as binding. I have even heard them say, "So what are you going to do, sue the Chinese government?" Even if a contract were negotiated in good faith with Mr. Lo, when Mr. Mo comes in to replace Mr. Lo, he might say, "Well, you signed the contract with Mr. Lo, not me. So to me this contract is void." I have seen this even if the contract was supposed to be binding for another five years.

Manager of contracts administration for a global payment services franchise

---

Your ability to get information is also influenced by the country involved. U.S. managers are accustomed to getting the information they need when they need it. Not so in many other cultures. If you are in countries such as Thailand, Nigeria, Poland, or Indonesia, you must do some real scrambling to get profile information on customers, competitors, the economy, suppliers, distributors, agents, import/export laws, and other routine data that U.S. negotiators take for granted.

The amount of bureaucracy in organizations also differs considerably from country to country. American managers sometimes complain about the red tape in their organizations. But whatever obstacles may be encountered in the United States are relatively manageable compared with countries like India or Russia, where even the most basic decisions can get bogged down for months in paperwork and confusing lines of authority. An American project manager notes her frustration related to an India-based project: "Prior to my trip I had requested a few critical items to follow through with a major contract. My Indian contact talked big about how well connected he was and how obtaining various governmental permits would be no problem. However, when I got to India, no permits were obtained. Of course, there were plenty of excuses. This is very typical when doing business in India."

Agendas are considered good business in the United States—a courtesy that provides participants a preview of key topics and focus for the discussion. In some countries, such as Mexico, Venezuela, and Saudi Arabia, an agenda is viewed as overly structured and restrictive.

Exhibit 5-8 summarizes the aspects of international negotiating that we have just discussed.

Exhibit 5-8. A summary of factors affecting international business.

1. Pace of Negotiations

2. Negotiating Strategies
   - Opening offers vis-à-vis final settlement
   - Presentation of issues (e.g., one at a time versus in a group)
   - Presentations (e.g., formality, level of detail)
   - Dealing with differences (e.g., argumentative, conciliatory)
   - Concession behavior

3. Emphasis on Personal Relationships

4. Emotional Aspects
   - Sensitivity
   - Degree of emotions
   - Loyalty (e.g., degree and to whom)

5. Decision Making
   - Overall method (e.g., amount of authority)
   - Areas of emphasis (e.g., logic, concepts)
   - Emphasis on group/team
   - Emphasis on face-saving
   - Influence of special interests on decision makers

6. Contractual and Administrative Factors
   - Need for an agent
   - Degree of contract specificity
   - Degree of paperwork/bureaucracy
   - Need for an agenda

Gender Issues in Global Business Negotiations

Workplace gender issues are increasingly sensitive in the United States and are even more complicated internationally. There are many countries where customs, attitudes, and religion are hostile to women in business, and there is no question that international business negotiations are still dominated by men. Resistance to international businesswomen comes from American firms as well as from foreign counterparts. When Carla Hills was first nominated for her job as U.S. trade representative in the Bush administration, one senator wondered whether she would appear as rigorous as the "tough" men who had preceded her.[10] Women account for only 5 percent of U.S. expatriate managers, though many more are sent on brief assignments, according to Banu Golesorkhi, the director of assessment and research at Moran, Stahl & Boyer International, a Colorado-based intercultural training and consulting firm. According to a survey of seventy American multinational companies, 80 percent of respondents said there were disadvantages to sending a woman on an international assignment. Exhibit 5-9 illustrates the variety of concerns expressed by U.S. companies regarding expatriate businesswomen. These reasons range from concerns about technical capabilities to host-country prejudices and family issues. Yet 93 percent of the companies that had female expatriates responded that women had been very effective in their international assignments. This same study found that when women are assigned internationally, there is a wide difference among locations: 54 percent to locations in Europe, 24 percent to Asia and the Pacific, 9 percent to Canada, and only 5 percent to Latin America.

The laws of a country are not always clear indications of how women are treated in actual practice. In Russia, for example, businesswomen are legally equal to men, but there is less parity among the genders in decision-making positions. In Sweden, on the other hand, where women make up almost half the work force (48 percent), there is equal rights legislation and men share home and work responsibilities—a situation that is reflected in the business world. A manager for the Swedish company Ewos Aquaculture illustrates this point: "Remember that your male counterpart might have to get the children from the day care center at 5:00

Exhibit 5-9. Reasons given by U.S. companies for not sending women on expatriate assignments.

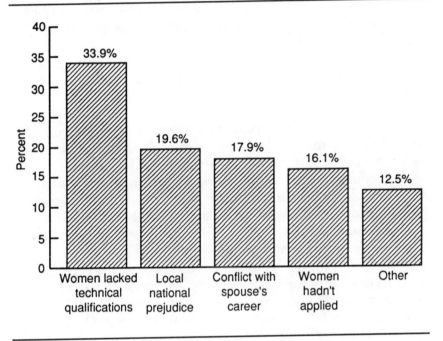

Source: "Status of American Female Expatriate Employees," Moran, Stahl & Boyer International, 1988.

P.M. If the meeting is supposed to end promptly at 4:30 P.M., this could be the reason." Generally, the genders are less equal in less developed countries. The Chinese, for example, continue to offer congratulations on the birth of a son; the birth of a daughter draws condolences.[11]

While it is important to consider the sexist attitudes of the host country, remember that what may be an unacceptable business role for local women in the host country may differ for women negotiators from the United States. An American businesswoman is likely to be seen first as a "foreign executive" and as an "American" than as a "woman" who may have a restricted role in the local society. In Spain, Venezuela, India, and Japan, for example, the "glass ceiling" for businesswomen is quite low: Few women are able to penetrate key professional or managerial jobs.

However, an American woman can be an effective negotiator in these countries, though the challenges may be formidable. Some women have adopted the slogan, "Think like a man, act like a lady, and work like a dog" as their guiding principle for international business conduct.

Here are practical tips for international businesswomen offered by Marlene L. Rossman, an international marketing consultant:

- Especially in developing countries, the fact that you look different from the locals helps your clients to see you as an "executive" rather than a "woman."
- If you are negotiating in a country where women are quite repressed, have a local male who is trusted and respected introduce you to the other party: "This is Linda Smith, our vice-president of finance. She will be handling the financing for our joint venture."
- If such a local person isn't available, ask a senior person from your home office to introduce you by telephone or in a letter: "Please give Joyce Trautman your usual cooperation. She will be responsible for Acme's interest in her discussions with you."
- When you enter a meeting room, stand tall even if you're only five feet high. Your height is unimportant; it's your posture that gives clues about your expertise and your general feeling about yourself.

Rossman also suggests that a woman take advantage of the fact that, as a professional businesswoman, you are an unknown quantity in many countries. She relates the story of a client in Milan, Italy, who "lit up like a Christmas tree when he saw that M. Rossman was a woman and spoke some Italian. He said he was expecting a tall man in a baggy suit and heavy oxfords who couldn't pronounce his name, wore a college ring, and shook his hand so hard that the crest of the ring imprinted on his finger."[12]

Many international businesswomen have found that they were able to overcome initial barriers by ably demonstrating their expertise. Susan Cherion, a manager who negotiates communications contracts in many parts of the world, relates her experience in Argentina: "I have found that Argentine businessmen prefer to do business with other men, but once they realize that I am competent and I have some authority to make decisions, we are able to establish excellent working relationships."

Global business negotiations are indeed different from domestic negotiations. For all the many challenges, however, there are also opportunities for you to achieve your goals when you follow some key guidelines. Let's now review more skills that will make you a world-class negotiator.

Notes

1. S. G. Redding, "Results-Orientation and the Orient: Individualism as a Cultural Determinant of Western Managerial Techniques," *International HRD Annual* 1 (February 1985: 45–60.
2. William B. Gudykunst and Young Yun Kim, *Communicating With Strangers: An Approach to Intercultural Communication* (New York: Random House, 1984), p. 131.
3. Ibid., pp. 12–13.
4. Lennie Copeland and Lewis Griggs, *Going International* (New York: Random House, 1985), p. 100.
5. Christophe DuPont, "International Business Negotiations," in Victor A. Kremenyuk, ed., *International Negotiation* (San Francisco: Jossey-Bass, 1991), p. 336.
6. Donald W. Hendon and Rebecca Angeles Hendon, *World-Class Negotiating: Dealmaking in the Global Marketplace* (New York: Wiley, 1990), pp. 25–33.
7. Nancy J. Adler, *International Dimensions of Organizational Behavior*, 2nd ed. (Boston: Kent Publishing, 1990), pp. 183–184.
8. Jeffrey Z. Rubin, "The Actors in Negotiation," in Victor A. Kremenyuk, ed., *International Negotiation* (San Francisco: Jossey-Bass, 1991), pp. 93–94.
9. Copeland and Griggs, *Going International*, p. 100.
10. Jolie Solomon, "Women, Minorities, and Foreign Postings," *Wall Street Journal*, June 2, 1989, p. B1.
11. Dusko Doder, "The Old Sexism in the New China," *U.S. News & World Report* (April 24, 1989): 37.
12. Based on discussions with Marlene L. Rossman. See also Marlene L. Rossman, *International Business of the 90s: A Guide to Success in the Global Market* (New York: Praeger, 1990), pp. 133–141.

Chapter 6

World-Class Negotiating Strategies

If I listen, I have the advantage: if I speak, others have it.

From the Arabic

• Ten Negotiating Strategies That Will Work Anywhere

There are many negotiating strategies that tend to work very well in one culture but are ineffective in other cultures. A case in point is the Miami-based project manager who put together a very detailed, thorough, research-oriented proposal and presentation for his Brazilian client. "I felt good that we had done our homework," he later noted. "I was very disappointed, however, to find that the Brazilian representatives were flatly uninterested in the details I was prepared to explain. A similar approach worked extremely well in Germany only four months earlier."

In spite of the many different negotiating approaches required among cultures, there are ten strategies that tend to be effective anywhere in the world. While there may be local variations in how these strategies are applied, their basic premises remain viable. You will recognize these strategies from "the American negotiator's report card" in Chapter 4.

Ten Negotiating Strategies That Will Work Anywhere

The ten strategies that tend to be effective in negotiations throughout the world are as follows:

1. Plan the negotiation.
2. Adopt a win-win approach.
3. Maintain high aspirations.
4. Use language that is simple and accessible.
5. Ask lots of questions, then listen with your eyes and ears.
6. Build solid relationships.
7. Maintain personal integrity.
8. Conserve concessions.
9. Be patient.
10. Be culturally literate and adapt negotiating strategies to the host country environment.

Strategy 1: Plan the Negotiation

Everybody wants to get a good deal, to get a sizable share of the pie, and to feel good about the negotiation. Everybody wants to be a winner. Yet not everyone is willing to do the homework necessary to achieve these ends. In Chapter 2, we discussed the essential steps necessary to plan your negotiation: (1) identify all the issues; (2) prioritize the issues; (3) establish a settlement range; and (4) develop strategies and tactics. Make this preparation a habit and you will set the stage for getting what you want.

There are ofter factors to consider prior to global negotiations. You can use the Tune-Up Checklist to ensure that you put yourself in the strongest possible position before the negotiation.

The Tune-Up Checklist:
Prior to the Negotiation

This is the data-gathering stage where you should get background information related to TOS, to his or her culture and its effects on the negotiating process, to TOS's organization and other potential players in the negotiation, and to the history of any past negotiations. *What do you know about:*

TOS
- [ ] Family status (e.g., married, single, children)?
- [ ] Leisure or recreational activities?
- [ ] Work habits (e.g., long hours, early to work)?
- [ ] Behavior style (e.g., perfectionist, "big picture"–oriented, task-oriented, people-oriented)?
- [ ] Number of years with current organization?
- [ ] Stability in current position?
- [ ] Overall reputation as a negotiator?
- [ ] What special interest groups might affect the negotiator?

TOS's Culture and its Effects on Negotiations
- [ ] Are meetings likely to be punctual?
- [ ] What can you expect the pace of the negotiations to be?
- [ ] How important is "saving face" likely to be?
- [ ] Are differences of opinion likely to be emotional or argumentative?
- [ ] Will TOS bring a large team?
- [ ] Will you need an agent or interpreter?
- [ ] Should you prepare a formal agenda?

TOS's Organization
- [ ] What is the organization's main product or service?
- [ ] What is its past, present, and projected financial status?
- [ ] What organizational problems exist (e.g., downsizing, tough competition)?
- [ ] Who is TOS's boss, and what do you know about him or her?
- [ ] Is the organization under any time pressures?

Past Negotiations
- [ ] What were the subjects of past negotiations?
- [ ] What were the main obstacles and outcomes of the negotiations?
- [ ] What objections were raised?
- [ ] What strategies and tactics were used by TOS?
- [ ] How high were the initial offers compared with the eventual settlement?
- [ ] How was the outcome achieved, and over what period of time?

There are many ways to plan negotiations. One study identified five approaches skilled negotiators share when planning their negotiations:

1. They consider twice as wide a range of action options and outcomes as do less skilled negotiators.

2. They spend over three times as much attention on trying to find common ground with TOS.
3. They spend more than twice as much time on long-term issues.
4. They set range objectives (such as a target price of $50 to $60 per unit), rather than single-point objectives (e.g., $55). Ranges give negotiators flexibility.
5. They use "issue planning" rather than "sequence planning." That is, skilled negotiators discuss each issue independently rather than in a predetermined sequence or order of issues.[1]

Strategy 2: Adopt a Win-Win Approach

We don't adopt the win-win approach simply because we are wonderful human beings. It helps us get what we want. There is a difference between how skilled and unskilled negotiators prepare for the win-win approach. Skilled negotiators, for example, tend to spend less time on defense/attack behavior and in disagreement. They also tend to give more information about their feelings and have fewer arguments to back up their position.[2] This last point may seem odd. It might seem that the more arguments one has for one's position, the better. Skilled negotiators know, however, that having only a few strong arguments is more effective than having too many arguments. With too many arguments, weak arguments tend to dilute strong arguments, and TOS often feels pressured or manipulated into settlement.

To achieve a win-win situation, you must tune in to the frequency with which TOS can identify: WIIFT ("What's In It For Them"). This means different things in different cultures. For example, in Saudi Arabia a certain amount of haggling back and forth on terms may indicate your sincerity about striking a deal. To refuse a somewhat expressive give-and-take would be an insult to many Saudi negotiators. A Dallas-based, commercial building contractor now experienced in Saudi Arabia discovered this on his first trip there. "I really got off-base in our early discussions in Riyadh. I felt we were being extremely polite as we patiently explained the reasonableness of our proposal. We fell flat on our faces. The Saudis felt we were inflexible and not serious about doing business. The next project we bid had a lot of fat built into it. We haggled back and forth for four meetings, and they ended up loving us. That's what they wanted—someone to bargain with back and forth. It showed them we cared." This negotiator adds, "I still get a knot in my stomach sometimes when I go through a Saudi negotiation, but at least I know what works now."

Fortunately for this negotiator, he quickly learned the win-win approach for his Saudi client. Yet the very idea of haggling would be a sure win-lose proposition in many parts of the world. In England, for example, it would be hard to come up with a worse idea than to engage TOS in an emotional afternoon of haggling back and forth. The British idea of win-win is a somewhat formal, procedural, and detailed discussion of the facts.

Achieving a win-win result also requires careful scrutiny of both parties' overall goals. You may be seeking short-term profit and cash flow, while your Japanese counterparts may be more interested in long-term viability. In many cases, different goals *can* lead to overall win-win results. Consider the company president negotiating a joint venture in Hungary in order to take advantage of a skilled, inexpensive work force, while her TOS is motivated to find business linkages outside Eastern Europe.

Wherever you negotiate, focusing on win-win results sharply increases your chances for success, particularly in the long term.

Strategy 3: Maintain High Aspirations

In the spring of 1978, the International Air Transport Association (IATA) discontinued its policy of airline ticket price compliance. IATA had been for many years a powerful enforcer that had maintained a firm grip on the airline ticket prices of the world's domestic and international airlines. Immediately after this announcement was made, Leroy Black, my boss, suggested I contact the airlines to determine what, if any, ticket price concessions we might extract as a result of this policy change. The Middle East Division where we worked was located in Dubai, United Arab Emirates, a small oil sheikdom adjoining Saudi Arabia. Our 3,500 workers and many of their family members collectively logged millions of air miles per year.

"That's a good idea," I remember telling Leroy. Shaving 5 or

10 percent—perhaps even 15 percent—would amount to substantial savings on our $4 million annual airline expenses. I was stunned, though, when Leroy suggested we ask for a 50 percent price decrease in ticket costs.

"Are you kidding?" I asked, quite shocked.

"I think that 50 percent is about right," Leroy said serenely.

Our first appointment was with representatives from British Airways. They told us, in a reserved, nice kind of way, to take a hike.

Then KLM, in a *not* particularly nice kind of way, suggested the same recourse as British Airways. The same with Lufthansa. "We really are being a bit chintzy on this thing," I thought to myself.

"Leroy, let's try asking for a little less and see what happens," I suggested.

"I don't know. Let's hang in there awhile longer," Leroy insisted.

Next was Alitalia. As in our appointments with the other airlines, I went through a short prologue explaining the company's position, and assertively put forth that we would like to see a 50 percent reduction in future fares. This caused quite a commotion with the Alitalia representatives, who waved their arms and with great conviction gave us several reasons why this was not possible.

"This is really a little embarrassing," I thought.

They then asked if they could privately telephone their regional headquarters staff. They returned in about ten minutes in a solemn mood.

"Mr. Acuff," one of the representatives said with a grave look on his face. "What you ask is quite impossible. The very most we can offer you is a 40 percent reduction," he said apologetically.

"Excuse me?" I asked. He repeated his offer.

"Unbelievable," I thought to myself. "Give us some time to think about it," I replied.

As soon as they were out of earshot, Leroy and I almost jumped for joy. As it turned out, this was the first of several key concessions we received from the various airlines, ranging from 15 to 45 percent discounts. British Airways, KLM, Sabena, and

Lufthansa all soon after reduced their rates well beyond my initial expectations.

This situation was a valuable lesson with regard to aspiration levels in negotiations. What at first seemed like a brash, overbearing approach to business turned out to be very positive. But was it win-win?, you ask. Didn't you just bleed the airlines at a time when they were vulnerable? Not at all. We later found out that the airlines were quite pleased with the new arrangements. They thought discounts might be greater than they were, and, of course, some of the airlines were delighted that they had negotiated better terms than their competitors.

We have all kinds of negative fantasies about high initial demands (HIDs):

"They won't like me anymore. I'll make them really mad and it will hurt the relationship."
"I'll price myself out of the market."
"Maybe we aren't being reasonable."
"This is embarrassing."

In spite of these concerns, there are compelling reasons to go for it, which are summarized in the following World-Class Tips.

World-Class Tips:
Seven Reasons Why You Should Have High Initial Demands

1. Don't take away your own power. TOS may do it to you, but don't do it to yourself.
2. HIDs teach people how to treat you.
3. They lower the expectations of TOS.
4. HIDs demonstrate your persistence and conviction.
5. You can always reduce your asking offer or demand. HIDs give you room to make concessions.
6. Remember that time is on your side. Making HIDs gives you more time to learn about your counterpart, and time heals many wounds.
7. There is an emotional imperative for TOS to beat you down. It's important for TOS to feel that they've "won."[3]

World-Class Tip 7 is especially important. Many negotiators find it hard to accept that there is an emotional imperative for TOS to beat you down. To illustrate this point, let's get in the other person's shoes to see how the TOS might feel. You are in Germany to negotiate the purchase of the Drillenzebit, a precision tool-making machine from a Munich-based firm. You say to yourself, "This time won't be like the other times. This time I'm going to do my homework—I will read appropriate industry periodicals and talk to consultants, clients, suppliers, and others who know a lot about the Germans, the German business environment, and the competitive market for precision tool-making machines." So you do your homework and begin to negotiate with the Germans for the Drillenzebit machine. When the subject of price arises, you are ready. You've got the facts, figures, and some *savoir-faire* about German negotiating practices. So you say, "Mr. Dietrich, today I'm going to offer you one price and one price only for this fine Drillenzebit machine. That final price is $74,000—that's U.S. dollars.

Dietrich looks at you for a moment and says, "Let me see if I have this right. That's $74,000—in U.S. dollars?"

"That's right," you repeat, proud that you're sticking by your guns.

"Seventy-four thousand dollars. You've got it. The machine is yours!" he beams.

How would you feel in this situation? Wonderful? Exuberant? If you are like most people, you would have a morbid, sinking feeling that you had just been taken. Your first thought would probably be. "Damn. I should have offered less." Is this reaction logical? No. You did, after all, get what you asked for. You reacted as you did because only part of your needs were met—the logical part—while the emotional part was not.

There are cultural differences as to how high our aspiration level should be with our foreign counterparts, but as a rule thumb, go for it! If you really want $30,000 for your widget machine, don't ask for $30,500. Ask for $60,000. Put TOS in the position of saying to his or her boss, "You know, this woman came in asking $60,000. This price was completely off-the-wall. Excellent negotiator that I am, I got her down to $38,000. I saved us $22,000." And if you are in a competitive bidding situation, stress the quality, service, and other aspects that make your price an excellent value.

Strategy 4: Use Language That Is Simple and Accessible

American English is filled with thousands of clichés and colloquialisms that make it very hard for others to understand. Phrases such as "getting down to brass tacks," "getting down to the nitty gritty," wanting to "zero in on problems," or "finding out where the rubber meets the road" only clog communication channels.

Don't assume that because your foreign counterpart speaks English, he or she fully understands it. This individual may know English as it was taught in school but may not be able to speak it or understand it in conversation with an American. An American executive who regularly travels to Taiwan makes this point. "When I first asked my Taiwanese client if he spoke English, he told me yes. I found out the hard way that his understanding was very elementary and that I used way too many slang expressions. We still do business together, but now I speak more slowly and simply, and I'm learning some Chinese."

This doesn't apply only to slang. Make sure you use the simplest, most basic words possible. Exhibit 6-1 provides examples of simplified words and terms you should use, even if you're speaking English.

Strategy 5: Ask Lots of Questions, Then Listen With Your Eyes and Ears

Asking good questions is vital throughout the negotiation, but particularly in the early stages. Your main goal is receiving information. Making a brilliant speech to TOS about your proposal may make you feel good, but it does far less in helping you achieve your ends than asking questions that give you data about content and the emotional needs of TOS.

Exhibit 6-2 illustrates the importance of asking questions. Skilled negotiators ask more than twice the number of questions as unskilled negotiators. They also engage in much more active listening than those who are less skilled.

There is one important consideration when asking questions:

Exhibit 6-1. Simplifying English words and terms.

Don't use this. . . .	*when this will do.*
annual premium	annual payment
accrued interest	unpaid interest
maturity date	final payment date
commence	start
utilize	use
acquaint	tell
demonstrate	show
endeavor	try
modification	change
proceed	go
per diem	daily

Don't do anything that would embarrass your international counterpart. Questions can be much more direct and open in cultures such as the United States, Canada, Australia, Switzerland, Sweden, and Germany than in Japan, Taiwan, Brazil, or Colombia, where indirectness is prized.

Judge a man by his questions rather than by his answers.

Voltaire

Effective listening is especially challenging when different cultures are involved. This can be the case even when English is the first language of TOS. Mike Apple, in American engineering and construction executive, found this to be the case in England and Scotland. Apple notes that even though English is spoken, one must listen very carefully to English and Scottish negotiators because of their dialects. "When I first got to Scotland, I wondered if some kind of challenge was in the making when a union

Exhibit 6-2. Questioning and listening in skilled and average negotiators.

Negotiating Behavior	Skilled Negotiators	Average Negotiators
Questions, as a percentage of all negotiating behavior	21.3%	9.6%
Active listening		
• Testing for understanding	9.7	4.1
• Summarizing	7.5	4.2

Source: Neil Rackham, "The Behavior of Successful Negotiators" (Reston, Va.: Huthwaite Research Group, 1976), as reported in Ellen Raider International, Inc. (Brooklyn, N.Y.) and Situation Management Systems, Inc. (Plymouth, Mass.), *International Negotiations: A Training Program for Corporate Executives and Diplomats (1982).*

negotiator told me he was going to 'mark my card.' I asked a colleague about it. As it turned out, the term is one used by Scottish golfers to explain the best approach to the course for those who haven't played there before. The union negotiator was only trying to be helpful," Apple notes. "The lesson learned here? When in doubt, ask for clarification."

If the communication pattern is from low-context countries, such as Japan, China, Saudi Arabia, Greece, or Spain, listening is even more challenging for Americans. In these cultures the message is embedded in the context of what is being said. Mike McMahon, a former managing director for National Semiconductor's Singapore plant, found Singaporeans reluctant to respond directly to questions. He notes, "I had to listen very carefully to figure out what was really on their minds."[4]

Here are some additional tips for effective listening:

- Limit your own talking.
- Concentrate on what TOS is saying.
- Maintain eye contact (but don't stare).
- Paraphrase and summarize TOS's remarks.
- Avoid jumping to conclusions. Be postjudicial, not prejudicial, regarding what TOS is saying.

- Watch for nonverbal cues.
- Listen for emotions.
- Ask for clarification: Assume differences, not similarities, if you are unsure of meaning.
- Don't interrupt.
- Pause for understanding; don't immediately fill the voids of silence.

Some of the rituals of international negotiating serve dual purposes of entertainment and information gathering. Foster Lin, director of the Taiwanese Far East Trade Service Office in Chicago, considers formal Taiwanese banquets and other entertainment as a prime opportunity to gain information on one's negotiating counterpart. Says Lin, "Entertainment demonstrates courtesy toward our foreign guests. It also helps us find out more about the individual person. Is this someone we can trust and want to do business with?" Such occasions can help you as well. Careful listening in this "offstage" time, away from the formal negotiating sessions, can give you another side to the negotiators. Use this time to gather additional data on your counterpart.

A key part of listening relates to body language. TOS may encode messages, making sophisticated, cogent arguments. However, one thing almost always happens during a moment of insecurity or deception: body movements change (e.g., the person literally squirms in his or her seat or blinks more rapidly). Also, be aware of the impact of your own nonverbal behavior. For example, if your gestures are quite expressive and TOS is from Sweden and quite reserved, tone it down a bit. Alternatively, if your facial and arm gestures are unexpressive and you are meeting a Brazilian who is very expressive, loosen up a bit—smile and use expressive hand and arm gestures.

World-Class Tips:
Five Positive Things You Can Do Without Saying a Word

1. *Smile!* It's a universal lubricant that can help you open the content of the negotiation. A genuine smile says very loudly, "I'd appreciate doing business with you."
2. *Dress appropriately and groom well.* Shined shoes, combed

hair, clean nails, and clothes appropriate for the occasion show that you respect yourself and your counterpart. It also communicates that you are worthy of your counterpart's business.

3. *Lean forward.* This communicates interest and attention in almost every culture.

4. *Use open gestures.* Crossed arms in front of your chest may be viewed as disinterest or resistance on your part. More open gestures send a signal that you are open to your counterpart's ideas.

5. *Take every opportunity to nod your head.* Don't you like it when people agree with you? Let TOS know that you are listening by this simple action.

Strategy 6: Build Solid Relationships

Stay away from value issues, which are full of potential landmines. When is the last time you won an argument on politics? On religion? That's right; you never have and you never will. Discussion of subjects such as politics, religion, race, and the role of women in the workplace will not help build a relationship with your negotiating counterpart, even if the other person brings up the subject or there is potential agreement. No matter what our particular view on these subjects, we tend to think that we have God, truth, and light on our side.

The personal relationship you develop with your counterpart provides the basis, or context, for the content portion of the negotiation. In many cultures it is the quality of the relationship more than the work accomplished that counts. There is more emphasis on building a solid personal relationship in some cultures than others. In Brazil, Japan, Greece, Spain, and Czechoslovakia, for example, a strong personal relationship almost surely precedes any deal. In other countries, such as Germany and Switzerland, the content portion of the negotiation usually precedes any substantial relationship building. In most cases, a strong relationship is critical to even short-term success. In all cases, it is critical to long-term success.

Be a pleasure to do business with. Even if you don't agree on the content part of the negotiation, you want TOS to have a positive view of you when they see you coming.

World-Class Tips:
Fifteen Statements That Will Help Build Solid Relationships
(Or at Least Keep You Out of Deep Soup)

1. "I'm very pleased to meet you."
2. "Could you tell me more about your proposal?"
3. "I have a few more questions I'd like to ask you."
4. "We might be able to consider X if you could consider Y."
5. "Let me try to summarize where we stand now in our discussion."
6. "I'm very happy to see you again."
7. "Could you tell me more about your concerns?"
8. "Let me tell you where I have a concern."
9. "I feel disappointed that we haven't made more progress."
10. "I really appreciate the progress that we've made."
11. "Thank you."
12. "Can I answer any more questions about our organization or proposal?"
13. "What would it take for us to close this deal?"
14. "I've enjoyed doing business with you."
15. "I haven't talked to you since we signed the contract. I just wanted to follow up with you to see how things are working out."

Even when you mean well, there are some terms and phrases that carry negative overtones. One study found that skilled negotiators used only 2.3 irritating words and phrases per hour in face-to-face negotiations, compared with 10.8 "irritators" per hour for average negotiators. Irritators included such phrases as "generous offer," "fair price," and "reasonable arrangement."[5] Exhibit 6-3 "is a "dirty word list" that details other phrases that tend to upset others, regardless of the culture involved.

There's another word that should be taken out of your business vocabulary: *negotiate.* Yes, we use it when discussing the sub-

Exhibit 6-3. Words and phrases to avoid.

These Words:	May provoke these reactions:
You always/You never . . .	I always, I never? Perhaps I *often* or *seldom* behave in that way, but not always or never.
What you need to understand . . .	I'll let you know if I *need* to understand it.
Be reasonable . . .	I didn't think I was being unreasonable. (*Have you ever met anyone in your whole life who told you, "I don't tend to be very reasonable, and I just thought I'd let you know?"*)
Calm down!	*If they were calm, they won't be after you tell them this!*
Needless to say . . .	Then why are you saying it?
Obviously . . .	You've somehow cornered the market on what is and is not obvious?
The fact of the matter is . . .	You know what is factual and I don't?
You can't tell me . . .	You bet I *can* tell you—that is, if you'll just listen!
Listen . . .	I may choose to listen, but I don't want to be directed to do so.
As you know . . .	Maybe I do and maybe I don't.
Most people would . . .	Are you suggesting that I'm some kind of oddball if I don't happen to agree with you?

ject, but in real-life situations, all kinds of images co
when you tell someone, "Let's negotiate this deal." ⌐ ⌐ ⌐ the
feeling that something manipulative is about to happen. Instead,
say something like. "Let's work out something that is good for
both of us" or "Let's discuss the concerns you have."

Reaching a deadlock or impasse is a common and often frustrating experience. This can happen even when both parties are
bargaining in good faith and are trying hard to reach an agreement. When you reach an impasse with TOS, take steps to break
the deadlock and yet keep the relationship strong. The following
list of World-Class Tips provides some helpful methods.

World-Class Tips:
Seventeen Ways to Break Deadlocks and Yet Keep the Relationships

1. Recap the discussion to ensure there really is a deadlock.
2. Emphasize mutual interests.
3. Stress the cost of not agreeing and situations you want to avoid.
4. Reach an agreement in principle, postponing difficult parts of the agreement.
5. Try to find out if the problem is based on something TOS isn't telling you.
6. Change the type of contract.
7. Change contract specifications or terms.
8. Add options to the contract.
9. Hold informal discussions in a different setting.
10. Make concessions that are contingent upon settling all of the issues.
11. Form a joint study committee.
12. Change a team member or team leader.
13. Discuss how both you and TOS might respond to a hy-pothetical solution, without committing either party to a course of action.
14. Tell a funny story.
15. Take a recess.
16. Consider setting a deadline for resolution. Deadlines cre-ate a sense of urgency and encourage action.
17. Be patient.

Keep in mind that both the tone and the content of the current negotiation will impact future negotiations with TOS. This is true even if you don't successfully conclude the current negotiation; sometimes you are really setting the stage for the next one. It's like arguing with the umpire in American baseball. Why do baseball managers do it? They never prevail. Aside from pleasing the crowd, the manager argues with the umpire for one simple reason—not for this call, but for the *next* call! So, too, in *your* negotiations, put markers in TOS's mind for the next time you sit down to do business. Leave him or her with two thoughts: (1) you're a good person for TOS to do business with; and (2) here are some expectations to keep in mind.

Strategy 7: Maintain Personal Integrity

A few years ago a businessman came up to me before I was about to make a speech on negotiations. He said that he was a good Christian and, as such, didn't know if he should stay for the speech since he assumed I'd be talking about scheming ways to manipulate other people. I told him that while I didn't know whether or not he should stay, negotiators who use manipulative, scheming, hidden agendas do not do very well in negotiations. He seemed somewhat shocked but relieved by my response.

Personal integrity is absolutely critical for your effectiveness as a world-class negotiator. My conviction on this point is not related to religion but to pragmatism. There are two reasons why personal integrity and trust are vital. The first reason has to do with information. No one tells you anything of importance if he or she doesn't trust you.* If you are not viewed as trustworthy, people will tell you only what they *must* tell you because of your position or title. For example, if you are trusted, after a negotiating session TOS may ask for some confidential "whisper time." She may confide in you as follows:

TOS: Look, I know we've been pressing for A, B, C, and D in there. But, off the record, what we're really interested in is only C and D.

You: But you've been really pushing hard for A and B.

*Herb Cohen talks about this effectively in his video *Persuasive Negotiating*.

TOS: I know. But if you can find a way to give us C and D, we've got a deal.

This is a rich disclosure. This is the stuff that will make you successful, not because you are technically brilliant, but because you are trusted. Risky, key data are shared with you only if your personal integrity is unquestioned.

Personal integrity is vital to building your negotiating strength for a second reason: *Issues of trust are the most difficult relationship problems to repair.* In fact, these are often irreparable. With some hard work, some skill, and a little luck, other types of relationship problems can be healed, but the trust issue hardly ever gets fixed. Think of the people you really don't trust in your professional or personal life. Is there *anything* they can do to repair the relationship and get back in your good graces? If you are like most people, the answer is "nothing."

American negotiators sometimes try to resolve issues of trust by formalizing the intent of the parties in an ironclad contract. We then hold TOS to the contract, regardless of how much we trust them. In many cultures, however, it is the person or the relationship that your counterpart trusts, not a piece of paper. Making and keeping contractual commitments is not a high priority for many of your international counterparts. Much of this view relates to the relative uncertainty felt by those from other cultures compared with Americans. Malaysians, for example, prefer to have exit clauses in their contracts in case things don't work out. They feel little control over future business events or even their country as a whole and want provisions for a respectable withdrawal should future circumstances make their compliance impossible.[6] In much of the Arab world, negotiators stress mutual trust and see themselves doing business with "the man" rather than a company or a contract.[7] In Britain, there are strong legal precedents but less reliance on formalized contracts than in the United States. Tom Wilson, a British management consultant, observes, "Detailed legal contracts are seldom the order of the day. The British feel aggrieved when outsmarted by clever contract language. Besides," he adds, "a legal decision will not enforce that for which there is no will to perform."

Building trust can be a long process, particularly in global negotiating, and it can be harmed in subtle ways. This is why you should avoid excessive use of phrases such as "to be honest with you . . ." (are you not normally honest?), "to tell you the truth . . ." (are you not normally truthful?), and "frankly . . ." (are you not usually candid?). Though TOS may not be conscious of why he or she doesn't trust you, too many of these phrases lead to a conclusion that you are not trustworthy, even if you are honest.

If you are viewed as trustworthy by TOS, protect this aspect of the negotiation at all costs. Remember, *lose the deal if you must, but keep the trust*. This will be vital for your next negotiation with TOS.

Strategy 8: Conserve Concessions

Concessions give valuable information about you, your style, and your resolve. How you use them sets the tone, not only for a current negotiation, but for future negotiations as well. Your current concession pattern teaches TOS how to treat you in the future.

Let's say you're in Budapest, involved in a tough negotiation with the Hungarians. You have traded data with them and made logical defenses of your negotiating position for five long meetings. The negotiation seems to be going nowhere. This particular negotiation is price-sensitive, and in the first meeting, you quoted $80 per unit for your product. The Hungarians have offered you $20. You know that building a good relationship is important in any negotiation. They haven't budged from the $20 since the first meeting.

In order to break the logjam, you show your good faith in working out this negotiation by making a counteroffer of $45. This, you think, shows that you mean business in resolving this issue and that you are acting in good faith. Besides, your "really asking" price is $40, and you will certainly have gone more than halfway. The Hungarians will surely do the same, and you can all conclude the session, have some vodka, and go home.

It may not work out this way. In fact, in the case related above, you can bet you are about to get clobbered. Like many negotiators, you might feel that making a concession will create goodwill or soften up TOS. Unfortunately, a much more likely scenario is that such a concession will suggest weakness on your part, make your counterpart greedy, or even make your counterpart suspicious. You must therefore be extremely careful in making concessions.

World-Class Tips:
Ten Guidelines on Making Concessions

1. Don't be the first to make a concession on an important issue.
2. Never accept the first offer.
3. Make TOS reduce a high initial demand; don't honor a high demand by making a counteroffer.
4. Make small concessions. Lower the expectation of TOS.
5. When you make concessions, make them slowly (like wine, they improve with time).
6. Make TOS feel good by making concessions of low value to you but of perceived high value to TOS.
7. Defer concessions on matters that are important to you.
8. Make contingent concessions (i.e., get something in return, or concede only on the condition that all issues be settled).
9. Celebrate the concessions you get. Don't feel guilty.
10. Don't feel that you must reciprocate every concession made to you.

The number of initial concessions differs among cultures. One study found that Japanese negotiators made fewer initial concessions per half-hour bargaining session (6.5) than did negotiators from the United States (7.1) or Brazil (9.4).[8] As a rule, the fewer the concessions, the better.

Also, beware when TOS asks for concession on the grounds of "fairness." Whenever your counterparts tell you that they want you to make a concession because their offer to you has been very "fair" or "reasonable," don't believe them. More often than not, this is a manipulative tactic to make you feel guilty.

Strategy 9: Make Patience an Obsession

Since almost every stage of a global negotiation tends to take longer than the domestic, patience is not only a virtue, but a necessity. Patience serves three vital functions: (1) It facilitates getting information from TOS; (2) it builds the relationship by sending out signals of courtesy; and (3) it increases your chances of effective concession making. Patience is linked to concession behavior because impatient negotiators tend to make both more counterproposals and more concessions. Skilled negotiators make fewer counterproposals than do less skilled negotiators.[9]

Patience may also be one of TOS's negotiating tactics, since TOS tries to wear you down with their patience. They are counting on your becoming anxious and making concessions that you otherwise wouldn't make. Don't be a victim. Take these countermeasures:

- Give yourself plenty of time.
- Relax and make yourself comfortable.
- Prepare your own people back home for a long negotiation.
- Recognize that it may be tougher on TOS than on you.
- Consider setting a deadline.

Patience, as important as it is, can be hard work. One manager from an American oil company illustrates this point in the Pacific Rim: "Negotiating in Indonesia is like drinking a thousand cups of tea—very challenging and very slow." Ted Cline, who has negotiated many large contracts in the Middle East, stresses the importance of persistence. "I tell my people: If you beat your head on the wall, it will get bloody. But if you keep constant pressure on the wall, some day it will fall down."

Strategy 10: Be Culturally Literate and Adapt the Negotiating Process to the Host Country Environment

By acquiring insight into the culture of TOS, as well as into your own cultural predispositions, you can bridge the cultural gap to become a more effective negotiator. You can be empathetic with TOS only if you understand the culture and environment in which TOS operates. Every step of the negotiating process must be seen through the lens of the host-country culture. Increasing your cultural IQ pays off in every step of the negotiating process, from the initial planning and greeting TOS right down to setting the stage for future business.

Cultural savvy takes many forms. Witness, for example, a supplier of oilfield technology that sent a program administrator to resolve the snags associated with a Russian joint venture. Despite the progress on technical details, the Russians continued to be very standoffish. Only later did the firm learn that sending a midlevel manager with the title of program administrator was an insult to the Russians, who felt that anyone with such a lowly title was unlikely to have the authority to negotiate a substantial deal, and that sending a midlevel manager was disrespectful of them. Such title and rank considerations are important to Russian negotiators. In this particular case, the firm's vice-president of international projects relates that now, when the program administrator travels to Russia, his title is revised to "managing director of special projects." The vice-president notes, "The title change makes the Russians feel like they are dealing with the right level of person, and all it costs us are new business cards."

Moira Crean, manager of contracts administration for MasterCard International, finds that cultural savvy takes the form of sensitivity to age in mainland China. "Age," she explains, "can be a key aspect in a big negotiation. Our Chinese partners have been known to dismiss a young person—let's say, a 35-year-old vice-president—and say, 'Send over the old guy.' "

Even concession making must be seen through a cultural perspective. Exhibit 6-4 illustrates different perceptions of your good intentions. The reaction to a large concession may range from pleasure (a U.S. negotiator) to dismay (a Swiss negotiator).

If you just remember the following two guidelines, you will

Exhibit 6-4. How a large concession from you might be perceived by negotiators from different countries.

Negotiators From	Likely Reaction
United States	"I gotcha."
Netherlands	"I cannot trust you."
Japan	"This has hurt the harmony."
Switzerland	"This person did not prepare well."
Saudi Arabia	"This is how business is done."

not only be culturally literate, but you will be a superb global negotiator.

1. *Adopt the Platinum Rule.* Most of us grew up with the Golden Rule or something similar: "Do unto others as you would that they do unto you." This works well when we are surrounded by people like us—whoever "us" might be. We know how to treat the other person because of shared backgrounds and traits. With our international counterparts, the Golden Rule is no longer very helpful, because how *you* want to be treated may indeed be very different from how Chin, Suresh, Ivan, Miguel, Mohammed, Isobella, or Isa wants to be treated. Instead, adopt what I call the Platinum Rule: "Do unto others as *they* would have done unto them." You might be comfortable with a firm handshake, with being direct and open, and with getting right down to business. But if the culture of TOS encourages other behaviors and your cultural savvy enables you to engage in them, you will be ahead of the competition. As you increase your comfort zone with others, so too will you increase your negotiating effectiveness.

Is there a place for common courtesy? You bet, as long as such courtesy isn't defined only on your terms. If common courtesy means a smile upon greeting or not interrupting others, this works almost anywhere. If it means inviting TOS to lunch, picking up the tab, complimenting TOS about his or her office, extending a firm handshake, or providing a gift as a token of your appreciation, then your courtesy may be another person's idea of irritating behavior. Tact has been called intelligence of the heart. In global business affairs, tact includes knowledge of the host-country culture.

2. *Conduct yourself as an effective foreigner.* The idea is not to go native,[10] but to be culturally savvy while remaining a foreigner. Don't worry about minor gaffes in the many rituals and customs associated with every culture. If your handshake is a little too firm in Rio de Janeiro, or you can't remember that phrase you learned in Polish, it is not the end of the world. TOS will normally give you an *A* for effort even if the details of the execution need a little work. Be culturally savvy, but also be authentic. If the sight of fish eyes makes you squeamish in Singapore, don't eat the fish

eyes if it means you're going to spend an hour being sick in the bathroom.

Let's now turn in Chapter 7 to some of the toughest problems you can expect to face as a global negotiator and explore strategies to deal with them.

Notes

1. Neil Rackham, "The Behavior of Successful Negotiators" (Reston, Va.: Huthwaite Research Group, 1976), as reported in Ellen Raider International, Inc. (Brooklyn, N.Y.) and Situation Management Systems, Inc. (Plymouth, Mass.), *International Negotiations: A Training Program for Corporate Executives and Diplomats* (1982).
2. Ibid.
3. See Phil Sperber, *Fail-Safe Business Negotiating: Strategies and Tactics for Success* (Englewood Cliffs, N.J.: Prentice-Hall, 1983), pp. 40–41; and Roy J. Lewicki and Joseph A. Litterer, *Negotiation* (Homewood, Ill.: Richard D. Irwin, 1985), pp. 75–79.
4. Frank L. Acuff, "What It Takes to Succeed in Overseas Assignment," *National Business Employment Weekly* (August 25, 1991): 17–18.
5. Rackham, "Behavior of Successful Negotiators."
6. Nancy J. Adler, *International Dimensions of Organizational Behavior* (Boston: Kent Publishing, 1986), p. 175.
7. Philip R. Harris and Robert T. Moran, *Managing Cultural Differences*, 2nd ed. (Houston: Gulf Publishing, 1987), p. 474.
8. John Graham, "The Influence of Culture on Negotiations," *Journal of International Business Studies*, vol. XVI, no. 1 (Spring 1985): 81–96.
9. Rackham, "Behavior of Successful Negotiators," p. 180.
10. Adler, *International Dimensions*, p. 187.

Chapter 7

The Six Most Difficult Problems Faced by International Negotiators (and How to Deal With Them)

Remember not only to say the right thing at the right time in the right place, but far more difficult still, to leave unsaid the wrong thing at the wrong moment.

Benjamin Franklin

- Overcoming Culture Shock
- Negotiating with the Boss and Headquarters Staff Back Home
- Dealing with Your Own Negotiating Team
- Resolving Bribery and Questionable Payment Issues
- Establishing an International Joint Venture
- Your Place or Mine? Where to Hold the Negotiation

Any negotiation presents problems, but there are unique challenges in international business negotiations. It is important that you learn about these challenges *before* they occur and then take preventive measures. Specifically, there are six key problems that are most likely to affect you as an international negotiator. Some of these problems are unique to international business negotiations (such as establishing an international joint venture), while others can occur domestically but are magnified internationally (such as dealing with a bribe). Let's review the impact of these problems and examine the action steps you must take to overcome them.

Six Key Problems

Problem 1: Overcoming Culture Shock

Culture shock occurs when we do not have the familiar signposts of how to conduct ourselves.* These signposts involve both our professional and personal lives and often guide us in activities that we normally take for granted. In international business negotiations, these might include how to shake hands; what forms of address to use; to whom your comments should be addressed; how direct to be with TOS; determining if TOS is really saying "no" when they use the word "yes"; and what, if anything, should be discussed over dinner.

Most individuals who work internationally go through four phases of adjustment to other cultures and negotiating situations. These phases of growth can be very troublesome and perplexing, but they are a normal and expected part of the intercultural journey. Each phase has its own unique characteristics and challenges. Let's review the four phases.

1. *Predeparture anticipation and enchantment at the new location.* The first phase is a time of great excitement and anxiety. There is excitement about the new opportunity to work in a foreign culture, coupled with anxiety about adjusting to the new situation. There is a desire to plunge in and enjoy every aspect of the host culture. You read about the surroundings, history, and architecture, and maybe take a tour as you celebrate differences between the host culture and the United States. You have a somewhat naive acceptance of the host culture without much critical analysis

*Dr. Michael Kane, a management consultant based in New Orleans, was particularly helpful in his thinking and writing on culture shock.

of its shortcomings. You feel buoyed by optimism about doing business with TOS. You begin thinking, "People all over are basically the same."

2. *Awakening.* This is known as the wake-up phase, when you begin slowing realizing that people from different cultures are not in fact the same as Americans. Annoyances begin to grind emotionally. For example, in South America it seems that your negotiating counterparts are never on time for meetings. They are overly friendly, always grabbing you and hugging you like you were their best friend; they seem more interested in talking about their brandy than about the negotiating issues; they won't give you straight answers to your questions; and four of them talk at once. It takes irritatingly long to get a long-distance call through back to the United States, and when you do, the price seems outrageous. In this phase, you come face-to-face with your own ethnocentrism. Initial culture shock can become permanent unless acknowledged and resolved.

3. *Disillusionment.* In this phase you become very specific about what is wrong with the host culture and with the individuals with whom you must deal. You begin thinking that if only you could extricate yourself gracefully from the negotiation, you would happily board an airplane in the morning and go home.

4. *Realization and productivity.* The final phase is characterized by serenity and a realization of what can and cannot be accomplished in the host culture. You realize that the host culture has existed in certain cases for centuries before your arrival—and will likely continue after your departure—and you begin to work creatively and enjoyably among its challenges and opportunities.

The time frame of these phases differs from person to person and may endure from one extended trip to the host country to several trips.

Action Steps for Dealing with Culture Shock

▪ *Find a cultural mentor.* Ask for advice from others who have negotiating experience in the areas of the world where you will be doing business. Talk with both people who have had successful negotiating experiences there and those who have had bad experiences there. In this way you can get a balanced view of the host country and its negotiators. The sooner you get this type of information, the better you will be when it comes to the later phases of adjustment.

- *Be flexible and patient with yourself and those in the host culture.* Events, services, issues, mechanical devices—in short, practically all aspects of your life—are not going to flow as smoothly and predictably as they do back home.

- *Withhold judgment about the new culture and its people.* Rather than being prejudicial about your new environment, be postjudicial. Try not to go overboard with either positive or negative reactions.

- *Recognize that the negative feelings you may have at the "awakening" and "disillusionment" stages are normal and appropriate for these phases of adjustment.* Annoyances, irritations, and letdowns are to be expected. After all, you have spent little or no time in the host-country environment.

- *Keep a sense of humor about yourself and your situation.* This doesn't mean joke telling, but rather, keeping a sense of proportion and a positive attitude about whatever culturally irritating situation you find yourself in.

- *Reduce stress by being as self-sufficient as possible with regard to business services.* "Routine business services" is an oxymoron in some countries. In mainland China, for example, there are often no secretaries, typewriters, copiers, faxes, and other business fundamentals. There may also be a confidentiality issue in many host-country business settings, so don't depend on TOS to type your bargaining position or other similar material. Take along a portable personal computer (with appropriate electrical adapters) for your notes, strategies, and other uses, or arrange for service at a hotel or other professional services provider where possible.

- *Process what has happened, and draw lessons for growth from your experience.* Learn from your cultural experiences, both good and bad ones. When you make mistakes, try to smile and learn from them. Continue to ask, "What is working well, and not well? And why is this the case?"

Problem 2: Negotiating With the Boss and Headquarters Staff Back Home

Negotiating with your international counterpart can be difficult, but experienced negotiators can tell you that negotiating with your own boss, legal staff, and others back in the home office can be brutal. Here's a likely scenario: You've been in Japan for two weeks, have had seven formal dinners with your counterpart, about 200 toasts and forty-seven sakes, and one less than impressed boss back home at headquarters.

"So what exactly is the status?" he asks you.

"Things seem to be on schedule. I feel we're building a good relationship with their negotiating team."

"Say what?"

"You know, building trust and all."

"Gosh, you don't know how happy that makes me. But let me remind you that I sent you over there to build a refinery." From there the discussion goes directly downhill.

In addition to dealing with your boss, you are likely to run into difficulties negotiating with your own legal staff or counsel. In many cases, you may get a lot more "help" with the negotiation than you want. Your legal counsel is likely to want more detail than will be acceptable to your foreign counterpart. Expect the legal staff to challenge, correct, and attempt to overrule portions of or even the entire agreement you are negotiating with TOS. They are only trying to keep you and the organization out of trouble.

Action Steps for Preparing the Boss and Headquarters Staff for the International Negotiation

▪ *Stress the protracted nature of international negotiations in most parts of the world.* Lower expectations as to the chances of a speedy agreement. Stretch out their time horizons.

▪ *Be clear as to who has the authority to negotiate on the organization's behalf.* The negotiation process will be undermined if TOS feels concessions can be gained from the home office that you wouldn't agree to.

- *Take time to educate the boss and others on the key cultural factors that influence the negotiation.* Contrast and compare specific instances overseas with how they would have been handled domestically (for example, the degree of emphasis put on the relationship aspects of the negotiation).

- *Cue the boss and legal staff to differences in contract length, specificity, and other matters, early on in the negotiation.* Try to determine the absolute necessities of protecting your side versus what would be in the "nice to have" category.

- *Keep your own attorneys away from the negotiating table in most other countries.* Their presence would be perceived as overly rigid and showing a lack of good faith.

- *Don't go around asking the corporate legal staff dozens of questions as to whether or not you can put various legal items in the agreement.* They will tell you no. It's their job to tell you no. It's your job to combine the necessary legal protections with the practicalities of achieving an agreement that is good for both parties.

- On the other hand, *don't surprise the technocrats with a big problem.* If you see that there is a potential legal, financial, or other problem, give ample notice to the appropriate person. By getting them involved early in the process, you have a chance to make your case to the technocrats before a final decision is made, and also to save yourself some potential problems with TOS.

- *Give your boss or other headquarters staff a lesson in International Negotiating 101.* If the boss or others make a trip with you, ensure that they are educated in detail regarding the status of the negotiations and the expectations associated with the culture of TOS.

Problem 3: Dealing With Your Own Negotiating Team

There are both advantages and disadvantages to team negotiations. Advantages include more complete preparation, since you get several viewpoints as to the course of events, and faster decision making, since the key parties are present for the negotiation. In addition, there can also be mental support (strength in numbers) and consequently, a slower erosion of your side's aspiration level. Team negotiations are also the norm in some nations.

These advantages are usually more than offset by liabilities. While team negotiations may meet the cultural expectations abroad, they can be very expensive, particularly if the negotiations are taking place in the host country. The travel, lodging, eating, and entertainment expenses could easily mount to $40,000 for a week in Japan, and this does not count the labor cost of those involved in the negotiation. Another disadvantage is having to manage the egos, roles, and expectations of the team members. You must negotiate with your own team before you can present your position to TOS. The opportunity for internal disagreement is substantial: differences regarding the priorities of your side and that of TOS; differences as to the roles of the team members; and differences in the overall negotiating skill of each team member. You may also find decision making more cumbersome, since breaks are frequent for discussions before team members reach agreement. The efficiency (though not necessarily the effectiveness) of making the decision yourself may be sacrificed. Finally, TOS may try to prejudicially influence the process if they sense the existence of dissension in your group.

Action Steps for Effectively Dealing With Your Team

▪ *Limit the size of your team.* There is no magic number there, but try to keep the team to no more than five people. When you get many more people than this together doing anything, little gets accomplished.

▪ *Clarify the roles you want the negotiators to play.* Ensure that all team members understand and accept roles such as spokesperson, technical expert, note taker, observer, or whatever other role may be required in the negotiation.

▪ *Ensure that all the team members are clear as to strategies and tactics.* All team members should understand how the team will handle first offers, concessions, caucuses, and other such matters.

▪ *Ensure that all members of the team are good negotiators.* You don't want to be at a critical point in the negotiations and have to negotiate with your own team members on matters like why it is vital to have aspirations or make concessions slowly.

Problem 4: Resolving Bribery and Questionable Payment Issues

What constitutes a bribe or payoff in the United States may be considered day-to-day business in many foreign countries. This point was brought home to me during negotiations for contract labor in the Philippines. I negotiated with Chito, a Filipino labor supplier, to contract for several hundred Filipinos to work mainly as welders, fitters, and other craftspeople on various projects throughout the Middle East. Chito delivered qualified people in remarkably short time frames, cutting through a labyrinth of Filipino administrative rules and regulations. Exactly what he had to do with governmental officials I didn't know then, and I don't know now. I did know, however, that he had repeatedly asked for a fee increase because his "government overhead" was increasing. (Yes, we gave him the increase.)

As always on my trips to Manila, Chito was engaging and gracious. One evening, as we walked a short distance from the restaurant where we had had dinner back to the hotel where I was staying, I briefly paused at an art show window to admire an oil painting of an old shack in an open field. Back at the hotel, Chito and I shook hands and said good-bye.

Four hours later, about midnight, the phone rang.

"Hello."

"Hello, Frank. This is Chito. How are you?"

"Fine," I lied. I had been asleep about an hour.

"Can I come up to your room?"

"Right now?" I asked, quite incredulously.

Chito came up to my room all right—with the painting about which I had remarked earlier that evening *and* the artist who painted it. I was certainly awake by now. As the engaging and gracious Chito and the proud, smiling artist stood there, clear thoughts rushed through my head about the Foreign Corrupt Practices Act and several internal company policies dealing with gifts. After awkward protestations that I really couldn't accept the gift, I in fact took the painting and thanked both of them.

After they left, I sat there for quite some time staring at the painting. Was I going to be sitting in some federal court two years from now, explaining why I had accepted a bribe from a company agent connected with a foreign government? Though I enjoyed a good working relationship with my boss, I was sure he would be singularly unimpressed with my new painting. As it turned out, our corporate legal staff approved of me keeping the painting, and to this day I somewhat defiantly have it hanging in my office.

What's in a Name?
International Names for Bribes

Backsheesh	Middle East
La busterella	
("envelope left on bureaucrat's desk")	Italy
Dash	West Africa
Grease	United States
La morbida ("bite")	Latin America
Kumshaw	Southeast Asia
Pot du vin ("jug of wine")	France

It has been acknowledged in the international business community for many years that gifts or money payments are necessary to obtain positive action from government officials, whether to secure a large order or to gain favorable treatment from customs officials, taxing authorities, and so on.[1] While U.S. negotiators tend to bargain over issues such as price, quality, and service and are not normally comfortable with considerations such as gifts or payoffs, gifts or payoffs are an important tradition in some countries. Members of the inner circle in communal cultures, such as those in many parts of Latin America and Asia, maintain their relationshps through a system of favors. It is assumed in these systems that any person who is obligated to another person or group has the duty to repay the favor at some time in the future. A lifetime cycle of obligations has thus been formed. Another factor is that to non-Westerners, Americans and other Westerners seem to be preoccupied with the business aspects of the negotiation rather than the important relationship aspects. Therefore, non-Westerners see gift giving as an appropriate way to increase social ties and to create a sense of obligation by the Western negotiator. Small gifts—such as pens, cups, and key rings engraved with your company logo—are not only acceptable, but virtually essential in global business. Home and office decorations and books and magazines are also popular.

You should be concerned about the legal issues concerning gifts, payments, or bribes from the perspectives of both the United States and the host country. Tips, commissions, and finder's fees may be legal abroad, but they are a legal nightmare within Uncle Sam's long arms of the law. During the 1970s, revelations of dubious or questionable payments made by U.S. companies to foreign officials rocked governments in the Netherlands and Japan. The U.S. Congress, considering corporate bribery "bad business" and "unnecessary," then passed the Foreign Corrupt Practices Act. The FCPA prohibits any U.S.-based company from "corruptly" offering or giving money or "anything of value to a foreign political official" for the purpose of obtaining or retaining business. On the other hand, the law allows *facilitating payments*—that is, payments made to expedite solely nondiscretionary official actions such as customs. This usually means routine promotional gifts, reimbursement of reasonable expenses for promotional meals or travel, and payments that are legal under the laws of the foreign country. It is not always clear, however, where illegal bribes end and facilitating payments begin. There are also uncertainties as to how far management must go in order to learn whether an employee has violated the FCPA. Also, while there are probably less stringent rules about bribes in the host country you are dealing with, it is vital that you know its laws in this respect.

Action Steps for Resolving Bribery and Questionable Payment Issues

- Above all, *check with your legal staff about any vague areas of home or host-country laws.* Here's a time when you want the legal staff's involvement. It may be necessary to get legal counsel in the host country as well.

- *Keep your boss informed.* This is no time to be the Lone Ranger. Be sure he or she is aware of any concerns you have.

- *If you must make a payment, find out how to do it.* Rather than make a direct money payment, it may be feasible for you to invest in community projects, such as building a school for the children of customs officials.

- *If a monetary payment must be made, don't make the payment yourself.* Use a go-between such as a "consultant" or someone's relative.[2]

Problem 5: Establishing an International Joint Venture

The term *joint venture* refers to many types of across-border alliances that may or may not involve equity participation. These arrangements are usually complex, with sometimes widely differing goals among the parties. For example, your company goal may be a quick return on its investment of capital, technology, and management, in perhaps three to five years. The local partner, on the other hand, may want to develop a growing business that yields satisfactory profits over a ten- to fifteen-year period. Too, the joint venture may be doomed to failure because of different motives regarding the source of supplies. For example, your company may want to use U.S. suppliers for key components to ensure quality and prompt delivery, while the national partner may want local suppliers to maintain competitive prices.

Joint ventures usually involve an arrangement by which the parties commit resources such as money, materials, and management to organize a jointly owned entity, generally for production purposes. Joint ventures, however, can also be organized around specific contracts (e.g., licensing or technology transfer) or loose alliances (e.g., sharing R&D expenditures or setting up a mutually beneficial organization) that serve as an "empty shell" partnership just to exchange information and trade a limited amount of technical data.[3] Here are a few examples of joint ventures:

- General Motors and Suzuki formed CAMI Automotive, Inc., a Canadian-based joint venture, to manufacture low-end cars for the U.S. market.
- A U.S. chemical company formed a joint venture in Nigeria with a local partner and financial investors to produce ag-

ricultural chemicals. The U.S. company invested 51 percent and the local partner and investors put in 49 percent.

- The Travelers and Nippon Life Insurance Co. formed a joint venture in which Travelers provides administrative services for Nippon's group life, health, and disability products in the United States.[4]

Joint ventures usually involve at least three major parties: (1) a multinational corporation, (2) a national partner, and (3) the government of the host country. Other parties may include national investors and the U.S. government (e.g., when the joint venture deals with national security). It is easy to see how joint venture negotiations can go astray, given the different possible goals of the major parties involved. Here, for example, are typical goals of joint venture partners for a manufacturing joint venture in a developing country:

A multinational corporation

- To increase market share where there is substantial market size.
- To maintain reasonable risk.
- To maintain a reasonable rate of return on investment.
- To take strategic initiative to use the company's specific advantages.

A national partner

- To enter into a profitable operation with a prestigious multinational corporation.
- To obtain technology.
- To gain business know-how.
- To obtain trademarks.

A host-country government

- To achieve industrialization and economic development.
- To increase national income and employment.
- To improve the balance of payments between the host coun-

try and home country of the multinational (e.g., the United States).

- To develop backward areas of the country.[5]

Forming a successful joint venture can be a good example of a win-win negotiation. In the CAMI Automotive joint venture noted above, Suzuki gained access to GM's dealer network and an expanded market for parts and components. GM avoided the cost of developing low-end cars and obtained the models it needed to regenerate the lower end of Chevrolet's product line and to improve GM's average fuel economy rating.[6]

Exhibit 7-1 provides a handy checklist of issues to be addressed in any joint venture negotiation. As you can see, there are many pivotal technical, management, financial, and legal issues to be addressed.

Action Steps for Establishing an International Joint Venture

- *Ensure that you and the other parties have similar goals with respect to the business.* For example, it is important to know short- and long-term goals and the rate of return that is expected over various periods of time. By clarifying such issues during the negotiations, you can eliminate a lot of problems later.

- *Try to maintain control of the critical management responsibilities.* This is important even if you have minority ownership. You want to retain the authority to appoint key managers and the right to veto important management decisions. In other situations, it may be feasible to have the national partner share in policy decisions, but you should retain the major operational decisions for your company.

- *Try to find suppliers from the host country.* It may not always be possible to find local suppliers, particularly in the early years of a joint venture since quality and delivery demands may eliminate local sources. When it otherwise makes good business sense to do so, however, use local suppliers to help form a strong relationship with the national partner and host government.

- As long as quality and delivery standards are met, *allow the joint venture operation to purchase materials, components, and other products from the lowest-cost available source.* This will reduce cost concerns on the part of the national partner.

- *Make training part of the package,* particularly if the joint venture is located in a developing country. Training is increasingly a selling point for your company with the host-country partners. The host country government usually emphasizes such provisions in a joint venture agreement, as it tries to make political points for adding or upgrading jobs and for the increased transfer of technology.

- *Maintain flexibility.* Over time there will be changes in the joint venture's objectives, resources, markets, and technologies and in the relative power of the partners.

Problem 6: Your Place Or Mine? Where to Hold the Negotiation

Where you hold the negotiation may in itself be a negotiation. There are several advantages to having the negotiation on your turf. First, you are more comfortable and probably more confident there. Second, it gives you an opportunity to treat TOS like a king or queen, thereby enhancing the relationship you want to build. Your playing the role of gracious host also does something else: It often makes TOS feel like the guests that they are. And how do guests normally treat you? That's right: with respect. Here's a chance to set the stage for concessions from TOS.

More likely than not, however, you will be conducting the negotiation in the host country. The main advantage of going to TOS's country is that you get information about TOS's way of life, concerns, and pressures. If you can visit the physical plant of TOS, this is even better. You obtain valuable data regarding the company's operations as well as insight into its modernity and professionalism. Additionally, your observations of TOS's relationship to other key people—the behind-the-scenes decision makers—are assets in the bargaining process.

There are, however, many major disadvantages to negotiating in the host country. There is not only the issue of culture shock discussed earlier, but being away from home can be expensive, frustrating, and time-consuming.

(text continues on page 136)

Exhibit 7-1. Outline of an international joint venture agreement.

A. Purpose of a Joint Venture

    1. Major goals and strategy of foreign partner
    2. Major goals and strategy of local partner
    3. Products, industries, markets, and customers served

B. Contributions of Each Partner

    1. Capital
    2. Existing land, plant, warehouse, offices, and other facilities
    3. Manufacturing design, processes, and technical know-how
    4. Product know-how
    5. Patents and trademarks
    6. Managerial, production, marketing, financial, organizational, and other expertise
    7. Management development and technical assistance and training
    8. Local relationships with government, financial institutions, customers, and suppliers

C. Responsibilities and Obligations of Each Partner

    1. Procurement and installation of machinery and equipment
    2. Construction and modernization of machinery and equipment
    3. Production operations
    4. Recruitment and training of workers and supervisors
    5. Quality control
    6. Relationships with labor unions
    7. Research and development
    8. General, financial, marketing, personnel, and other management

D. Equity Ownership

    1. Equity granted to foreign partner for manufacturing and product technology and industrial product rights
    2. Equity granted to local partner for land, plants, warehouses, and facilities
    3. Ownership share of foreign partner
    4. Ownership share of local partner

E. Capital Structure

1. Equity capital
2. Loan capital (national and foreign)
3. Working capital
4. Provisions for raising future loan funds
5. Loan guarantees by partners
6. Future increase in equity capital
7. Transfers of shares of stock, including limitations

F. Management

1. Appointment, composition, and authority of the board of directors
2. Appointment and authority of executive officers
3. Expatriate managers, technicians, and staff
4. Right of veto of appointment of officers and key decisions
5. Development of local managers, including time schedule
6. Organization
7. Strategic and operational planning
8. Information system

G. Supplementary Agreements

1. Licensing and technology agreements
2. Management contracts
3. Technical service agreements
4. Allocation of foreign partner's corporate overhead to affiliate

H. Managerial Policies

1. Declaration of dividends
2. Reinvestment of earnings
3. Source of supply of materials and components, including price, quality, and assurance of delivery
4. Major marketing programs, including product lines, trademarks, brand names, distribution channels, promotion, pricing, service, and expenditures
5. Export markets and commitments
6. Executive compensation and bonuses

(continues)

Exhibit 7-1. Continued.

I. Accounting and Financial Statements

1. Accounting standards
2. Financial statements in currencies of host and foreign countries
3. Reporting requirements
4. Audit and review of financial statements

J. Settlement of Disputes

1. Board of directors and executive committee
2. Mediation
3. Arbitration

K. Legal Matters

1. Relevant local laws, regulations, and policies
2. Required government approvals
3. Articles and bylaws of incorporation
4. Antitrust considerations
5. Tax law considerations
6. Selection of legal counsel
7. Use of host-country courts

Note: This outline represents a comprehensive list of factors that could be included in a joint venture agreement. Not all of these aspects necessarily apply to every joint venture agreement.

Source: "Arrangements Between Joint Venture Partners in Developing Countries," no. 2, UNCTC Advisory Services (New York: United Nations, 1987).

Action Steps for Dealing With Where to Hold the Negotiation

- *Invite TOS to your location.* This may be more difficult if you are the seller, or if you are a buyer who must physically see the product or service involved. If TOS visits you, however, you can bet that they will not be quick to walk out. The pressure will be on them to make extra concessions.
- If you're the visitor, *don't necessarily divulge the timing of your return trip.* If you do, this may give TOS the edge on how to

pace the negotiation, waiting until you are ready to leave—and vulnerable—before key issues are discussed.

- If you're the visitor, *don't let the time, money, and goals you've invested in the trip dissuade you from the planning you did.* Be sure not to exceed the deal breaker in your settlement range. The best deal may be no deal at all.
- If you're the visitor, *don't be a prisoner to fatigue.* Jet lag is real. Eat light and drink alcohol in moderation on the way over, and be sure to give yourself a day or two to rest up before entering a key negotiation. You will not be at your best if you leave New York in the afternoon, arrive in London about 6:00 A.M., and begin negotiations later that morning.

We are now ready to begin your country-by-country journey, examining specific negotiating strategies along the way.

Notes

1. Donald A. Ball and Wendall H. McCulloch, Jr., *International Business: Introduction and Essentials,* 4th ed. (Homewood, Ill.: BPI/Irwin, 1990), p. 289.
2. Lennie Copeland and Lewis Griggs, *Going International* (New York: Random House, 1985), p. 177–178.
3. Victor A. Kremenyuk, ed., *International Negotiation* (San Francisco: Jossey-Bass, 1991), p. 338.
4. Joel Bleeke and David Ernst, "The Way to Win in Cross-Border Alliances," *Harvard Business Review* (November–December 1991): 130; "Arrangements Between Joint Venture Partners in Developing Countries," No. 2, UNTC Advisory Series (New York: United Nations, 1987) pp. 9, 24; "Travelers and Nippon Join Forces," *MCEBO Update* (Travelers newsletter), November 15, 1991, p. 1.
5. "Arrangements Between Joint Venture Partners," p. 14.
6. Bleeke and Ernst, "The Way to Win," p. 130.

Part Four

Negotiating Around the World

In Part Four, we examine the specific skills required for effective business negotiations throughout the world. In Chapters 8 through 14, you will learn the how, what, when, and where of international negotiating on a regional and country-by-country basis. Six regions of the world are profiled, with key information on the business environment, the specific cultural factors that affect negotiating, and practical do's and don'ts.

The discussion of each of the six regions is divided into four sections:

1. The Business Environment
2. Cultural Factors That Affect Negotiating
3. How Negotiations Work
4. Your Negotiating Primer

These sections consist of a great deal of practical, relevant information that will help you become a world-class negotiator. Keep in mind that the guidelines throughout these sections are primarily from a U.S. perspective and that such guidelines are relative. For example, when we say that the pace of negotiations in Western Europe is moderate, this is from a U.S. viewpoint. The Japanese might consider these negotiations to be quite fast-paced.

The "Cultural Factors" section in each chapter encompasses the four factors discussed in Chapter 5: (1) use of time;

(2) individualism versus collectivism; (3) role orderliness and conformity; and (4) patterns of communication. The section on "How Negotiations Work" is patterned after the six aspects of global negotiations also outlined in Chapter 5: (1) pace of negotiations; (2) negotiating strategies; (3) emphasis on personal relationships; (4) emotional aspects; (5) decision making; and (6) contractual and administrative factors.

A Negotiating Primer has been prepared for forty-one countries, divided into regions:

Western Europe (Chapter 8)

- Belgium
- France
- Germany
- Greece
- Italy
- The Netherlands
- Spain
- Sweden
- Switzerland
- United Kingdom

Eastern Europe (Chapter 9)

- Czechoslovakia
- Hungary
- Poland
- Russia

Latin America (Chapter 10)

- Argentina
- Brazil
- Colombia
- Mexico
- Venezuela

North America (Chapter 11)

- Canada
- United States

The Middle East (Chapter 12)

- Egypt
- Israel
- Saudi Arabia
- The United Arab Emirates

The Pacific Rim (Chapter 13)

- China
- Hong Kong
- Indonesia
- Japan
- Malaysia
- Philippines
- Singapore
- South Korea
- Taiwan
- Thailand

Other Important Countries (Chapter 14)

- Australia
- India
- New Zealand
- Nigeria
- Pakistan

The Primers consist of practical do's and don'ts and other important day-to-day information. The focus for each country is on five areas:

1. *Fast Facts:* trading partners, key imports and exports, and other profile information on the country. This is based on 1990 data unless otherwise noted, and monetary figures are given in U.S. dollars.
2. *Reducing Communication Noise:* techniques for getting your message through.
3. *Key Negotiating Pointers:* country-specific negotiating guidelines.

4. *Day-to-Day Pointers:* business entertainment and related matters.
5. *Gender Issues:* sensitivities and guidelines.

In addition, there is a section at the end of each Primer called *Also Remember This* . . . , which provides further important background information to help you negotiate in that country.

The points that are emphasized within each of these categories differ from country to country. For example, a particular tactic is highlighted only if it seems of consequence in a particular country. Similarly, the ritual of "toasts" is mentioned under Day-to-Day Pointers only when this behavior is a key part of business entertainment. In some cases, a particular point is included because the information was available for that country and not for others.

Some issues are mentioned in almost all the Primers. For example, the importance of being punctual is highlighted almost everywhere, even if TOS keeps you waiting. This is because there is usually an expectation from TOS that you be on time, even if TOS is not. Popular sports are mentioned under "Conversation" in most Primers because many individuals find it easy to discuss such matters. In all cases, use your own judgment on how to use this information. For example, many Canadians are rabid ice hockey fans, but if you sense that TOS has no interest in the subject, or if you clearly feel like a phony discussing it, then leave it alone. ("Conversation" also covers such topics as personal space and touching.) Some guidelines, such as the avoidance of political or religious discussions, can generally be followed anywhere, but are emphasized in those countries where these can be especially sensitive topics.

Let's continue our intercultural journey by stopping in Western Europe.

Chapter 8
Negotiating in Western Europe

The Business Environment of Western Europe

While you may be more comfortable doing business in Western Europe than in many other places, remember that negotiating there can sometimes be quite difficult and that negotiating styles differ from country to country. If your experience in Europe is limited to vacations, you will probably find that behavior in business situations is quite different from what you have experienced.

The most important business development in Western Europe is the emergence of the European Community (EC). The core twelve-member European Community consists of Belgium, Denmark, France, Germany, Greece, Ireland, Italy, Luxembourg, the Netherlands, Portugal, Spain, and the United Kingdom. It is likely that other countries will join the EC, among them Hungary, Poland, and other Eastern European countries. The EC is a powerful new economic and political force whose goals are to reregulate a Europe that is a single market: a Europe without frontiers, where there will be an unrestricted movement of money, products, services, and people.

The EC is seen by Europeans as a critical step in regaining their competitive position with the United States and Japan. There are reasons for the Europeans to be optimistic. By July 1993, projected gross national product and gross world trade will be more than double the levels in North America (United States and Canada) and triple the levels in Asia and the Pacific.[1] The biggest opportunities for member countries may lie in the ability to exploit economies that are available in the widely expanded "home" market.

The most likely impact of the EC on your business activities is in the area of common standards, deregulation, economic research and development, fiscal harmony, open government procurement, and taxation and tariff reforms.

Those who are optimistic about the growth of the EC as a powerful economic force make some underlying assumptions. Among them are that:

- Europe will succeed as an economic unit and as a political confederation, with perhaps a supernational federal entity that will provide a loose government for Europe as a whole.
- Europe is likely to establish both a federal bank and a common currency.
- At least half of all key legislation affecting economic, political, and technological decisions will be determined by Euro-wide institutions rather than by national institutions.[2]

Many important strategic decisions remain to be made to realize the fruition of these assumptions. Much of the decision making will be influenced by the European Commission. The Commission is the executive of the EC (not its government). It is responsible for EC policy and legislation for discussion and adoption by the Council of Ministers (made up of the foreign secretaries of each member country), as well as for implementation of approved policies. But regardless of the degree of unity achieved, various national differences are almost certain to endure.

What all this means in practical terms is that, among many other things, workers from member countries will be able to work anywhere in the EC, sales taxes and value-added taxes (VATs) will be made more uniform, foreign exchange controls will be discontinued, and property laws will be standardized. Products will be sold anywhere in the EC as long as they meet home-country standards. Flexible manufacturing will produce standard products (regarding packages and sizes) that will cater to local markets. But again, realize that member countries will almost certainly retain key national differences when it comes to negotiations.

Cultural Factors That Affect Negotiating in Western Europe

Use of Time

The Western Europeans, more than any of the other cultures that we examine, share common views of time with North Americans. Business life is generally quite fast-paced, and meetings almost always start and end on time. Expect negotiations to move crisply in most of Western Europe.

Individualism vs. Collectivism

Western Europeans are generally quite individualistic. There is generally a distinction between one's core of intimate associates and those outside that core. Status and class consciousness are prevalent. One joins groups that are within one's class status. Friendships usually take a long time to develop. As with other high-individualism parts of the world, the individual is emotionally independent from the work organization. The emphasis is on individual initiative and achievement.

Role Orderliness and Conformity

Order, discipline, and responsibility are highly valued in the family and at work. The path to the corporate world is a mixture of education and connections. Leisure time with the family is extremely important, and monthlong summer holidays (vacations) are typical.

Power in organizations flows from the top down, and the hierarchy is important. Top managers usually have a great deal of technical expertise and tend to dislike power-sharing and delegation of responsibility. In addition, top managers do not communicate regularly with lower management. Consequently, lower-level managers may not have much information about the corporate goals or mission. An exception is Scandinavia, where top management communicates regularly with middle management, and substantial power is delegated for key decisions.

Though Western Europeans have high occupational mobility,

long tenures exist within the same company. Job-hopping tends to be viewed with disfavor, and loyalty and hard work are rewarded.

Patterns of Communication

Verbal Communication

Articulate speakers are valued. Many Western Europeans have a low tolerance for ambiguity. The communication is generally formal, understated, and subtle. It is expected that there will be face-to-face communication on initial contact. Emotional outbursts are looked upon very unfavorably.

Nonverbal Communication

Western Europeans are typically more reserved in their body language than North Americans, and much more so than Latin Americans or Middle Easterners. Wide, rapid gestures are almost always inappropriate in either a business or social setting.

Expect most Western Europeans to have about the same personal space as do North Americans in business settings—usually about 3 feet. Physical contact is usually limited to a brief handshake in business situations.

Notes

1. Lynne Hall, *Latecomer's Guide to the New Europe: Doing Business in Central Europe* (New York: American Management Association, 1992), p. 31.
2. Ibid., pp. 12–13.

HOW NEGOTIATIONS WORK IN WESTERN EUROPE

Negotiating Factors

1. Pace of Negotiations   Moderate

2. Negotiating Strategies
   Opening Offers vis-à-vis
      Settlement   Moderate initial demands
   Presentation of Issues   One at a time
   Presentations   Formal
   Dealing With Differences   Polite, direct
   Concessions   Fairly slow

**3. Emphasis on Personal
   Relationships**   Low

4. Emotional Aspects
   Sensitivity   Moderate
   Degree of Emotions   Moderate

5. Decision Making
   Overall Method   Planned, organized
   Emphasize   Logic
   Emphasis on Group/Team   Moderate: Decisions from top
                                              management
   Emphasis on Face-Saving   Moderate
   Influence of Special
      Interests on Decision
      Maker(s)   Moderate

**6. Contractual and
   Administrative Factors**
   Need for an Agent   Average
   Degree of Contract
      Specificity   High
   Degree of Paperwork/
      Bureaucracy   Moderate
   Need for an Agenda   High

BELGIUM

Fast Facts

Population:	10.0 million
GNP:	$154.7 billion
Per Capita Income:	$15,440
Monetary Unit:	Belgian franc
Major Industries:	engineering, metal products, processed foods, beverages, chemicals
Main Trading Partners:	
Exports:	other EC members (74%), U.S. (5%)
Imports:	other EC members (72%), U.S. (5%), oil-exporting developing countries (4%)
Key Exports:	iron, steel, transportation equipment, tractors, diamonds
Key Imports:	fuels, grains, chemicals
Major Cities:	Brussels (cap.) (970,300), Antwerp (476,000), Ghent (232,600), Charleroi (208,900)
Ethnic Groups:	Flemish (55%), Walloon (33%), mixed or other (12%)
Main Religions:	Roman Catholic (75%), Protestant or other (25%)
Language(s):	Flemish (Dutch), French

Reducing Communication Noise

Greetings

- Shake hands quickly with light pressure upon meeting. When leaving, shake hands again and bid farewell to each member of the group.
- The local custom is to kiss three times on alternate cheeks. You need not do so unless you know the other person very well.

- First names are not used in business settings, unless among close friends. Address French-speaking people as *Monsieur, Madame*, or *Mademoiselle*. For Dutch-speaking people, use *Mr., Mrs.*, or *Miss*.

Conversation

- Belgians enjoy talking about their fine food, art, and architecture. Artistic masters such as van Eyck, Rubens, and Van Gogh lived in Belgium.
- Participant sports are very popular. Cycling and soccer are the most prominent.

Sensitivities

- Avoid personal questions about private lives. Belgians guard their privacy.
- Avoid discussing language, political, and cultural distinctions between the Dutch and French in Belgium, and try not to confuse the two groups.
- The Belgians sometimes tell "Dutch" jokes (and vice versa). Stay out of this rivalry.
- Don't flaunt wealth.

Key Negotiating Pointers

- Belgians exhibit business savvy and are tough negotiators.
- Be punctual. Expect the negotiation to proceed at a rapid pace. Be friendly but to the point in your discussions.
- Be reserved and respect formalities. The personal relationship generally follows the business relationship.
- Back up your information with lots of facts and figures.
- Have written materials translated into both French and Dutch.

Day-to-Day Pointers

Business Entertainment Guidelines

- Meals are a social and cultural event and are usually protracted. You may discuss business during a meal, but let your host initiate the subject.
- Dinner is usually served at 7:00 P.M. or 8:00 P.M.
- Avoid sending chrysanthemums as a thank you for an invitation, since they are a reminder of death.
- In restaurants, normally pay your bill at the table. Tips are included in the bill, but you can leave a bit extra if you wish.

Table Manners and Food

- Finish your food. Belgians are thrifty and despise waste.
- Pork, game birds, fish, cheese, fruits, vegetables, breads, and soups are favorite foods. Wine, beer, or mineral water is usually served with meals.
- Belgians prefer bottled water to tap water.

Gender Issues

- Although there is still a traditional view of female careers in business, Belgium is a good place for U.S. women to do business.

Also Remember This . . .

- Belgium is sometimes considered the *de facto* capital of Europe.
- Belgium's strong foreign trade is aided by Antwerp, the third largest seaport in the world, and its central location among EC countries.
- Belgians have a reputation for working and playing hard. They are cosmopolitan and appreciate culture.

FRANCE

Fast Facts

Population:	56.2 million
GNP:	$1,099.8 billion
Per Capita Income:	$19,480
Monetary Unit:	French franc
Major Industries:	steel, machinery and equipment, textiles and clothing

Main Trading Partners:	
Exports:	Germany (16%), Italy (12%), Belgium-Luxembourg (9%), the Netherlands (9%), U.S. (7%)
Imports:	Germany (19%), Italy (12%), Belgium-Luxembourg (9%), U.S. (8%), U.K. (7%)
Key Exports:	machinery and transportation equipment, chemicals, food, agricultural products
Key Imports:	crude petroleum, machinery and equipment, agricultural products, chemicals
Major Cities:	Paris (cap.) (2.2 million), Marseilles (878,700), Lyons (418,500), Toulouse (354,300)
Ethnic Groups:	Celtic and Latin, with Teutonic, Slavic, North African, Indochinese, and Basque minorities
Main Religions:	Roman Catholic (90%), Protestant (2%), Jewish (1%)
Language(s):	French

Reducing Communication Noise

Greetings

- Shake hands with a single, quick shake and light pressure upon meeting. When leaving, shake hands again with all those to whom you were introduced.
- Women do not normally offer their hands to men, so men should initiate the greeting. Don't offer your hand to a person of superior authority.
- First names are used only among close friends. The use of first names is initiated by the person who is older and superior in rank.
- Until told to do otherwise, address people as *Monsieur, Madame,* or *Mademoiselle,* without adding the surname.
- Common greetings are *Bonjour* (Hello), *Comment allez-vous?* (How are you?), and *Ca va?* (a casual How are you?).

Conversation

- Try talking about French art, architecture, food, and history.
- Soccer and rugby are popular spectator sports. Fishing, bicycling, tennis, hiking, skiing, and sailing are popular individual sports. The annual Tour de France is a major international cycling event.

- The business language in France is most certainly French. Though knowledge of English is commonplace, your counterpart may or may not want to speak it to accommodate you. If you speak little or no French, your best bet is to speak English (except for greetings or toasts) or have a French-speaking representative.
- Don't take it personally if you sense that your French counterparts are shocked by your inept French (they are also often shocked by the way other French people speak French). The French are as ethnocentric as Americans—extremely proud and self-centered about their culture.
- There tends to be a lot of touching in France compared with many other Western European countries.

Sensitivities

- Avoid discussing politics, money, and personal matters.
- Prepare yourself for graceful responses to challenges between French and U.S. wines, and between soccer and American football.
- The American *okay* sign (with the thumb and index finger forming a circle) means "zero" to the French. The French gesture for *okay* is the American "thumbs up" sign.

Key Negotiating Pointers

- Avoid a hard sell. The French are rather formal and conservative in business.
- Make prior appointments and be punctual.
- After a brief exchange of pleasantries, get to the point of your discussions. Let your host take the lead on this. The personal relationship is normally solidified after the business relationship has been formed.
- New ideas should be well-researched and conceptually strong. The French apply reason and logic to negotiations.
- Presentations should be formal, informative, rational, and subdued.
- Allow plenty of time; decisions are made after much deliberation.
- Be aware that though the French are often reserved, the team may be argumentative, disagreeing for the sake of discussion. Expect them normally to state their intentions directly and openly.
- An agreement may be reached orally, with written contracts to follow.
- A local representative or agent is advised. Joint ventures or branch offices, or even a network of distributors throughout France, may be needed for success.

Day-to-Day Pointers

Business Entertainment Guidelines

- Most entertaining is done in restaurants. You are generally invited to someone's home only if you become very good friends as well as business associates.
- Business lunches and dinners may last over two hours, with more than ten courses.
- Cultural conversation is as important as fine food in France. Avoid talking about business over a meal until your host gives a signal.
- Eat something light before a formal dinner since guests are likely to arrive late.
- Lunch (*déjeuner*), is the main meal of the day, eaten at noon.
- Whether you are entertained at home or in a restaurant, telephone the next day or write a brief note to express your thanks.
- When a key negotiation is completed, the heads of the two negotiating groups usually toast each other and wish each other a long, fruitful relationship.
- Logo gifts with your company name should be reserved and unobtrusive.

Table Manners and Food

- Etiquette in eating is important.
- Keep your hands (but not elbows) above the table.
- French restaurants are often very expensive. Avoid ordering the most expensive item on the menu, overeating, and overdrinking.
- Be sure to compliment the fine cuisine.
- Always ask permission before you smoke. Smoking in public places is frowned upon.
- French cuisine is world-famous, with French standards often the gauge of fine cooking. Expect large multicourse meals and *nouvelle cuisine* (lighter foods).
- Have only one helping of cheese. Fold lettuce into small pieces, but do not cut it.

Gender Issues

- France is generally a good place for U.S. women to do business, though they should expect to be treated with some gallantry and flirtatiousness.
- Women increasingly occupy professional and management positions, such as in the areas of retail, service, media, advertising, law, finance, and human resources.
- Women make up about 43 percent of the French work force.

Also Remember This . . .

- Although the French are quite formal in their "onstage" business dealings, they usually have an off-the-record web of informal networks that help them get what they want done in their organizations.
- The French tend to be family-oriented in their private life and company-oriented in their business life.
- Most French workers take five weeks of vacation: four in the summer, and one during Christmas.

GERMANY

Fast Facts

Population:	78.6 million
GNP:	$1,411.3 billion
Per Capita Income:	$22,730
Monetary Unit:	Deutsche mark
Major Industries:	iron, steel, coal, cement, chemicals, metal fabrication
Main Trading Partners:	
Exports:	France (12%), U.S. (10%), the Netherlands (9%), U.K. (9%)*
Imports:	France (12%), the Netherlands (11%), Italy (10%), U.K. (7%), Belgium-Luxembourg (7%)*
Key Exports:	manufactured goods (machinery and machine tools, chemicals, motor vehicles, iron and steel products)*

*Based on data for West Germany before reunification.

Key Imports:	manufactured goods, agricultural products, fuels, raw materials
Major Cities:	Berlin (cap.) (3.3 million), Bonn (seat of government) (291,000), Hamburg (1.6 million), Munich (1.2 million)
Ethnic Groups:	predominantly German, with small Slavic and Danish minorities
Main Religions:	Protestant (45%), Roman Catholic (37%)
Language(s):	German

Reducing Communication Noise

Greetings

- Shake hands firmly upon meeting and leaving.
- Do not use first names unless invited to do so. Address people as *Herr, Frau,* or *Fräulein,* with the last name. Anyone with a doctorate (such as a lawyer) is addressed as Herr Doktor X, and a professor is Herr Professor X. It is important to know a person's proper title.
- Common greetings are *Guten morgen* (Good morning), *Guten tag* (Good afternoon), and *Guten abend* (Good evening).

Conversation

- Try talking about the weather, your trip over, hobbies (many Germans have one or more), or travel (many Germans like to vacation abroad). German wines and beers are world-famous.
- Soccer, hiking, and bicycling are popular sports.
- Germans tend to be formal and reserved at first meetings and may seem unfriendly. It takes time for them to get on a first-name basis.

Sensitivities

- Avoid personal questions other than general, polite inquiries about one's family. The German sense of privacy is very strong.
- Avoid discussing politics and World War II.

- It is considered impolite to keep your hands in your pockets while talking with someone.

Key Negotiating Pointers

- Germans have a reputation as hard bargainers.
- Make appointments well in advance at the highest possible level. Be punctual.
- Prepare an agenda for the meeting. Germans conduct business with great attention to order and planning and tend to be uneasy with ambiguity. The tone of negotiations is formal.
- Dress neatly and maintain a formal decorum. Practice restraint. Remain silent rather than offer an uninformed opinion.
- Do not try to establish personal relationships beyond normal courtesies. Germans tend to remain aloof until business is completed, though younger Germans are a bit more informal. Avoid joke telling to break the ice.
- Try to arrange smaller meetings if you can, where the atmosphere tends to be less formal.
- Avoid surprises and a hard sell. Don't spring a startling new proposal on your counterpart at a formal meeting.
- Be well prepared. Proposals and presentations should be detailed, logical, and filled with appropriate technical data. Be thoroughly knowledgeable in product and contract details.
- Negotiating proposals should be concrete and realistic, presented in a clear, orderly, and authoritative manner.
- Decision making in Germany involves a thorough analysis of all the facts and may take longer than in the United States. A top manager may make even minor decisions.
- Follow up with a fax or letter that summarizes discussions. Germans like to have things in writing.
- Be aware of last-second demands. If you must make a concession, do it conditionally.
- This is one of the few places in the world where contracts tend to be more specific than those in the United States. German contracts spell out what U.S. contracts might leave to standard trade practice. Also, there are two kinds of signing authority. The marks *p.p.* or *ppa* (per procura) indicate someone with restricted authority, while *i.V.* (in Vertretung) indicates a manager with full authority.
- Participate in German trade fairs and contact the chambers of commerce. Both are prestigious institutions in Germany.

Day-to-Day Pointers

Business Entertainment Guidelines

- A customer should be invited to a business lunch or dinner. But if your customer insists on being the host, readily accept the invitation.
- Lunch is normally the main meal of the day. The evening meal is generally simple, except on special occasions.
- A gift of flowers should be brought if invited to a private home for an evening meal or party. The visitor is expected to make the first move to terminate the visit and should never stay too late.
- Germans have great respect for social formalities. Much handshaking takes place on social occasions.

Table Manners and Food

- It is customary to say *Guten appetit* before eating and not to start drinking before the host has toasted the guest with *Prost, Prosit,* or *zum Wohle.* If someone raises the glass to you personally, reciprocate sometime during the meal.
- Keep your hands above the table.
- Do not smoke during a meal until after the last person has finished eating and coffee or brandy is being served.
- Potatoes, noodles, dumplings, sauces, vegetables, and pastries are common foods. Germans also enjoy sausages, pork, chicken, and other meats.

Gender Issues

- Germany is one of the hardest places for U.S. women to do business in Europe. Chauvinism is alive and well.
- Germans are more resistant to women working than people in some other European countries. Women who do work are unlikely to obtain key professional or management positions. Almost no sex discrimination laws exist.

Also Remember This . . .

- Germany is one of the world's top five economic powers.
- Money from the economically powerful Western states is being used to revive the Eastern states.

• Germany is one of the world's largest exporters of cars, steel, aluminum, and televisions.

GREECE

Fast Facts

Population:	10.0 million
GNP:	$60.2 billion
Per Capita Income:	$6,000
Monetary Unit:	drachma
Major Industries:	food and tobacco processing, textiles, chemicals
Main Trading Partners:	
Exports:	Germany (24%), Italy (14%), non–oil developing countries (12%), France (10%), U.S. (7%)
Imports:	Germany (22%), non–oil developing countries (14%), oil-exporting countries (13%)
Key Exports:	manufactured goods, foods, live animals, fuel lubricants
Key Imports:	machinery and transportation equipment, light manufactured goods, fuels, lubricants, foods
Major Cities:	Athens (cap.) (885,800), Salonika (406,400), Piraeus (196,400)
Ethnic Groups:	Greek (98%), Turkish (1%)
Main Religions:	Greek Orthodox (98%), Muslim (1%)
Language(s):	Greek; English and French are widely understood

Reducing Communication Noise

Greetings

- Shake hands upon meeting and leaving.
- The Greek custom is to embrace and kiss each other on the cheek. As a Westerner you are not expected to do so.
- Upon first meeting, use the title *Kyrie* (Mr.) or *Kyria* (Mrs.) with the last name.
- The Greeks are generally formal with names but use first names with colleagues of similar age and status. Do not use first names until you are invited to do so.
- Common greetings are *Kalimera sas* (Good morning) and *Kalinixta* (Good evening).

Conversation

- Greeks enjoy talking about their history, culture, families, and sports. Many Greeks are movie and theater fans. Men often spend their leisure time talking with friends in coffeehouses.
- Soccer, basketball, swimming, and sailing are popular sports.
- Don't be surprised if you are asked personal questions about your family.
- Don't praise an object too much. Your Greek host may insist on giving it to you.
- Be aware that a head nod can mean *no* as well as *yes*. Tilting (not shaking) one's head to either side usually means *yes* or *of course*. However, be careful because Greeks also adopt gestures used in North America.

Sensitivities

- Avoid discussing Cyprus and other political issues.

Key Negotiating Pointers

- In Greece, connections with the right people are critical. The *xorio,* or close network of family alliances, extends into business considerations.
- Prior appointments are not necessary but are appreciated. Be punctual, though your meeting probably won't start on time. Meetings are also not likely to have a specified ending time. Greeks are generally casual about time.
- Don't expect a formal agenda to be followed.

- Build a solid relationship. Trust is more important than expertise. Any suspicion that you are trying to exploit or dominate a relationship could cost you the deal.
- Expect discussions to be spirited. Greeks like to debate, usually with expressive words and body language. What might seem like a major confrontation is really just a normal exchange of views. Be more concerned if your counterpart becomes silent and withdrawn rather than engaging in a somewhat boisterous exchange.
- Be firm and persistent, yet patient and courteous.
- Try to do your negotiating in person, the preferred method of communication in Greece. If possible, avoid the telephone and written communication.
- Keep contracts simple. They are generally distrusted.

Day-to-Day Pointers

Business Entertainment Guidelines

- Don't discuss business during meals. Meals are a social occasion.
- Lunch is usually the main meal of the day, served between noon and 2:00 P.M. Dinner is usually a small meal, served from 7:00 P.M. to 9:00 P.M.
- Greeks are very generous and sincere hosts. You may be invited home for dinner. If so, take flowers or a cake.
- In restaurants, a service charge is usually included in the bill for the server; a tip may be left for the busperson.

Table Manners and Food

- The elderly, who carry an usual amount of respect in Greece, are served first.
- It is typical for a group to order several dishes that everyone shares.
- Having a second helping is considered a compliment to your host.
- Lamb, chicken, seafood, olives, cheese, potatoes, rice, beans, fruit, and vegetables are common foods. Many foods are cooked in olive oil. Spices are popular.
- Salads are usually eaten with the main meal. A popular dish is *souvlaki,* a shish kebab with cakes of meat (usually lamb) and vegetables.

Gender Issues

- Greece is a good place for U.S. women to do business.
- Although Greek society is generally male-dominated, women are well represented in business and politics.

- Business success in Greece depends more on one's connections than on one's sex.

Also Remember This . . .

- Although the industrial sector is growing, Greece has a strong agricultural base. Over 25 percent of the labor force is employed in agriculture.
- The industrial sector now accounts for about half of all export earnings.
- The key unit in Greek business has traditionally been large conglomerates run by dynastic families, closely affiliated with the banks. Many large conglomerates have been socialized, with family managers replaced by political appointees.

ITALY

Fast Facts

Population:	57.6 million
GNP:	$970.6 billion
Per Capita Income:	$16,850
Monetary Unit:	lira
Major Industries:	machinery and transportation equipment
Main Trading Partners:	
Exports:	other EC members (57%), U.S. (9%), OPEC (4%)
Imports:	other EC members (57%), U.S. (6%), OPEC (6%)
Key Exports:	textiles, clothing, metals, transportation equipment, chemicals
Key Imports:	petroleum, industrial machinery, chemicals, metals, foods, agricultural products

Major Cities:	Rome (cap.) (2.8 million), Milan (1.4 million), Naples (1.2 million), Turin (1.0 million)
Ethnic Groups:	primarily Italian, with small clusters of German-, French-, and Slovene-Italians in the North and Albanian-Italians in the South; Sicilians
Main Religions:	nominally Roman Catholic (almost 100%)
Language(s):	Italian; French and English are spoken by some businesspeople in large cities

---

Reducing Communication Noise

Greetings

- Shake hands upon meeting and leaving. Guests are introduced first.
- Address people by their formal titles. Use *Dottore* if you are unsure of the title. First names are used only among close friends.
- Common greetings are *Ciao* (Hi or Good-bye), *Buon giorno* (Good morning or Good afternoon), and *Buona sera* (Good evening).
- Bring plenty of business cards.

Conversation

- Italians enjoy talking about international events, their fine food and wine, and their many museums, art galleries, and historical sites. Italy has been the center of the arts for centuries.
- Italians are avid sports fans, particularly when it comes to soccer. (Italy has won the World Cup several times.) Bicycling, horse racing, skiing, tennis, boxing, and swimming are other popular sports. Basketball and American football have recently attracted an Italian following, but most Italians remain partial to soccer and other traditional sports.
- Italian are very family-oriented, and general discussions about one's family are common.
- Don't be surprised if you see persons of the same gender walking arm-in-arm in public.

Sensitivities

- Italians like discussing politics. Do more listening than talking.

Key Negotiating Pointers

- Make appointments well in advance. Punctuality is not a preoccupation with Italian businesspeople, so you may occasionally be kept waiting.
- Avoid making a cold call. Announce yourself first by sending a letter or fax. This helps make you a known quantity.
- Take every opportunity before, during, and after the negotiating session to build a relationship with your Italian counterpart. Italians like to deal with people they know well.
- Expect to get down to business after a few minutes of small talk. Let your host take the lead on this.
- Italy's negotiating style gets more informal as you move south.
- Make your presentations factual and relevant to local applications.
- Avoid any sense of urgency. Italians often exhibit a calculated nonchalance. For example, a common tactic is to unexpectedly close a negotiating session, pretending the whole thing is of minor importance. Conversely, the deal can come together quickly when all seems lost. Urgency on your part may send a signal that you are desperate to do the deal.
- Get a local agent and consider getting an attorney.

Day-to-Day Pointers

Business Entertainment Guidelines

- Except in Milan, there is not a lot of business entertaining in Italy.
- Business entertaining is usually done in a restaurant.
- Don't discuss business during meals or social events.
- Lunch is the main meal of the day, usually served around 1:00 P.M. A light dinner is eaten in the evening, usually around 8:00 P.M. or 9:00 P.M.
- Meals may last from one to four hours.
- If you are invited to a private home, take wine, flowers (not chrysanthemums, used only for funerals), or chocolates.
- Gift giving among business associates is common.
- In restaurants, a service charge is usually included in the bill. A small tip for the waiter is also appropriate.

Table Manners and Food

- Keep your hands above the table, not in your lap.
- Compliment your host on the fine cuisine.
- When finished eating, place the utensils parallel to each other on the plate.

- Lunch usually consists of three courses: pasta, fish or meat with vegetables, and fruit.
- Wine is a common drink at meals.

Gender Issues

- Italy has a male-dominated business environment, but U.S. women can successfully do business.
- U.S. women should expect some gallant behavior from their Italian male counterparts—for example, having doors opened for them with some flair. Such actions should be accepted graciously.
- A woman traveling with a male colleague should define clearly what her role is. If the male is her superior, the male should define her role.
- Women make up about 34 percent of the Italian work force, among the lowest percentages in Western Europe. With the exception of the fashion industry, there are few Italian women in professional positions and almost none in decision-making positions.
- There is no equal employment opportunity legislation for working women, even though there are generous maternity benefits and a well-developed system of free day care.

Also Remember This . . .

- The Italian economy is based on agriculture in the South and industry in the North.
- Italy is one of the world's largest wine producers. Tourism is another major source of revenue.
- Milan is the leading business city.

NETHERLANDS

Fast Facts

Population:	14.9 million
GNP:	$258.8 billion
Per Capita Income:	$17,330
Monetary Unit:	guilder
Major Industries:	agro-industries, metal and engineering products, electrical machinery and equipment
Main Trading Partners	
Exports:	Germany (28%), Belgium-Luxembourg (14%), France (11%), U.K. (10%), U.S. (5%)
Imports:	Germany (27%), Belgium-Luxembourg (23%), U.S. (8%)
Key Exports:	agricultural products, processed foods and tobacco, natural gas, chemicals, metal products
Key Imports:	raw materials and semifinished products, consumer goods, transportation equipment, crude oil
Major Cities:	Amsterdam (cap.) (694,700), Rotterdam (576,200), The Hague (443,800), Utrecht (230,600)
Ethnic Groups:	Dutch (99%), Indonesian and other (1%)
Main Religions:	Roman Catholic (40%), Protestant (31%)
Language(s):	Dutch

Reducing Communication Noise

Greetings

- Shake hands with everyone present, including women and children, upon meeting and leaving. Women are insulted if men do not shake hands with them.

- The Dutch are fairly informal. First names are common, but do not use them until you are invited to do so. Until that time, address people as *Mr.*, *Mrs.*, or *Miss*. If the other person is much older or very senior in position, be careful about using first names even if invited to do so; this invitation may be extended out of courtesy, and you will be perceived as being overly familiar if you accept it.

Conversation

- The Dutch enjoy talking about their art, music, museums, beautiful country, and international affairs. Many famous artists are from Holland, such as Rembrandt, Vermeer, and Van Gogh. The Dutch also appreciate compliments on their homes and their flowers, and they like to talk about traveling.
- The Dutch are sports-minded. Soccer is the most popular sport, followed by tennis, bicycling, field hockey, swimming, sailing, and ice skating.
- Maintain eye contact during conversation. Personal space is about the same as in the United States.

Sensitivities

- Avoid discussing religion.
- If you discuss politics, do more listening than talking. The Dutch see their politics as very plain and down-to-earth compared with the relative glamour of U.S. politics.

Key Negotiating Pointers

- Make prior appointments and be punctual.
- The pace of negotiations is fast, similar to in the United States.
- Make your proposals conceptually strong as well as quantitatively correct. The Dutch pay attention to the bottom line but are not obsessed with numbers.
- Presentations should be professional-looking, practical, and factual. Consider using charts and graphs. Sloppiness is hard to overcome.
- Leave yourself some room to negotiate, but make your first offer fairly close to your "really asking" price. The Dutch are not hagglers. You may lose points if you start making large concessions.
- Be straightforward and downplay humor. Even informal business discussions tend to remain serious. The Dutch prize plain speaking.
- Comply with the details of your promises. Failure to do so hurts your credibility. The Dutch are practical and efficient and expect results.

Day-to-Day Pointers

Business Entertainment Guidelines

- Business entertaining is less common than in the United States, but when done, usually takes place in restaurants.
- It is appropriate to discuss business during a business lunch. (Most Dutch feel somewhat guilty if they have fun during working hours.)
- The main meal of the day is dinner.
- If invited to a Dutch home, shake hands with everyone, including children. Leave after coffee is served, usually before 10:00 P.M.
- In restaurants, tips are usually included in the bill, but leave a small additional tip if the service is good.

Table Manners and Food

- The Dutch tend to pay attention to table manners.
- Men usually wait until all the ladies are seated before sitting down.
- Before eating, the host or hostess usually says *Eet smakelijk* (ATE-smaahk-AY-lick), meaning "Eat deliciously."
- Keep your hands (but not elbows) above the table.
- Dinner usually consists of meat or fish and potatoes and gravy, with vegetables of the season. Herring, smoked eel, oysters, pea soup, and *hutspot* (mashed potatoes mixed with various vegetables) are typical dishes.

Gender Issues

- U.S. women can successfully conduct business with the Dutch. However, in spite of the social responsibility of the Netherlands as a nation, the Dutch are sometimes chauvinistic about women in business.
- There is a powerful Old Boy Network in industry and a male-dominated aristocracy within banking and the diplomatic service.
- Women seldom have professional careers, and married women tend to end their careers when they have children.
- Women make up only about 35 percent of the work force, somewhat low by Western standards.

Also Remember This . . .

- The Dutch welcome foreigners and are generally open to new ideas.
- The Netherlands has a strong economy that is based on commerce, indus-

try, and agriculture. Banking and tourism are also key sectors of the economy.

- The Netherlands produces food for export and is responsible for over 60 percent of the world's flower exports.

SPAIN

Fast Facts

Population:	39.3 million
GNP:	$429.4 billion
Per Capita Income:	$10,920
Monetary Unit:	peseta
Major Industries:	textiles, clothing, footwear, foods and beverages, metals
Main Trading Partners:	
Exports:	other EC members (66%), other developed countries (9%), Switzerland (8%)
Imports:	other EC members (57%), other developed countries (13%), U.S. (9%), Middle East (3%)
Key Exports	food, live animals, wood, footwear, machinery, chemicals
Key Imports:	petroleum, footwear, machinery, chemicals, grains, soybeans, coffee
Major Cities:	Madrid (cap.) (3.1 million), Barcelona (1.7 million), Valencia (732,500), Seville (655,400)
Ethnic Groups:	composite of Mediterranean and Nordic backgrounds
Main religions:	Roman Catholic (99%)

| **Language(s):** | Castilian Spanish; second languages include Catalan, Galician, and Basque; English and French are also spoken in business |

Reducing Communication Noise

Greetings

- Shake hands upon meeting and leaving. Men should wait for women to extend their hands first.
- *Abrazos,* or hugs, are reserved for friends.
- Titles—*Señor, Señora,* or *Señorita*—are usually used with the last name in business. *Don* and *Doña* are used with the first name to show respect. The mother's family name is attached to a person's name in written communication (e.g., Sr. Franco Martinez Rodriquez)
- Though a senior person may address you by your first name, do not reciprocate unless you are invited to do so.

Conversation

- Spaniards enjoy talking about Spain's history, culture, and rapid economic growth and their families.
- Soccer is a very popular national sport. Many Spaniards are also involved in tennis, basketball, swimming, skiing, and hunting. Bullfighting is a popular spectator sport and is seen as both an art and a sport.
- There tends to be a lot of touching in Spain compared with many other Western European countries.

Sensitivities

- Spaniards like discussing politics. Do more listening than talking.
- Avoid comparisons with the United States.
- Don't be critical of bullfighting. Spaniards see it as an important part of their culture.

Key Negotiating Pointers

- Be punctual, though you may be kept waiting. Business meetings generally start fifteen or so minutes after the designated time.

- Expect a relaxed pace of negotiations.
- Establish a solid relationship. Trust, rapport, and compatibility are essential in order to do business in Spain.
- Never embarrass your counterpart. Pride and honor are very important to Spanish negotiators.
- Leave yourself room for concessions. Though bargaining is part of everyday life in Spain, don't haggle so much that you jeopardize the relationship.
- Make your proposals detailed and practical. Grandiose schemes are not likely to be well accepted.
- Business is not conducted during the afternoon *siesta* (break), from 1:30 P.M. to 4:30 P.M.
- Don't be put off by occasional "advice giving" or "corrections." Spaniards often consider it their duty to correct "errors" by others.
- Dress well and speak with as much flair and eloquence as you can. Appearances are important.

Day-to-Day Pointers

Business Entertainment Guidelines

- Business entertaining is usually done in restaurants. Invitations to one's home may be extended only as polite courtesy. Accept only if the host insists.
- Lunch is eaten around 2:00 P.M. and is usually the main meal of the day. A snack (*merienda*) is eaten about 5:00 P.M. or 6:00 P.M. Dinner is very late—normally around 9:00 P.M. or 10:00 P.M.—and is not as substantial as lunch.
- Your host indicates seating arrangements if the dinner is formal. Take a small gift if invited to a private home.
- The national toast is *Salud* (To your health), usually spoken before sipping a glass of *jerez* (sherry), the national drink.
- In restaurants, a 15 percent service charge is often added to the bill. If not, leave a 10–15 percent tip.

Table Manners and Food

- Compliments on meals are well received.
- Keep your hands (but not elbows) above the table.
- The continental style of eating is used, with the fork in the left hand and

the knife in the right. The knife is used to push food onto the fork. (Don't use other food or fingers to do so.)

- Place the utensils side-by-side on the plate when you are finished eating. Leaving them any other way indicates that you want to eat more.
- Fresh vegetables, meat, eggs, chicken, and fish are typical foods. Most foods are cooked in olive oil.
- There are several regional Spanish dishes: *gazpacho* (a cold vegetable soup), from the Southern province of Andalusia; *paella* (a stew of seafood, rice, and vegetables), from the Eastern province of Valencia; and *marmitako* (fisherman's stew), from the Basque region.
- Wine is usually served with meals.

Gender Issues

- U.S. women can expect *macho* and chauvinistic attitudes toward women in business from many male Spanish counterparts.
- Although changes are taking place, there are few career-oriented Spanish women, and even fewer in management or key decision-making positions. The Spanish business community is polarized regarding the appropriate role of women in business.

Also Remember This . . .

- Spain is one of the poorest countries in Western Europe, though its economy has been steadily improving.
- Industry has been expanding, though agriculture and mining are important sectors of the economy.
- Spain is a leading wine producer.

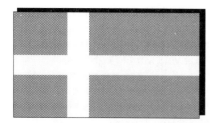

SWEDEN

Fast Facts

Population:	8.5 million
GNP:	$205.5 billion
Per Capita Income:	$23,680
Monetary Unit:	Swedish krona
Major Industries:	iron and steel, precision equipment (bearing radio and television parts), paper and pulp
Main Trading Partners:	
Exports:	Germany (12%), U.K. (11%), U.S. (10%), Norway (9%), Denmark (7%)
Imports:	Germany (21%), U.K. (9%), U.S. (8%), Denmark (7%), Norway (6%)
Key Exports:	machinery, motor vehicles, paper products, pulp and wood, iron and steel products
Key Imports:	machinery, petroleum and petroleum products, chemicals, motor vehicles, foods
Major Cities:	Stockholm (cap.) (666,800), Goteborg (431,500), Malmö (230,800), Uppsala (160,000)
Ethnic Groups:	homogeneous Caucasian population (88%), foreign-born or first-generation immigrants (12%)
Main Religions:	Evangelical Lutheran (94%), Roman Catholic (1%)
Language(s):	Swedish; there are small Lapp and Finnish-speaking minorities; English is widely spoken

Reducing Communication Noise

Greetings

- Shake hands firmly upon meeting.
- First names are used quite quickly, but do not use them until you are invited to do so. Titles and last names are usually reserved for very formal occasions.
- Typical greetings are *God dag* (Good day) and *God morgon* (Good morning).

Conversation

- Swedes enjoy talking about Sweden's accomplishments, the theater, movies, and sports.
- Soccer, skiing, ice hockey, tennis, and golf are popular sports. Many Swedes are also involved in hiking, fishing, and bird watching.
- Sweden is the home of the Nobel Prize.
- Try to learn a few words of Swedish. This is appreciated.
- Avoid very expressive hand gestures when speaking. Swedes tend to be very friendly, but reserved.
- Maintain eye contact during conversation.

Sensitivities

- Avoid discussing politics or personal matters.
- Don't praise one area of Sweden over the one you are visiting. Swedes have a strong regional loyalty.
- Swedes are very concerned about the environment and typically have strong opinions about the disappearing ozone layer, global warming, and pollution.
- Avoid lumping the cultural distinctions of Sweden with those of other Scandinavian countries.

Key Negotiating Pointers

- Swedes have a reputation as tough negotiators—not hagglers who enjoy the process, but methodical, detailed individuals who are slow to change positions. On the other hand, expect your Swedish counterpart to push for concessions.
- Make prior appointments. Punctuality is important.

- Negotiations are similar to those in the United States in that they move crisply and are task-oriented.
- Make presentations factual, practical, precise, and reserved. Showy behavior is not rewarded.
- Be friendly, but get to the point of your discussions. Use a modest and direct communication style.
- Remember that strong personal relationships follow a solid business relationship.
- Look for decision makers to be at middle to lower levels of the organization. Swedish senior management often delegates key decisions. Expect to negotiate with middle managers most of the time.
- Expect decision making to be rather slow. Alternatives are often worked out with middle management before a decision is made. This can be a time-consuming process, but once a decision is made, implementation is usually rapid.
- Dress well. As in other Scandinavian countries, public presentation is considered very important.
- Contracts are detailed.

Day-to-Day Pointers

Business Entertainment Guidelines

- Swedes do not usually combine business and entertainment, though business lunches are not unusual.
- Business may be discussed over meals.
- Toasting is quite formal. Don't toast your host or those senior in rank or age before they first toast you. Don't touch your glass until your host says *Skoal.*
- Gift giving is not typical in business.

Table Manners and Food

- Be punctual for the meal, which is usually served right away.
- Keep your hands (but not elbows) above the table.
- Try to eat everything on your plate.
- The continental style of eating is used, with the fork in the left hand and the knife in the right.
- Use a separate knife for the butter rather than your dinner knife.
- Place the utensils side-by-side on the plate when you are finished eating.
- The Swedish diet has traditionally been heavy on meat, fish, and cheese,

but it now includes fresh vegetables and fruits as a result of Swedes' efforts to eat more healthfully. Potatoes are eaten a few times a week.
- The *smorgasbord* (a large buffet) is not an everyday meal, but eaten at parties or during the Christmas season.

Gender Issues

- Sweden is a good place for U.S. women to do business.
- Swedes are somewhat more conservative in their views toward women in the professions and management than their sexually liberated reputation might indicate.
- Women make of 48 percent of the work force—one of the highest percentages in the world.

Also Remember This . . .

- Sweden has one of the world's most prosperous economies and has a very high standard of living. The country is highly industrialized, has an excellent distribution system, and has an educated and skilled work force.
- The economy has been somewhat sluggish in recent years. Various economic reforms have been introduced to stimulate it.
- Swedish income taxes are among the highest in the world (recently reduced from 72 percent to 50 percent). These taxes maintain a comprehensive social welfare system. Most Swedes are quite supportive of the tax structure.

SWITZERLAND

Fast Facts

Population:	6.7 million
GNP:	$219.3 billion
Per Capita Income:	$32,790

Monetary Unit:	Swiss franc
Major Industries:	machinery, chemicals, watches, cheeses, textiles
Main Trading Partners:	
Exports:	EC (56%), U.S. (9%), Japan (4%)
Imports:	EC (70%), U.S. (5%)
Key Exports:	machinery and equipment, precision instruments, metal products, foods
Key Imports:	agricultural products, machinery and transportation equipment, chemicals, textiles
Major Cities:	Bern (cap.) (135,100), Zurich (345,200), Basel (170,100), Geneva (164,000)
Ethnic Groups:	German (65%), French (18%), Italian (10%)
Main Religions:	Catholic (49%), Protestant (48%)
Language(s):	German, French, Italian; English is widely spoken

---

Reducing Communication Noise

Greetings

- Shake hands firmly with both men and women upon meeting and leaving.
- Address people by their title and last name. Address German-speaking people as *Herr* and *Frau;* French-speaking people as *Monsieur, Madame,* or *Mademoiselle;* and Italian-speaking people as *Signor, Signora,* or *Signorita.* First names are usually used only among close friends.
- For people of German and Italian backgrounds, use the person's surname, as in "Good morning, Herr (or Signor) Johnson." For the French a simple "Good morning, monsieur" will do.
- Verbal greetings vary because Switzerland is a multilingual society. English greetings are usually acceptable, though the Swiss appreciate attempts to speak the language of the region you are visiting.
- Give your business card to the receptionist when visiting a company.

Conversation

- The Swiss enjoy talking about Switzerland's nature and beauty and their travels.
- Soccer and bicycling are the most popular sports. Hiking, skiing, and other outdoor sports are also popular.

- If you are fluent only in English, try to learn a few phrases in the language of the region you're visiting.

Sensitivities

- Avoid personal questions about one's job, salary, age, or family.
- The Swiss like discussing politics. Do more listening than talking.
- Don't flaunt wealth. Despite their high standard of living, the Swiss are conservative.

Key Negotiating Pointers

- The overall conduct of Swiss negotiations is similar to in the United States in that negotiations are somewhat impersonal, brisk, orderly, planned, and task-oriented. Swiss negotiations tend to be a little more formal than in the United States, however.
- Make prior appointments and be punctual. This is particularly important to the Swiss.
- Pay attention to formalities and courtesies. Be conservative in your dress.
- Expect a brief amount of small talk before getting to the task at hand. The personal relationship tends to follow the development of a solid business relationship.
- Make proposals practical, detailed, precise, and reserved. The Swiss value hard work, sobriety, and thrift.
- Presentations should be orderly and well prepared. Consider the use of slides, graphs, and charts. If you have a laser-jet printer, use it.
- Be thoroughly knowledgeable in product and contract details.
- Leave yourself some room to bargain, but make your initial offer fairly close to your "really asking" price. The Swiss are not hagglers.
- Be patient in both the negotiations and the project details that are discussed. The Swiss are often cautious and pessimistic about achieving project deadlines.
- Expect decision making to be methodical, with many questions and requests for information. Decisions are usually centralized and slow.
- Deemphasize deals that stress Swiss production of labor-intensive items. Swiss manufacturers must overcome high wages and very low unemployment.
- Follow up with a fax or letter that summarizes discussions. The Swiss like to have things in writing.
- Contracts are detailed.

Day-to-Day Pointers

Business Entertainment Guidelines

- Lunch, the main meal of the day, is the most common business meal. Dinner is usually light and is served around 6 P.M. or 7 P.M.
- Business is often discussed over meals.
- If you are invited to a Swiss home, wipe your feet before entering. Candy and unwrapped flowers are appropriate gifts. Avoid red roses, however, since they imply romantic interest. Shake hands with all members of the family when leaving.
- Gift giving is not common for business acquaintances.
- In restaurants, the bill usually includes the service charge and is paid at the table.

Table Manners and Food

- Don't drink until a toast is made. Typical Swiss toasts are the German *Prost,* the French *Sante,* and the Italian *Cincin.*
- Asking for salt and pepper is sometimes interpreted as an insult because it implies the food is improperly spiced.
- Keep you hands (but not elbows) above the table.
- Asking for a second helping of food is a great compliment to your host.
- Place the utensils side-by-side on the plate when you are finished eating. Leaving them any other way may indicate that you are still hungry.
- Lunch usually consists of meat and potatoes or pasta and salad. Dinners consists of an open-faced sandwich.
- Sausages, leek soup, cheese, fish, and wines are regional specialties.

Gender Issues

- Switzerland is generally a good place for U.S. women to do business.
- Although banking and finance are dominated by men, women get a fair hearing and are treated professionally.

Also Remember This . . .

- Switzerland has one of the world's strongest economies with the highest per capita income in the world.

- Banking, finance, tourism, and industry are all strong segments of the economy.
- Switzerland has four distinct ethnic communities: German, French, Italian, and Romansh.

UNITED KINGDOM

Fast Facts

Population:	57.2 million
GNP:	$924.0 billion
Per Capita Income:	$16,070
Monetary Unit:	British pound
Major Industries:	machinery and transportation equipment, metals, food processing
Main Trading Partners:	
Exports:	other EC members (50%), U.S. (13%)
Imports:	other EC members (53%), U.S. (10%)
Key Exports:	manufactured goods, machinery, fuels, chemicals, semifinished products, transportation equipment
Key Imports:	food, manufactured goods, machinery, semifinished products
Major Cities:	London (cap.) (6.7 million), Birmingham (993,700), Glasgow (703,200)
Ethnic Groups:	English (82%), Scottish (10%), Irish (3%), Welsh (2%)
Main Religions:	Anglican (47%), Roman Catholic (9%), Presbyterian (3%)
Languages:	English, Welsh, Scottish form of Gaelic

Reducing Communication Noise

Greetings

- Shake hands with men upon meeting and leaving. Women don't have to shake hands, so wait for them to extend their hands first.
- When introduced, both parties say, "How do you do?" It is also polite to add some form of expression of pleasure about getting to meet the other person.
- Address people as *Mr., Mrs.,* or *Miss,* until you are invited to use their first names.

Conversation

- The British enjoy talking about their rich cultural heritage. They also love animals and like to talk about them.
- Football (soccer), rugby, cricket, and tennis are very popular sports. Badminton, sailing, swimming, darts, and squash are also favorite sporting activities. The British are proud of the Wimbledon tennis tournament, an international sporting event.
- Remember that many "English" words have a totally different meaning than they do in the United States—for example, *vet* (to check or appraise, such as "to vet a contract"), *lift* (elevator), *chemist* (druggist), *intercourse* (friendly conversation, such as "I had intercourse with my negotiating team before the session began").

Sensitivities

- Avoid discussing politics or religion. Don't criticize the status, role, or wealth of the Royal Family.
- Avoid personal questions and demonstrative touching. Many British consider Americans pushy and aggressive.
- Be careful with humor. While the British enjoy a good joke, they often "don't get" American jokes, and vice versa.
- Avoid poking fun at the British affection for their dogs (it is not unusual to see dogs accompany the British on visits to restaurants or pubs).
- Be conspicuously polite to older people.
- Tone down discussion of genealogy. If you are British by heritage, this is of less interest to your counterpart than it might be to you.
- Use the term *British* rather than *English.* Remember that while people may live in London, they may have Welsh, Irish, or Scottish backgrounds. Also,

people from Scotland are called Scots or Scotsmen (or British). Scotch is what you drink.
- Avoid comparisons with the United States.
- Don't talk loudly or gesticulate wildly. Project your voice to reach only your conversational counterpart.

Key Negotiating Pointers

- Make connections with the traditional power brokers. The old class system still influences business, particularly in England. Traditions are important.
- Make prior appointments and be punctual.
- Most British negotiators are less competitive in style than U.S. negotiators. Bargaining is not a usual fact of everyday life for the British. Expect formalities and attention to protocol, especially in London. Northern England, Scotland, Wales, and Northern Ireland are less formal.
- Be friendly, but keep your small talk impersonal and to a minimum.
- Expect the pace of negotiations to be crisp, but slower than in the United States.
- Presentations should be matter-of-fact, detailed, and subdued.
- Leave yourself room for movement, but you needn't build a large amount of "fat" into your proposal. The British tend to have moderate initial demands.
- Try not to push for agreement or appear to be in a hurry. Avoid doing most of the talking.
- Delivery time may be a sticking point if you are the buyer. Be sure to include a contract clause that imposes hefty payment penalties for late deliveries.
- Financing and quality are lesser problems. Chances are the British will be helpful with financing, and generally their goods are of high quality.
- Be aware of the political and union context of the negotiation. Bureaucratic requirements can be cumbersome, political signals mixed, and unions powerful. Seek counsel on finding the "right" union if you are negotiating the start-up of a new facility that is likely to be unionized.

Day-to-Day Pointers

Business Entertainment Guidelines

- Most business entertaining is done in pubs and restaurants.
- The business lunch is an institution. It is customary to discuss business over the meal if there are no spouses present.

- A night at the theater or ballet are good entertainment options.
- Tea is often the main meal of the day and is eaten between 5:00 P.M. and 7:00 P.M.
- You are likely to be offered coffee or tea when calling on a business associate. The U.K. is one of the few places in the world where declining a beverage is not an offense.
- An invitation reading "black tie" or "smoking" means men must wear dinner jackets and women, long dresses.
- A small gift (flowers or chocolates) is appropriate if invited to a home and you are likely to be the only guest.
- Gift giving is prevalent. Logo gifts with your company name should be unobtrusive. Be careful not to leave an impression that you are trying to bribe your counterpart.

Table Manners and Food

- Do not smoke before a meal is finished and not without asking the permission of your host. Smoke only after the toast to Her Majesty's health, subsequent to the main course.
- Beef, mutton, potatoes, and vegetables are part of the British diet. Tea and beer are popular drinks. Fish and chips (French fries) are as popular as the American hamburger.

Gender Issues

- Although U.S. women find a very acceptable business climate in the U.K., the Old Boy Network is still very much alive.
- While women make up about 42 percent of the work force, there are few British women in management positions.

Also Remember This . . .

- There has been increased privatization of industry since the early 1980s.
- Great Britain consists of England, Scotland, and Wales. When Northern Ireland is added, the correct name is United Kingdom.

Chapter 9

Negotiating in Eastern Europe

The Business Environment of Eastern Europe

Though definitions vary in the fast-changing European political and economic landscape, Eastern Europe is considered to be Czechoslovakia, Poland, Hungary, Romania, Bulgaria, and Russia and the other countries that formerly constituted the Soviet Union. Russia is the world's largest nation, spanning eleven time zones.

Eastern Europe can be a very tough part of the world for a negotiator. The business environment is characterized by fundamental changes in economic and political structures. There are, however, also great opportunities. Reported investment strategies in Eastern Europe are summarized in Exhibit 9–1.

An emphasis is likely to be put on the creation of an auto industry in Hungary, Poland, and Czechoslovakia to meet projected domestic and international demand. "Feeder" industries will involve the mechanical engineering, electronics, electrotechnical, chemicals, glass, and sheet metal subsectors.[1]

You should give consideration to investing in Eastern Europe if your company is involved in selling to priority areas such as the auto industry, consumer goods, processed food, health, telecommunications, or computers. Investment viability will be enhanced by improvements in business conditions. In 1991, multinational corporations were allowed to repatriate profits generated in local currencies in Hungary and Czechoslovakia, and zloty

Exhibit 9-1. Reported investment strategies in Eastern Europe in 1990.

Notes: Based on overall risk analysis, including such factors as commitment to reform by both populace and politicians; experience and scope of reforms; quality of leadership in both public and "private" sectors; and overall cultural readiness and receptivity to change. Also based on such factors as physical and service (including communications) infrastructure; overall indebtedness; natural resource base; industry development, skill base, and status; and hard currency capability (i.e., exportable produce/products).

Source: Adapted from Lynne Hall, *Latecomer's Guide to the New Europe: Doing Business in Central Europe* (New York: American Management Association, 1992).

profits were partially transferable from Poland.[2] From the perspective of a global procurement strategy, Eastern Europe offers major cost advantages, mainly because of inexpensive labor. The attractiveness of Eastern Europe is also enhanced by active involvement by the World Bank, United Nations, International Monetary Fund, and New European Bank for Reconstruction and Development.

The business arrangements favored in Eastern Europe in the 1990s by many multinational companies are joint ventures, direct investment, or start-ups, rather than the barter/countertrade approaches of the 1970s and 1980s. Joint ventures are popular because of their export and hard currency potential.

There are key obstacles to overcome in much of this part of the world. First, the concept of "profit" is still not understood in many parts of Eastern Europe. Another obstacle is that of currency. As a rule, Eastern currencies are considered worthless in the West. Alternative financial arrangements must therefore be found to circumvent this problem. This is sometimes done through bartering arrangements, with the U.S. organization paid in a commodity such as oil, rather than in currency.

The "P" Word

Despite the new bullishness, there are still plenty of obstacles to doing business in the former Soviet Union. Under the old command economy, the costs of production routinely exceed the price of oil. "We have to begin by discussing the concept of profit," says one frustrated American executive. "We have to tell the Soviets that a lot of their oil isn't worth getting out of the ground at $21 a barrel."

Many foreigners in this high stakes business are dismayed to find that "profit" is still a dirty word in the former Soviet Union. "The Soviets are looking for bank-style returns of 6 or 7 percent," says Gordon Andrus, vice-president of Houston's Anglo-Suisse. "In our industry we expect to see something in the 20 percent range. That's commensurate with the risk." Chevron is still stinging from local charges that it negotiated an unfair share of profits from its $25 billion deal with Kazakhstan to develop the enormous Tengiz oil fields. As a result, Western companies now shy away from exclusive negotiations and instead enter bids for coveted projects to reduce the appearance of favoritism.[3]

Cultural Factors That Affect Negotiating in Eastern Europe

Use of Time

Expect Eastern Europeans to be punctual, or at most, to begin meetings no more than ten to fifteen minutes past the appointed time.

Individualism vs. Collectivism

As one would expect given the strong influence of a Communistic political system over the past several decades, a "we" consciousness, or collectivist orientation, still predominates. Group ideals are prevalent in many business discussions.

The group emphasis may help explain the limited authority of most Eastern European negotiators. Checking with headquarters, even on minor points, is typical. In addition, one can almost always expect team negotiations. There is also often lack of clarity about the decision-making process, leaving questions as to who is in charge. These factors tend to make negotiations slow and tedious.

Role Orderliness and Conformity

There is on the one hand a predictability as to one's place and strict rules and regulations surrounding organizational behavior. On the other hand, it is not always clear who exactly is in charge. This is probably the result in large part of the cumbersome bureaucracies that generate duplication of effort and occasionally blurred lines of authority. Decisions generally flow from the top down.

Patterns of Communication

Verbal Communication

Eastern Europeans are generally direct in their communication, making straightforward, firm requests and demands. Once past any language barrier, there is little guesswork regarding their point of view. Though they are very gracious as hosts, the communication styles of Eastern Europeans may sometimes seem abrupt and aggressive, even to North Americans.

Nonverbal Communication

Personal space in Eastern Europe is generally closer than in North America. Hand and arm gestures are usually quite expressive. Handshakes are firm and brief. An exception are hand-shakes between men and women, which can be quite lengthy in countries such as Poland or Czechoslovakia, with the man kissing the woman's hand.

Notes

1. Lynne Hall, *Latecomer's Guide to the New Europe: Doing Business in Central Europe* (New York: American Management Association, 1992), p. 75.
2. Ibid., p. 46.
3. Karen Breslau, "Exploring Siberia, with a Texas Accent," *Newsweek* (October 21, 1991), p. 52. © 1991, Newsweek, Inc. All rights reserved. Reprinted by permission.

HOW NEGOTIATIONS WORK IN EASTERN EUROPE

Negotiating Factors

1. Pace of Negotiations   Slow

2. Negotiating Strategies
  Opening Offers vis-à-vis
    Settlement   High initial demands
  Presentation of Issues   Group of issues may be presented
  Presentations   Fairly formal
  Dealing With Differences   Argumentative
  Concessions   Slow

**3. Emphasis on Personal
   Relationships**   Very low

4. Emotional Aspects
  Sensitivity   Not highly valued
  Degree of Emotions   Moderate

5. Decision Making
  Overall Method   Somewhat impulsive
  Emphasize   Logic
  Emphasis on Group/Team   Moderate: Decisions from top
                                         management
  Emphasis on Face-Saving   Fairly high
  Influence of Special
    Interests on Decision
    Maker(s)   Usually not condoned

**6. Contractual and
   Administrative Factors**
  Need for an Agent   Average
  Degree of Contract
    Specificity   Moderate
  Degree of Paperwork/
    Bureaucracy   High
  Need for an Agenda   Moderate

CZECHOSLOVAKIA

Fast Facts

Population:	15.7 million
GNP:	$49.2 billion
Per Capita Income:	$3,140
Monetary Unit:	koruna
Major Industries:	iron and steel, machinery and equipment, cement
Main Trading Partners:	
Exports/Imports:	USSR (former), Germany, Poland, Hungary, Yugoslavia, Austria, Bulgaria
Key Exports:	machinery and equipment, industrial consumer goods, minerals and metals
Key Imports:	machinery and equipment, fuels, minerals and metals, agricultural and forestry products
Major Cities:	Prague (cap.) (1.2 million), Bratislava (435,700), Brno (389,800), Ostrava (330,600)
Ethnic Groups:	Czech (64%), Slovak (31%), Hungarian (4%)
Main Religions:	Roman Catholic (77%), Protestant (20%), Orthodox (2%)
Language(s):	Czech, Slovak, Hungarian

Reducing Communication Noise

Greetings

- Shake hands with men upon meeting and parting. Men should wait for women to extend their hands first.
- Address people by a title (such as *Doctor, Professor, Director, Mr., Mrs.,*

or *Miss*) with the last name. First names are usually used only among friends.

- Common greetings are *Dobry den* (Good day) and *Tesi mne?* (pronounced teh-shee-mnye, for How do you do?). The word for "Thank you" is *Dekuji* (de-ksee).

Conversation

- Czechs enjoy talking about their cultural heritage. Czechs have a history of great composers and famous authors such as Dvořák, Kafka, and Čapek. Czech gothic and baroque architecture is superb. Czechs also like to discuss their many fine regional wines.
- Soccer is the most popular sport, followed by ice hockey and tennis. Czechs have their own Olympics, called Spartakiade, every five years.

Sensitivities

- Avoid discussing politics, religion, or social conditions.

Key Negotiating Pointers

- Make prior appointments far in advance and be punctual.
- Be patient. Negotiations are likely to be time-consuming. Decision making is slow. Czech organizations are bureaucratic and cumbersome.
- Stress your company's link to the global economy. Access to Western economies is key to Czech organizations.
- Emphasize your company's ability to transfer business skills and technological know-how.
- If you are negotiating the purchase of a business, don't expect many clues about what the business is worth (asset valuations, cash flow analyses, or marketing plans).
- Use an interpreter unless you speak Czech or Slovak.

Day-to-Day Pointers

Business Entertainment Guidelines

- The main business meal is lunch, eaten about noon.
- Toasting is often part of both formal and informal meals.

- If you are invited to a private home, bring flowers (except for red roses, which signify romantic affection), wine, whiskey, or cognac.

Table Manners and Food

- Keep your hand (but not elbows) above the table.
- Pork roast, dumplings, and sauerkraut are a popular meal. Prague specialties include roast goose, ham, and sausages. Fruits and vegetables must be imported.
- Wine and beer are typical beverages. Water is served in restaurants, though mineral water can be ordered.

Gender Issues

- Western women must contend with almost exclusively male-dominated organizations at almost every decision-making level.

Also Remember This . . .

- For Eastern Europe, Czechoslovakia has a high standard of living.
- Until 1990 the economy was centrally controlled, and trade was conducted mainly with other Communist countries. The private sector was virtually nonexistent before 1989.
- There are serious conflicts between the Czechs and the Slovaks, which could lead to the breakup of the country.

HUNGARY

Fast Facts

Population:	10.6 million
GNP:	$30.0 billion
Per Capita Income:	$2,780

Monetary Unit:	forint
Major Industries:	mining, metallurgy, engineering
Main Trading Partners:	
Exports:	USSR (former) (48%), other Eastern Europe (25%), developed countries (16%)
Imports:	USSR (former) (43%), other Eastern Europe (28%), less-developed countries (23%)
Key Exports:	capital goods, foods, consumer goods, fuels, minerals
Key Imports:	machinery and transportation equipment, fuels, manufactured consumer goods
Major Cities:	Budapest (cap.) (2.1 million), Debrecen (219,200), Miskole (207,800)
Ethnic Groups:	Hungarian (97%), German and other (3%)
Main Religions:	Roman Catholic (68%), Calvinist (29%), Lutheran (5%)
Language(s):	Hungarian (called Magyar in Hungary)

Reducing Communication Noise

Greetings

- Shake hands upon meeting and parting. Men should wait for women to extend their hands first.
- Address people by a title (such as *Doctor, Professor, Director, Mr., Mrs.,* or *Miss*) with the last name. First names are usually used only among close friends.

Conversation

- Hungarians are proud of their artists, composers, folk music, food, and fine wines. Franz Liszt and Béla Bartók are two famous Hungarian composers.
- Hungary is called a "nation of horsemen." Hungarians were historically known for their horsemanship, and even today horses are a prominent part of recreation and tourist activities.
- Soccer is the most popular sport, along with swimming, tennis, fencing, and sailing.

Sensitivities

- Avoid discussing politics, religion, or social conditions.

Key Negotiating Pointers

- Make prior appointments and be punctual.
- Be patient. Negotiations are likely to be time-consuming. Decision making is slow. Hungarian organizations are still bureaucratic and cumbersome.
- Stress your company's links to the global economy.
- Emphasize your company's ability to transfer business skills and technological know-how.
- If you are negotiating the purchase of a business, don't expect many clues about what the business is worth (asset valuation, cash flow analyses, or marketing plans).
- Use an interpreter unless you speak Magyar (Hungarian). Few Hungarian businesspeople speak English.

Day-to-Day Pointers

Business Entertainment Guidelines

- Most business entertaining is done in restaurants.
- Lunch is the main meal of the day, usually eaten between noon and 2:00 P.M. Dinner is normally eaten after 7:00 P.M.
- In restaurants, a 10–15 percent tip is appropriate.

Table Manners and Food

- The continental style of eating is used, with the fork in the left hand and the knife in the right.
- Many ethnic cuisines are available because of Hungary's central European location. A famous Hungarian specialty is *goulash,* a stew of meat, potatoes, onions, and paprika.
- Pork and chicken are common meats. Popular side dishes are noodles, potatoes, and dumplings. Most dishes include spices and sauces. Other common dishes include *halaszle* (fish soup), stuffed paprika (sweet peppers), stuffed chicken, strudel, and pancakes.

Gender Issues

- Western women must contend with almost exclusively male-dominated organizations at almost every decision-making level.

Also Remember This . . .

- Hungary is one of the most prosperous and politically open countries in Eastern Europe.
- Foreign investment is welcomed to build the economy and to gain hard currency.
- The World Bank, International Monetary Fund, and other international organizations influence Hungary's business development. Heavy debt hinders further economic development.

POLAND

Fast Facts

Population:	38.0 million
GNP:	$64.5 billion
Per Capita Income:	$1,700
Monetary Unit:	zloty
Major Industries:	machine building, iron and steel, extractive industries
Main Trading Partners:	
Exports:	USSR (former) (25%), West Germany (former) (12%), Czechoslovakia (6%)
Imports:	USSR (former) (23%), West Germany (former) (13%), Czechoslovakia (6%)
Key Exports:	machinery and equipment, fuels, minerals and metals, manufactured consumer goods

Key Imports:	machinery and equipment, fuels, minerals and metals, agricultural and forestry products
Major Cities:	Warsaw (cap.) (1.7 million), Lodz (851,500), Cracow (743,700), Wroclaw (637,400)
Ethnic Groups:	Polish (99%), Ukranian and Byelorussian (1%)
Main Religions:	Roman Catholic (95%)
Language(s):	Polish

Reducing Commuinication Noise

Greetings

- Shake hands upon meeting and parting. Poles sometimes kiss the extended hand of a woman when meeting.
- Address men by the title *Pan* (pronounced pahn) with the last name. For women, the term is Pahni (pronounced pahn-ee). First names are used only among close friends.
- A common greeting is *Dzien dobry* (pronounced jean du-bree, meaning Hello or Good morning.)

Conversation

- Try talking about Poland's cultural history, life in the United States, and your family.
- Soccer is a very popular sport. Bicycling, table tennis, skiing, and basketball are also poplar. Bridge is a favorite card game.

Sensitivities

- Avoid discussing politics, social conditions, or German or Russian involvement in World War II.

Key Negotiating Pointers

- Poles are generally outgoing and outspoken.
- Make prior appointments and be punctual.
- You will meet mainly with representatives from state-owned and operated businesses.

- Be patient. Negotiations are likely to be time-consuming. Decision making is slow. Polish organizations are still bureaucratic and cumbersome.
- Stress your company's links to the global economy.
- Emphasize your company's ability to transfer business skills and technological know-how.
- If you are negotiating the purchase of a business, don't expect many clues about what the business is worth (asset valuations, cash flow analyses, or marketing plans).
- Explore options with regard to a wide variety of business arrangements such as liquidations, joint ventures, and sales to foreigners.
- Focus on small and midsize enterprises as possibilities for joint ventures.
- Use an interpreter unless you speak Polish. If your counterpart speaks English and you conduct the negotiation in English, speak slowly and distinctly. Avoid jargon.

Day-to-Day Pointers

Business Entertaiment Guidelines

- The main meal of the day is eaten after 3:00 P.M.
- You may be entertained in a *kawiarna* (cafe), where the local specialty and French pastries are usually available.
- Pace yourself with alcohol. The Poles tend to drink a lot of hard liquor. Toasting is often part of both formal and informal dinners.
- If you are invited to a private home, bring flowers (except for red roses, which signify romantic affection).

Table Manners and Food

- Keep your hands above the table.
- The continental style of eating is used, with the fork in the left hand and the knife in the right.
- Typical meals consist of foods such as soup, fish, salad, potatoes, and tea. *Pierogi* (dumplings with cream cheese and potatoes), *uszka* (a kind of ravioli), and braised pork and *bigos* (cabbage) are popular foods.

Gender Issues

- Western women must contend with almost exclusively male-dominated organizations at almost every decision-making level.

Also Remember This . . .

- Poland has a strong industrial sector and is a major producer of minerals and steel.
- Until 1989 the economy was centrally controlled, and trade was conducted mainly with other Communist countries.
- Foreign investment is welcomed to help build the economy and to gain hard currency.

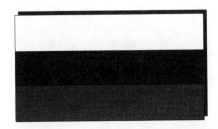

RUSSIA

Fast Facts

Population:	148.4 million (est.)
GNP:	$2,659 billion (est.)*
Per Capita Income:	$1,780†
Monetary Unit:	ruble
Major Industries:	ferrous and nonferrous metals, fuels and power, building materials
Major Trading Partners	
Exports:	Eastern Europe (49%), EC (14%), Cuba (5%), U.S. (5%)*
Imports:	Eastern Europe (54%), EC (11%), Cuba (11%), China (11%), U.S. (11%)*
Key Exports:	petroleum and petroleum products, natural gas, metals, wood, agricultural products*
Key Imports:	grains and other agricultural products, machinery and equipment, steel products*
Major Cities:	Moscow (cap.) (9.0 million), St. Petersburg (5.0 million), Novosibirsk (1.4 million), Sverdlovsk (1.4 million)

*Based on 1989 Soviet Union data.
†Based on 1990 Soviet Union data; estimates of per capita income vary widely.

Ethnic Groups: Russian
Main Religions: Russian Orthodox, Jewish
Language(s):   Russian

Reducing Communication Noise

Greetings

- Shake hands with a firm grip upon meeting and leaving. Introductions tend to be direct and informal.
- The Russians are very status-conscious, so address people by a title (such as *Director, Minister, Mr., Mrs.,* or *Miss*) with the last name.
- Use business cards printed in both Cyrillic (the Russian script) and English.

Conversation

- Russians are proud of their art, architecture, literature, ballet, theater, and other cultural achievements. Museums are also a safe topic of conversation. Russians are often interested in life in the United States, but you should be careful not to appear boastful.
- Hockey, soccer, basketball, volleyball, and cross-country skiing are popular sports. Chess is also a popular leisure activity.
- The public image of Russians is sometimes stiff and dull, largely because of their unexpressive hand and arm gestures and facial expressions.
- There tends to be a lot of touching in Russia compared with many other countries.

Sensitivities

- Avoid discussing politics, social conditions (such as the alcoholism problem), or the negative aspects of Russian history, such as Stalinism.
- Listen, rather than give lots of opinions, regarding the hardships currently taking place.

Key Negotiating Pointers

- Russians have a reputation for being warm and intelligent people, but not hard workers who show a lot of initiative.
- Make prior appointments and be punctual.

- Business dealings go through the appropriate ministry and are likely to move quite slowly through the bureaucratic machinery.
- Be prepared to devote a lot of senior executive time. Russians are very status-conscious and want to deal with your key decision makers. Use the most impressive title allowed you by your organization.
- Business presentations should be factual and full of technical details. Be prepared to defend technical aspects and performance standards, particularly of high-tech products. Russians want to know exactly what they are buying. Consider bringing along a specialist.
- Compared with negotiators in many cultures, no long-term personal relationship is necessarily desired or expected by your Russian counterpart.
- Give yourself a lot of room to negotiate. Russian initial demands are often extreme.
- If you are the seller, try to determine if there is genuine interest and ability to pay for your product or service. Beware of giving detailed information if you sense that your counterpart seeks only the information, and not the deal.
- If your counterpart needs your product, particularly if it is high-tech, price may be less of a sticking point than in other countries. Russia lags far behind the West in high technology.
- Be patient. Russian negotiators typically have limited authority, so they frequently check with headquarters. You can also expect Russians to be slow in making concessions.
- Expect considerable time to pass before you get a response to a proposal. Delaying tactics are common.
- Another common Russian tactic is to stress the tough competition you face as a seller. Quotations from competitors are sometimes revealed. If your counterpart uses these tactics, be sure to point out those areas where your product is of higher quality and all-around better value.
- You may also find that Russian negotiators obtain concessions from the weakest competitor first, then demand that you make the "required concessions."
- Get help with the financial aspects of your deal. One of your biggest problems in doing business in Russia is how you will get paid. Nobody wants the ruble.
- Expect to make at least one trip to Russia before a negotiation is finalized. Several years may be required to establish a business or joint venture.
- Check and recheck to ensure that all items have been considered before making a final agreement. Last-minute demands are common after you think all the details have been resolved.
- You can expect compliance with the spirit, if not the letter, of the agreement.

Day-to-Day Pointers

Business Entertainment Guidelines

- A typical night of entertainment might involve a visit to the circus or a concert or dinner in a restaurant. It is rare to be invited to a Russian's home.
- Lunch is the main meal of the day, while supper is usually light and eaten late in the evening.
- After 8:00 P.M., an orchestra often plays music in restaurants while patrons dance.
- Be aware of multiple toasts, and be prepared to return them. Unless you can handle large amounts of alcohol well, fill your glass with mineral water (usually provided at the table).
- Almost any modest gift is appreciated, especially those items not readily available in Russia, such as printed T-shirts, quality ballpoint pens, picture books of America, chewing gum, and audiocassette tapes.

Table Manners and Food

- Keep your hands above the table.
- Sit at the table for a while after the meal to compliment your host.
- Typical Russian foods include bread, potatoes, cabbage, and, to some extent, meat. *Borscht* (beet soup) and various kinds of *goulash* (stew) are popular.

Gender Issues

- Western women must contend with almost exclusively male-dominated organizations at almost every decision-making level.
- In spite of egalitarian principles, Russian women have limited access to key professional positions.

Also Remember This . . .

- Russia is the world's largest country.
- Russians are experiencing radical political, social, and economic changes. Almost any business deal should be viewed against this backdrop. This period of transition has resulted in a lower standard of living and longer lines for foods and other basic items.
- Trips to Russia should be planned months in advance to arrange visas, contacts, and travel arrangements.

Chapter 10

Negotiating in Latin America

The Business Environment of Latin America

Latin America generally refers to Mexico, Central and South America, and the Spanish-speaking Caribbean. Business practices differ in the many different cultures collectively referred to as "Latin."

With over 400 million people, a large market exists in Latin America. In addition, vast natural resources make Latin America a potentially strong economic force in the world. Political and economic policies have heretofore hampered progress.

There are generally huge differences in the distribution of wealth. Though the small middle class is growing in countries such as Brazil and Mexico, economic and political power remains concentrated in the hands of a few people.

Cultural Factors That Affect Negotiating in Latin America

Use of Time

The typical Latin American sees time as abstract—more a series of events than in terms of hours or minutes. There is no sense of urgency in the traditional way of life, rooted in the seasons of agriculture. It is natural in Latin America to consider a 10:00 A.M. appointment as meaning roughly 10:30 A.M. or 11:00 A.M.; in fact, it is "prompt" there.

Latin Americans are more present-oriented than future-oriented. They accept many things as "just happening," rather than applying logical or technical analysis and planning.

Individualism vs. Collectivism

A key to understanding Latin negotiators is to understand the Spanish-Portuguese culture. Both Spain and Portugal dominated colonial Latin America, and status could be achieved only by adapting to their standards. While North Americans came to the New World to flee the oppression of the Old, the Spanish and Portuguese brought their traditional system with them, and they considered themselves still part of the mother country rather than colonizers. Their social and economic style was based on the manorial lifestyle of Europe, a system where status is connected to birth and bloodlines, and where loyalty is primarily to individuals rather than to laws or the constitution of the land. Overall, you will find Latin Americans very ethnocentric—intensely proud of their own country more than the region as a whole.

The Latin view of individualism is quite different from that in the United States. We believe in the dignity of the individual as defined by what he or she does or accomplishes in life—for example, what occupation a person chooses. The Latin American emphasizes the inherent uniqueness of each person. The individual is valued not for what he or she does, but for whom he or she is.

It is also important to understand the concept of *machismo* in the role of the Latin American negotiator. North Americans usually connect this concept with sexual overtones. In Latin America, it is more the "essence of being masculine." Whether the male is tall, short, skinny, fat, ugly, or handsome, a *macho* is confident. He has charisma and is a good talker, both eloquent and witty. He is a man for whom no task is impossible. You will encounter him often during your negotiations.

Macho Man

"Enough of this harassment. It's time to fight back."
Words to that effect were uttered by speaker after speaker
at a convention held in Brazil recently. Feminists would
have found the sentiments familiar, but this time all the
speakers were men. And the convention was the founding
act of the Brazilian *Macho* Movement.

With slogans like "the best feminine movement remains that of the hips," the movement's aim is to combat
what it calls the excesses of feminism. In the name of
equality, the movement members say, women are losing
their femininity.

Contrary to the conventional image of the Latin American *macho*, however, these men—or at least most of
them—say a true *macho* is a gentleman, albeit a sexist
one who believes decisions belong to the men. Predictably, many women are outraged. "I hope you have no success," says a female journalist as she leaves the meeting.
"You represent the worst in Brazilian society."

The men say their wives agree with them. But one has
to take their word for that, because not one of the *machos*
bothered to bring his wife along. "She would have gotten
in the way," says one man. "I would have had to give her
attention, and this isn't the time for that."[1]

Role Orderliness and Conformity

There is generally low need for role orderliness and conformity in
Latin America. In negotiations, a *macho* shows his dislike of plans,
schedules, and legal details and a preference for ad hoc and free-
wheeling decisions.

Latin Americans have a strong sense of dignity. Words and
actions are easily interpreted as insults to the individual's inner
worth and are highly explosive in their effects. To promote harmony among different social strata, a complicated system of etiquette and diplomacy has evolved for interpersonal relations.
This may lead to "group think" in some negotiating situations,
where the negotiating team follows the leader's choices. This re-

lates to the traditional patterns where a lower-status person does not correct the high-status person openly or put forward conflicting ideas.

Personal relationships are the key to negotiations, as they are to most functions in Latin America. People take priority over institutions, laws, and regulations. When negotiating with Latin Americans, this need for a personal relationship is critical before anything else can be accomplished. The only way to get anything done in Latin America is through a "friend" or a "friend of a friend."

Don't be surprised if your negotiating counterpart asks you for a favor—part of the Latin American tradition of starting a personal relationship. The very fact that the favor was asked shows that he or she feels a personal relationship is started, and you are expected to produce. If you refuse bluntly to help ("No, I can't do that, there's a company policy . . ."), then the friendship tie is broken. If you really cannot accommodate the request, give a "Latin no." You might say, "I'll see what I can do." This means that you will try and that you care. If the person asks about it again, or indirectly brings up the subject, continue the indirect no: "I'm still trying." This will usually not be an offense to the person.

Patterns of Communication

Verbal Communication

Latin negotiators are likely to have a lot of voice inflection, gestures, and emotion. While individuals from the United States tend to consider softer tones, fewer gestures, and less emotion as the sign of a poised individual, in Latin America expressiveness and emotion in talking is tied to the Latin concepts of individualism and *machismo*.

Expect to get interrupted frequently. This is not seen as being impolite so much as eagerness to share points of view with you.

Nonverbal Communication

You can expect the physical space to be quite close among Latin Americans compared to the United States. While people in the United States stand at arm's length when conducting business face-to-face, Latin Americans stand much closer. Latins often complain than North Americans are impersonal and don't want to get close to them—personally or figuratively. Embracing is common among men who are established business acquaintances; similarly, women may briefly kiss the other's cheek.

You will probably shake hands unless you get to know your counterpart quite well. Handshaking is softer than in the United States; firm handshakes may be perceived as hostile. U.S. negotiators sometimes mistakenly think that the soft Latin handshake is an indication that the Latin negotiating counterpart is unassertive and will not negotiate a very effective agreement on his or her own behalf. Only later does the U.S. negotiator learn that the Latin American negotiator was in fact very effective.

There is no general rule on eye contact, though some Latin Americans are taught that it is respectful to look down when with someone in a position of authority. This can sometimes look shifty to a North American who does not know the cultural influence at work. On the other hand, sustaining eye contact is considered important in Argentina.

Latin America is a good place to be expressive in your hand, arm, and facial gestures. Smiles are valued in Latin America.

Note

1. Thomas Kamm, "Besieged Brazilian Machos Battle Advance of the Amazon Feminist," *Wall Street Journal*, December 4, 1991, p. B1. Reprinted permission of *Wall Street Journal*, © 1991 Dow Jones & Company, Inc. All Rights Reserved Worldwide.

HOW NEGOTIATIONS WORK IN LATIN AMERICA

Negotiating Factors

1. Pace of Negotiations   Slow

2. Negotiating Strategies
    Opening Offers vis-à-vis
      Settlement   Moderate initial demands
    Presentation of Issues   One at a time
    Presentations   Informal
    Dealing With Differences   Argumentative, whether right or
                                        wrong; passionate
    Concessions   Slow

**3. Emphasis on Personal
Relationships**   High

4. Emotional Aspects
    Sensitivity   Valued
    Degree of Emotions   Passionate

5. Decision Making
    Overall Method   Impulsive, spontaneous
    Emphasize   Concepts
    Emphasis on Group/Team   Low: Decisions from top person
    Emphasis on Face-Saving   Extreme
    Influence of Special
      Interests on Decision
      Maker(s)   Expected, condoned

**6. Contractual and
Administrative Factors**
    Need for an Agent   Average
    Degree of Contract
      Specificity   Moderate
    Degree of Paperwork/
      Bureaucracy   Moderate
    Need for an Agenda   Low

ARGENTINA

Fast Facts

Population:	32.3 million
GNP:	$76.5 billion
Per Capita Income:	$2,370
Monetary Unit:	peso
Major Industries:	food processing (especially meat packing), motor vehicles, consumer durables
Main Trading Partners:	
Exports:	U.S., Russia, Italy, Brazil, Japan
Imports:	U.S., Brazil, Germany, Bolivia, Japan
Key Exports:	meat, wheat, corn oilseed, hides
Key Imports:	machinery and equipment, chemicals, metals, fuel lubricants
Major Cities:	Buenos Aires (cap.) (2.9 million), Córdoba (980,000), Rosario (950,000)
Ethnic Groups:	Caucasian descendants of Spanish-Italian immigrants (85%), Mestizo Indian and other non-Caucasian groups (15%)
Main Religions:	nominally Roman Catholic (90%, with less than 20% practicing)
Language(s):	Spanish; English, German, French, and Italian are spoken by many people

Reducing Communication Noise

Greetings

- Greet each person present, not the group as a whole. A handshake and a slight nod to show respect is also appropriate.

- In some areas, such as Buenos Aires, an embrace with a peck on both cheeks is common among friends.
- Address people as *Señor, Señora,* or *Doctor* when being introduced.
- When approaching someone such as a customs official for information, greet the official before asking questions.
- A common greeting is *Buenos días,* or *Buen día* in Buenos Aires (Good day). Say good-bye by using common phrases such as *Adiós* or *Hasta luego.*

Conversation

- Argentines appreciate compliments about their children and the meal, and they like to talk about the beauty of local parks and gardens.
- Many Argentines are opera fans. Buenos Aires is on the world's opera circuit, and the Colón is one of the finest opera houses in the world. In addition, the tango originated in Argentina, and many Argentines appreciate American jazz.
- Soccer is the national sport and Argentines love to talk about it. Horse racing, rugby, tennis, and polo are also popular.
- Though your counterpart may speak English, give serious consideration to learning Spanish. Argentines are very proud, and an effort to learn Spanish—at a minimum, a few phrases—will be appreciated.
- Maintain eye contact during conversation as you would in the United States.

Sensitivities

- Avoid discussing politics and religion, even though you can expect urban Argentines to be cosmopolitan, progressive, and often vocal about politics and social conditions.
- Avoid comparisons with the United States. Argentines are proud and often view Brazilians, those from the United States, and others as uncultured.

Key Negotiating Pointers

- Argentines have a reputation as tough negotiators. Be patient and expect concessions to come very slowly and grudgingly.
- Make prior appointments and be punctual, though your counterpart may arrive up to thirty minutes late without being inappropriate.
- Nurture the relationship with your counterpart. Argentines are very social, and friendship is a key part of the negotiating process.

- Find a contact who can introduce you to the top person in the organizational unit where you want to do business. Dealing with midlevel managers is very time-consuming and usually fruitless. Decisions are made from the top down.
- Avoid behavior that might be construed as personal criticism of your counterpart.
- Get a written agreement. Try to close key loopholes. Expect contracts to be fairly lengthy and detailed.

Day-to-Day Pointers

Business Entertainment Guidelines

- Meals are a social event. Don't discuss business during meals.
- Meals are likely to start very late (8:00 P.M. or 9:00 P.M.). There are many late-night restaurants, theaters, and clubs in Buenos Aires.
- If you are invited to a private home for dinner, bring a small gift such as flowers or candy. Avoid personal items such as a tie or other articles of clothing.
- Tipping is not required but is becoming more common in many restaurants.

Table Manners and Food

- Keep your hands (but not elbows) above the table.
- It is considered poor manners to clear one's throat or blow one's nose at the table.
- Vegetarians have a hard time here. Beef is an Argentine staple; Argentines lead the world in per capita beef consumption.
- Baked stuffed beef and *empanadas* (meat pies) are favorite foods. French cuisine is widely available.

Gender Issues

- Argentine men show great respect for women in their conversation. However, this doesn't necessarily translate into doing serious business with U.S. women.
- Argentine men may be easy to warm up to on a personal level, but difficult on a business level. U.S. women often find Argentine men chauvinistic—for example, they do not discuss business over dinner with Argentine women present.

Also Remember This . . .

- Argentina can be a tough place to do business. There is a long history of Fascism, political instability, foreign debt, and inflation. Recent political developments indicate a strong movement toward a free-market economy, however.
- Argentines are proud, educated, and sophisticated, and they identify very strongly with European traditions. Many Argentines believe Buenos Aires is the cultural counterpart of Paris.
- Agriculture has always been the mainstay of the Argentine economy, though industry is developing. The country is a major exporter of beef, hides, and wool.

BRAZIL

Fast Facts

Population:	150.2 million
GNP:	$402.8 billion
Per Capita Income:	$2,680
Monetary Unit:	cruzado
Major Industries:	textiles and other consumer goods, footwear, chemicals
Main Trading Partners:	
Exports:	U.S. (28%), EC (26%), other Latin America (12%), Japan (7%)
Imports:	Middle East and Africa (24%), EC (22%), other Latin America (12%), Japan (6%)
Key Exports:	coffee, metallurgical products, chemical products, foods, iron ore
Key Imports:	crude oil, chemical products, foods, coal

Major Cities:	Brasília (cap.) (1.6 million), São Paulo (10.1 million), Rio de Janeiro (5.6 million)
Ethnic Groups:	Caucasian, mainly of Portuguese descent (55%), mixed heritage (38%), black (6%)
Main Religions:	nominally Roman Catholic (90%)
Language(s):	Portuguese; Spanish, English, German, and French are widely spoken

---

Reducing Communication Noise

Greetings

- Shake hands upon meeting. When leaving a small group, shake hands with all who are present.
- When greeting, good friends often embrace. Women often kiss each other on alternating cheeks.
- Brazilians tend to use first names, but do not do so until you are asked. Brazil differs from Spanish-speaking Latin America in the use of formal names. You can usually address people by a title and last name instead of middle name (e.g., Paulo Pedro Alvares is Senhor Alvares). Often you can address people by a title and their first name (e.g., Dōna Maria).
- A common greeting is *Come vai?* (How are you?).
- Bring plenty of business cards.

Conversation

- Brazilians enjoy talking about their country's rapid development, industry, and beautiful beaches.
- Soccer and basketball are popular sports. Pele, the legendary soccer player, is from Brazil.
- Be expressive in your speech. Brazilians enjoy conversation and are likely to be very expressive and passionate in their viewpoints. They are comfortable with showing emotion and like good jokes and love to laugh. Though Brazilians tend to be warm, friendly, and outgoing, don't ask personal questions (such as age or salary). Don't be surprised, however, if you are asked personal questions.
- Learning a few Portuguese phrases can earn you points.
- Try to get comfortable with the closer physical distance in Brazil than in

the United States. Your counterpart may be only about a foot from you if you are talking while standing up.

Sensitivities

- Avoid discussing politics or religion.
- Avoid voicing your opinions on the deforestation of Brazilian forests.
- Don't refer to yourself as an American, since Brazilians also see themselves as Americans.
- Avoid speaking in Spanish to Brazilians; this may be offensive even though they understand the language.
- Don't refer to Brazilians as Latin or South Americans. Brazilians consider themselves independent from the rest of South America. Avoid talking about Argentina.
- Avoid ethnic jokes.
- Avoid using the American *okay* sign, with the thumb and index finger forming a circle. This is an obscene gesture in Brazil.

Key Negotiating Pointers

- Brazilians like to bargain. Like U.S. negotiators, they tend to make concessions slowly and grudgingly.
- Be punctual for your negotiating session though your counterpart will probably arrive a few minutes after the appointed time. An exception is in São Paulo, where punctuality is practiced.
- Negotiators generally move at a faster pace in São Paulo than in Rio.
- Engage in general conversation before you get down to business.
- Develop a solid relationship with your Brazilian counterpart.
- Put some flair into your presentations. Try to be expressive.
- Avoid public statements that could possibly embarrass your counterpart.
- Be aware that some use of "phony facts" may occur at the early stages of the negotiation. Brazilians expect more deception among negotiators who do not know each other than do Americans.
- Don't mistake for anger the passion with which Brazilians may argue their points.
- Get a written agreement. Be clear about delivery times and payment details.
- Speak English or use an interpreter unless you speak Portuguese.
- A knowledgeable local is essential to help you maneuver through the government bureaucracies.

Day-to-Day Pointers

Business Entertainment Guidelines

- Meals are considered a social event. Business is occasionally discussed during meals in São Paulo or Rio.
- If you are invited to a private home for dinner, bring a small gift such as candy, wine, or a small figurine.
- In restaurants, the check is requested with the phrase *A conta, por favor.* Tips are usually included in the bill. If not, 10–15 percent is appropriate.

Table Manners and Food

- Avoid touching food with your fingers while eating. Wipe your mouth before taking a drink.
- Conversation after the meal often takes place over a cup of strong black coffee *(cafezinho).*
- In Rio, the favorite dish is *feijoada,* consisting of black beans with beef, pork, sausage, tongue, and—yes—sometimes a pig's ears, nose, and tail. *Feijoada* is the Brazilian national dish.

Gender Issues

- Overall, U.S. women find a favorable business climate in Brazil.
- There is less *machismo* in Brazil than in Mexico. Brazilian women often fill professional jobs in education, medicine, and journalism and are sometimes small business owners. Brazilian women are slowly starting to attain managerial positions.
- Brazilian men tend to stare at and make comments about women passing by on the street.

Also Remember This . . .

- Brazil is a good long-term market with over 150 million people. U.S. goods are highly valued and sought after, and there is generally a positive attitude toward doing business with the United States.
- Brazil has a large national debt and high inflation.
- Brazil has recently removed restrictions on importing computer technology and other goods.

COLOMBIA

Fast Facts

Population:	32.8 million
GNP:	$40.8 billion
Per Capita Income:	$1,240
Monetary Unit:	peso
Major Industries:	textiles, food processing, oil
Main Trading Partners:	
Exports:	U.S. (36%), EC (21%), Japan (5%), Netherlands (4%), Sweden (3%)
Imports:	U.S. (34%), EC (16%), Brazil (4%), Venezuela (3%), Japan (3%)
Key Exports:	coffee, petroleum, coal, bananas, fresh-cut flowers
Key Imports:	industrial equipment, transportation equipment, food, chemicals
Major Cities:	Bogotá (cap.) (4.8 million), Medellín (1.7 million), Cali (1.6 million), Barranquilla (1.0 million)
Ethnic Groups:	*Mestizo* (mixed Spanish-Indian) (58%), Caucasian (14%), mulatto (black-Caucasian mix) (14%)
Main Religions:	Roman Catholic (95%)
Languages:	Spanish; English is widely spoken in business.

Reducing Communication Noise

Greetings

- Shake hands with men upon meeting, but not too vigorously. Women offer a verbal greeting and may kiss each other on the cheek if they are acquainted.

- *Abrazos* (hugs) are common only among close friends or relatives.
- Address people by title (such as *Señor, Señora,* or *Doctor*) when being introduced. First names are not used among strangers.
- Individuals bear two family names: The last name is the mother's family name, and the middle name is the father's family name and the official surname. Therefore, Pedro Muñoz Gomez is called Señor Muñoz.
- Common phrases are *Buenos días* (Good day), *Cómo está?* (How are you?), and *Adiós* (Good-bye). Smiles are particularly valued in Colombia.
- Bring plenty of business cards.

Conversation

- Colombians are proud of their country's history of democracy and independence. Other good topics of conversation include Colombian art, coffee, and the beautiful countrysides.
- Soccer is the most popular sport. Bicycle racing, swimming, track and field, auto racing, and bullfights are also popular. Wealthy Colombians belong to golf or tennis clubs.

Sensitivities

- Avoid discussing politics or drugs.
- Don't be critical of bullfighting.
- U.S. foreign policy is often seen as overbearing.

Key Negotiating Pointers

- Colombian negotiators are gracious and formal. They are generally receptive to U.S. businesspeople.
- Be punctual even though your counterpart may not be. Individuality more than punctuality is stressed by Colombian negotiators.
- Be prepared for sometimes long discussions over black Colombian coffee before serious business is transacted.
- The pace of negotiations is slow.
- Focus on the top person in the negotiating team, probably the head of the family firm.
- Avoid embarrassing your counterpart in front of others. Try to find ways to make him look good.
- Put flair into your presentations.
- Get a written agreement that summarizes the key aspects of agreed-to points. Expect contracts to be fairly lengthy and detailed.

Day-to-Day Pointers

Business Entertainment Guidelines

- Courtesy and etiquette are emphasized. Business is sometimes discussed over meals, but let your Colombian counterpart bring up the subject.
- Lunch is the main meal of the day, usually eaten between noon and 2:00 P.M. Many businesses and schools close during this time, and family members eat lunch together.
- Supper is usually served between 7:00 P.M. and 8:00 P.M.
- In restaurants, a 10 percent tip is usually included in the bill. If not, leave a tip at the table.

Table Manners and Food

- Social conversation over meals is prized.
- Overeating is considered impolite. Though your host may offer more helpings, politely refuse them.
- Colombians generally eat starchy foods, such as potatoes, rice, and noodles, and enjoy stews and thick soups. A popular dish is chicken with rice.

Gender Issues

- The overall receptivity to U.S. businesspeople helps U.S. women doing business in Colombia.
- There are very few Colombian women in professional or management positions.
- Some traditional values prevail, with the father the provider for the family. The mother is usually responsible for home duties.

Also Remember This . . .

- Colombia is a developing country whose economy has been heavily dependent on agriculture. Inflation continues to be a major challenge. A very small number of Colombians hold most of the country's wealth and political power.
- Colombia is a leading coffee producer, but Colombians drink less coffee than Americans.
- Many wealthy Colombians send their children to U.S. colleges and universities.

MEXICO

Fast Facts

Population:	86.2 million
GNP:	$214.5 billion
Per Capita Income:	$2,490
Monetary Unit:	peso
Major Industries:	foods and beverages, tobacco, chemicals
Main Trading Partners:	
Exports:	U.S. (66%), EC (16%), Japan (11%)
Imports:	U.S. (62%), EC (18%), Japan (10%)
Key Exports:	crude oil, oil products, coffee, shrimp, engines, cotton
Key Imports:	grains, metal products, agricultural machinery, electrical equipment
Major Cities:	Mexico City (cap.) (9.4 million), Guadalajara (3.2 million), Monterrey (2.9 million), Puebla (1.7 million)
Ethnic Groups:	Mestizo (60%), Amerindian or predominantly Amerindian (30%), Caucasian (9%)
Main Religions:	Roman Catholic (97%), Protestant (3%)
Language(s):	Spanish; English is spoken by many business-people

Reducing Communication Noise

Greetings

- Shake hands with business acquaintances upon meeting or when you are introduced to someone for the first time. A full embrace is common with closer acquaintances or friends. Women often kiss each other on the cheek.

- First names are not used unless you know the person well. Address men by the title *Señor,* unmarried women by the title *Señorita,* and married women by the title *Señora,* followed by the surname. *Doña* is a term of respect before a first name, somewhat like "Dame" in Britain.
- Individuals usually bear two family names: The last name is the father's family name, and the middle name is the mother's family name and the official surname. Therefore, Franco Martinez Rodriquez is called Señor Martinez.
- Bring plenty of business cards.

Conversation

- Mexicans are very proud of their country and appreciate compliments on its culture, history, and achievements. Try talking about Mexico's geography, art, archeology, museums, and beautiful scenery.
- Praise Mexico's economic accomplishments. Mexicans are proud of their progress, independent of U.S. influence.
- Remember in conversation that Mexicans are geographically North Americans, though they are of the Latin culture.
- Your counterpart will appreciate it if you try to speak a few phrases of Spanish.
- Try to get comfortable with the closer physical distance in Mexico than in the United States. Your counterpart is likely to stand much closer to you than you are used to.

Sensitivities

- Some Mexicans still resent the U.S. annexation of the Southwest.
- Avoid comparisons with the United States or issues related to immigration of Mexicans into the United States.

Key Negotiating Pointers

- A half-hour or more past the designated meeting time is considered prompt in Mexico, so don't expect meetings to start at the precise time (*hora Americana,* or American time, as it is sometimes jokingly called). In extreme cases, don't be shocked if meetings are delayed, cancelled, forgotten, or occasionally ignored.
- Don't worry about establishing a formal agenda.
- Be prepared to take a while before the content of the negotiation is ad-

dressed. Building rapport and friendship is essential. Take time to build a solid relationship.

- Your host might do business with an unexpected visitor even if you arrived first and are in the middle of a meeting.
- Mexicans like to bargain. Don't make your initial offer an insult, but give yourself some room for movement from your original offer.
- You will probably deal with the top person in the organizational unit (perhaps a family member). Pay attention to the issue of face; embarrassing your counterpart could be very costly.
- Mexicans are expressive in their verbal communication. Don't take it personally if there are loud exchanges.
- Use lots of detail in your presentations—charts, graphs, and models—to overcome initial suspicions.
- Get your agreements confirmed in writing, but try to stay away from detailed contracts. Contracts are considered a goal to be strived for more than a binding obligation.
- Ask in advance if you can speak English during the negotiation. Your negotiating counterpart may speak very good English but staunchly refuse to use it in a negotiation. Consider the use of an interpreter if you don't speak Spanish.

Day-to-Day Pointers

Business Entertainment Guidelines

- You are generally invited to a person's home only if you are known very well.
- Lunch breaks may be as long as three hours, and business is often conducted during this time.
- The main meal of the day is eaten in the early afternoon. A light dinner is usually eaten between 8:00 P.M. and 9:00 P.M.

Table Manners and Food

- Keep both hands above the table.
- Guests do not usually leave directly after a meal.
- Corns, beans, and chiles are staple foods. They are combined with spices, vegetables, and meats or fish. *Tortillas,* made from cornmeal, are eaten either alone as bread or as part of a meal. Other popular foods are *frijoles refritos* (refried beans), *torta* (tortilla roll stuffed with meat or cheese), *que-*

sadilla (tortilla baked with cheese), and *taco* (folded tortilla filled with meat, cheese, and onions).

- Avoid tap water. It is usual to order mineral water even in better restaurants.

Gender Issues

- U.S. women must work hard for acceptance in business circles. They must be cordial, but firm. *Macho* attitudes predominate.

Also Remember This . . .

- Mexico is a large and growing market of almost 90 million people, right next door.
- In recent years the government has sold state-owned companies, attracted foreign investment, and liberalized trading regulations.
- Tourism is important for foreign exchange and employs many people.

VENEZUELA

Fast Facts

Population:	19.7 million
GNP:	$50.6 billion
Per Capita Income:	$2,560
Monetary Unit:	bolivar
Major Industries:	petroleum, iron ore mining, construction materials
Main Trading Partners:	
Exports:	U.S. (50%), Germany (5%), Japan (3%), Netherlands (3%)

Imports:	U.S. (44%), Germany (9%), Japan (6%), Italy (5%), Brazil (4%)
Key Exports:	petroleum, bauxite, aluminum, iron ore, agricultural products
Key Imports:	food, chemicals, transportation equipment
Major Cities:	Caracas (cap.) (3.4 million), Maracaibo (1.4 million), Valencia (1.2 million)
Ethnic Groups:	Mestizo (67%), Caucasian (21%), black (10%), Indian (2%)
Main Religions:	nominally Roman Catholic (96%), Protestant (2%)
Languages:	Spanish; Portuguese is spoken in many areas

Reducing Communication Noise

Greetings

- Shake hands and smile politely upon meeting. Men greet close friends with an *abrazo* (a full embrace), while patting each other on the back. Women greet each other with an *abrazo* and a kiss on the cheek. *Abrazos* are given between men and women only if they are close friends or relatives.
- Venezuelans are very title-conscious. Address people as *Señor, Señora, Señorita,* followed by the surname. Be sure to use the person's professional title when introducing them in public.
- Common greetings are *Buenos días* (Good morning), *Buenas tardes* (Good afternoon), and *Buenas noches* (Good evening). Greetings often include polite inquiries about the other person's health.
- Bring plenty of business cards.

Conversation

- Baseball is Venezuela's most popular sport. Horse racing, bullfighting, soccer, fishing, and hunting are also popular.
- Be respectful in conversation of religious or historical figures.
- English is widely understood among businesspeople.
- Maintain eye contact during conversation.
- Try to get comfortable with the closer physical distance in Venezuela than in the United States. Your counterpart is likely to stand much closer to you than you are used to.

Sensitivities

- Don't sit in a slouched position or put your feet up on any object.

Key Negotiating Pointers

- The pace of Venezuelan business is relaxed. Venezuelans prefer an easy-going, informal approach to business relationships.
- Be punctual even though your counterpart may not be.
- Get to know your counterpart on a casual, personal basis before business aspects are approached. Be aware, however, that many Venezuelan businesspeople are very busy and may cut the small talk shorter than you think. Let your host take the lead in this.
- Make your presentations factual. Venezuelans are shrewd businesspeople and do not want to be left with any doubts about the deal.
- Be patient and keep a sense of humor. The negotiations are likely to be slow and interrupted.
- Be consistent in your answers to questions. You may be asked the same questions repeatedly.
- Avoid embarrassing your Venezuelan counterpart publicly.
- You will be served *un cafecito* (thick, black coffee in a small cup) when visiting a home, a business, or the office of a government official. Accept it graciously or you will offend your host.
- Appearances are important in Venezuela. Dress fashionably to give an aura of success.

Day-to-Day Pointers

Business Entertainment Guidelines

- Business entertaining is usually confined to restaurants.
- Meals are considered a social event and business is seldom discussed.
- Dinner is usually late (about 8 P.M. or 9 P.M.).
- After an evening out, call or send a thank you note or a good quality pen or flowers (orchids are the national flower).

Table Manners and Food

- Don't sit at the head of the table. Those seats are for the mother and father of the family.

- Most of the food consists of casseroles, meat pies, stews, and pasta dishes. *Arepa,* a thick fried pancake made from white corn flour and filled with butter, meat, and cheese, is a favorite dish.
- Hot chocolate is almost as popular as coffee.

Gender Issues

- The concept of *machismo* is alive and well in Venezuela, but U.S. women can still operate effectively there.

Also Remember This . . .

- Venezuela is the most urban country in Latin America.
- Family continues to be a dominant factor in business, with nepotism a way of life.
- Petroleum is the cornerstone of the economy.

Chapter 11

Negotiating in North America

The Business Environment of North America

The economy of North America (the United States and Canada) is the largest in the world. There is a climate of free enterprise where most laws are designed to promote competition rather than restrict it. Big corporations dominate the business environment, particularly in the manufacturing and oil sectors. Small and medium-size businesses are prevalent in the service, retail, and construction industries.

North Americans tend to take business quite seriously compared with most of the rest of the world. U.S. businesspeople in particular often view themselves as being "professional"—technically proficient individuals with an ability to get the job done. They tend to be quite knowledgeable in the latest management techniques and ideas. Anyone planning to do business with North Americans should be aware of such management trends as total quality management, customer service, and participative management and empowerment (giving nonsupervisory employees more power to participate in decision making). In the United States, management gurus such as Peter Drucker, W. Edwards Deming, Joe Juran, and Tom Peters strongly influence management thinking.

Fixed ideas about the behavior of North American negotiators are particularly dangerous because of the enormous heterogeneity in the backgrounds of the negotiators themselves. How one might behave in Manhattan may be quite different from one's behavior in Jackson, Mississippi, or Calgary, Alberta, or Montreal, Quebec. The gender, racial, and ethnic mix of the U.S. work force is going through unprecedented demographic changes. Women are projected to be almost half the U.S. work force by the year 2000, there are vast increases in the Hispanic and Asian populations, and large numbers of immigrants are entering the country. Caucasian males, who once dominated the U.S. work force, are now a minority and are expected to be increasingly so in the future.

The most prized job in North American organizations is that of the CEO, or chief executive officer. This person can also be the president or chairperson of the board. Even if this individual reports to the chairperson of the board, the CEO has the power status, and day-to-day decision-making ability to have the greatest impact on the company. The chief operating officer, or COO, who can also be the president, has important strategic responsibilities.

Employees are routinely dismissed individually or in large groups for economic or performance reasons. A scene feared by a U.S. employee is being called into the boss's office on a Friday afternoon, being terminated, and then being asked to clear out his or her desk immediately before being escorted out of the building.

U.S. businesses are organized by state rather than at the federal level, but once a business is established in one state, it can operate in any of the other forty-nine states. It is generally advisable to organize in the state where you do the most business. However, liberal incorporation laws, tax breaks, and other considerations make states such as New York and (especially) Delaware favorite incorporation sites. In Delaware there is no need for any one of the incorporators to be a U.S. citizen.

There are usually few unusual problems for foreign investors in the United States (unless there are security-related reasons, such as in the defense, communications, and airline industries). In fact, a French company has the same status as a Delaware company incorporated in the state of Ohio.

Cultural Factors That Affect Negotiating in North America

Use of Time

The pace of business is vigorous in North America, particularly in the United States. Whether a negotiation takes place over the telephone, in an office, or over a business meal, emphasis is put on getting through the content of the negotiation as efficiently as possible. Don't be surprised however, if final decisions are occasionally bogged down in detailed analysis by financial, strategic planning, legal, or other managers. This slow, exhaustive review is sometimes irreverently referred to as a "paralysis of analysis." Financial analysis of one- to five-year returns on investment are typical.

There is often more of an emphasis on short-term profits than on long-term growth, though this is more the case in the United States than Canada. Many shareholders demand quick results.

Individualism vs. Collectivism

Individualism is prized in North America. With no aristocracy in either Canada or the United States, one earns social status largely through individual competitiveness that leads to business success. Though family commitments and outside interests are extremely common and deeply held, a preoccupation with business success is usual, particularly in the United States. The fierce competition of New York City executives typifies this preoccupation, though executives in the Midwestern, Southern, and Western parts of the United States, and most of Canada, do not stress individualism to the same degree.

Team negotiations with, say, seven or more individuals are very unlikely unless the negotiation is very complex and critical to the company's future. Even with several team members present, there are normally only one or two key decision makers on whom you should focus most of your attention. These one or two key players usually "call the shots"—that is, they have the authority to make decisions that can consummate a business deal, or consummate the deal subject to the review of various financial, legal, and other technical experts in the company. Be aware that while many U.S. and Canadian companies are trying to find ways to involve workers in key decisions through participative management techniques, any such involvement normally impacts operational decisions rather than business negotiations.

Role Orderliness and Conformity

There is a low need for role orderliness and conformity in North American organizations compared with those in other regions of the world. More emphasis is put on the content than on the form of the negotiation. *How* business is done tends to get less emphasis than getting it done efficiently. U.S. negotiators sometimes say, for example, "Let's not stand on ceremony—let's just get on with it."

North Americans are generally quite informal in their business dealings, though in French-speaking Canada there is a bit more formality than elsewhere in North America. The use of first names in business characterizes North America informality.

Please Watch Your Positive Attitude

The thing Brits hate most in Yank associates is their infernal *optimism*. This reads to them as the worst kind of naivete. Brits often cultivate, for business purposes, the image of those who are world-weary with experience and have been around all the houses at least once. There is a common reluctance to entertain new ideas, make special efforts, or even miss the 5:46 [train] to Weybridge. Instead, one earns corporate Brownie points for "making the best of a bad job."

Enter the fresh-faced Yank, brimming enthusiasm and fiscal fitness. The Irresistible Force has met the Immovable Object. He's reinvented the wheel and seems bent on talking about it. He comes on like a corporate adolescent as he rabbits about "more cost-effective ways" and "simpler solutions." Brits have mixed emotions when they appear to work.[1]

Patterns of Communication

Verbal Communication

North American verbal communication is direct and open. This means that a U.S. or Canadian negotiator is likely to tell you directly, "I'm sorry, but we can't accept your offer." If your North American counterpart is unwilling to make further concessions, she may tell you, "This is our bottom line—our final offer."

The English language as used by North Americans has many slang expressions that make understanding difficult. Each region of the United States and Canada has its own forms of expression. Be sure to ask for clarification if you do not understand what is being said.

Silence is avoided in conversation, and interruptions are common. Don't be surprised or take it personally if a North American negotiator, particularly one from the United States, finishes your sentence for you if you hesitate when you are speaking.

Nonverbal Communication

North Americans like more space in their organizational lives than individuals in most other regions of the world. A distance of 3 feet is typical between people in business situations. Very little touching takes place. Handshakes, for example, are usually firm and brief. You rarely see two North American businesspeople hugging each other upon greeting or leaving (an exception is in French-speaking Canada).

Some North American executives are known to be back slappers—those who give others a light slap on the back to show camaraderie or encouragement. Even this gesture is brief and often not appreciated by others.

Note

1. Jane Walmsley, *Brit-Think, Ameri-Think* (London: Harrap, Ltd., 1986), p. 27.

HOW NEGOTIATIONS WORK IN NORTH AMERICA

Negotiating Factors

1. *Pace of Negotiations*   Fast

2. *Negotiating Strategies*
    Opening Offers vis-à-vis
      Settlement   High initial demands
    Presentation of Issues   One at a time
    Presentations   Formal
    Dealing With Differences   Direct
    Concessions   Slow

3. *Emphasis on Personal*
   Relationships   Fairly low

4. *Emotional Aspects*
    Sensitivity   Moderate
    Degree of Emotions   Moderate

5. *Decision Making*
    Overall Method   Group consensus
    Emphasize   Logic
    Emphasis on Group/Team   Moderate: Decisions from Middle
                                         Managers
    Emphasis on Face-Saving   Moderate
    Influence of Special
      Interests on Decision
      Maker(s)   Low

6. *Contractual and*
   Administrative Factors
    Need for an Agent   Low
    Degree of Contract
      Specificity   High
    Degree of Paperwork/
      Bureaucracy   Moderate
    Need for an Agenda   High

CANADA

Fast Facts

Population:	26.5 million
GNP:	$542.8 billion
Per Capita Income:	$20,450
Monetary Unit:	Canadian dollar
Major Industries:	processed and unprocessed minerals, food, wood and paper products
Main Trading Partners:	
Exports:	U.S., Japan, U.K., Germany, other EC
Imports:	U.S., Japan, U.K., Germany, Taiwan, South Korea, Mexico
Key Exports:	pulp, timber, grains, crude petroleum, ores
Key Imports:	processed foods, beverages, crude petroleum, chemicals, industrial machinery
Major Cities:	Ottawa (cap.) (819,300), Toronto (3.4 million), Montreal (2.9 million), Vancouver (1.4 million)
Ethnic Groups:	British Isles origin (40%), French origin (27%), other European (20%)
Main Religions:	Roman Catholic (46%), United Church (16%), Anglican (10%)
Languages:	English (predominates in Ontario, Manitoba, and other Western provinces), French (predominates in Quebec)

Reducing Communication Noise

Greetings

- Shake hands firmly upon meeting and leaving. *Hello* is a common greeting for English-speaking people. In the French parts of Quebec, the hand-

shake should be a little less firm, and *Bonjour* is the appropriate greeting; exchanging light kisses on each cheek is typical.
- First names are not usually used in business situations, except by close friends.
- Use business cards printed in both French and English for French-speaking clients.

Conversation

- Canadians enjoy talking about the history, culture, and geography of their individual province and of Canada as a whole.
- Canadians are sports-minded. Ice hockey is the most popular sport. Curling, boating, swimming, baseball, football, skiing, fishing, hunting, lacrosse, soccer, and rugby also have large followings.
- Try to become familiar with the Canadian political system, geography, and current events. Also recognize that Canada is the biggest trading partner of the United States.
- Most Canadians speak English, and many speak French. French-speaking associates appreciate your efforts to speak French.
- Maintain eye contact during conversation as you would in the United States.

Sensitivities

- Don't behave in any way that might be perceived as condescending. Canadians are conscious about being "talked down to" by Americans.
- Avoid taking sides on the issue of partition: separation into different English-speaking and French-speaking states.
- Avoid comparisons with the United States. Canadians are proud of their accomplishments and independence.

Key Negotiating Pointers

- Canadians tend to be restrained in their negotiating style, keeping their emotions in check. Don't come on too strong. Hard sells do not work well in Canada.
- Make prior appointments and be punctual.
- Be friendly but get to the point of your discussions.
- Etiquette is important. Perhaps because of their British and French heritage, Canadians tend to be more patient and genteel than many U.S. negotiators.

- Expect the pace of negotiations to be quite fast in the larger cities, such as Toronto or Montreal, and a bit slower in the Western provinces where the atmosphere is more friendly and relaxed.
- Focus attention on your counterparts in top management.
- Expect your counterpart to ask you to "split the difference," a common tactic by Canadian sellers when asking the buyer to pay more.
- Leave yourself ample room to make concessions. Canadians tend to have high initial demands as both buyers and sellers.
- Canadians tend to make concessions in a deescalating pattern: generous at first, then tapering off.
- Respect deadlines. The Canadians are time-conscious.
- Expect detailed and lengthy contracts.
- Be sure to translate documents into French for French-speaking associates.

Day-to-Day Pointers

Business Entertainment Guidelines

- Business entertaining normally takes place in restaurants or clubs.
- Dinner is usually the business meal, served between 5:00 P.M. and 7:00 P.M. and often continuing for two or three hours.
- Dress well for dining in restaurants: usually a coat and tie for men, and dresses or nice pants for women.
- *Cheers* is the traditional toast in most situations. In French-speaking areas, use *Sante* (To your health).
- If you are invited to a private home, bring an inexpensive gift or flowers or send flowers to your host.

Table Manners and Food

- In French-speaking areas, keep your hands (but not elbows) above the table.
- Place the utensils together on the plate when you are finished eating.
- The Canadian cuisine reflects the country's multicultural heritage. In the Western provinces, there is fish, beef, Pacific salmon, ethnic dishes, and a variety of foods similar to those in the United States. In Quebec, there is a definite French influence, with pea soup, meat pies, French pastries and breads, cheese, and lamb. In Newfoundland and Nova Scotia, the most important foods are fish, lobster, and crab.

Gender Issues

- U.S. women are in a comfortable business climate in Canada.
- Except in some of the more rural parts of Quebec where there are strong family traditions, U.S. women in managerial and professional positions are welcomed.
- Canadian women make up about 44 percent of the work force and occupy key professional and managerial positions.

Also Remember This:

- Canada has one of the strongest economies in the world and is the United States' largest trading partner.
- Canada is the second largest country in the world, after Russia.
- Canada is a leading supplier of metals: second in the world in gold and uranium, third in silver, and fourth in copper.

UNITED STATES

Fast Facts

Population:	250.9 million
GNP:	$5,445.8 billion
Per Capita Income:	$21,700
Monetary Unit:	U.S. dollar
Major Industries:	petroleum, steel, motor vehicles, aerospace, telecommunications, chemicals, electronics

Main Trading Partners
Exports:	Canada (23%), Japan (12%)
Imports:	Japan (20%), Canada (20%)

Key Exports:	capital goods, automobiles, consumer goods, industrial raw materials, foods and beverages
Key Imports:	crude and partly refined petroleum, machinery, automobiles, consumer goods, industrial raw materials
Major Cities:	Washington, D.C. (cap.) (606,900), New York City (7.3 million), Los Angeles (3.5 million), Chicago (2.8 million)
Ethnic Groups:	Caucasian (80%), black (12%),* Hispanic (9%), Asian or Pacific Islander (3%)
Main Religions:	Protestant (61%), Roman Catholic (25%), Jewish (2%)
Languages:	English; there is a sizable Spanish-speaking minority

---

Reducing Communication Noise

Greetings

- Shake hands firmly and briefly with both men and women upon meeting and leaving, and smile. American greetings are informal. A peck on the cheek or a hug may be used between women or between men and women who have been acquaintances for a long time.
- First names are used in most business situations. Possible exceptions would be to use *Mr., Mrs., Miss,* or *Ms.* for a very senior person in age and rank, or in formal situations.
- Common greetings are *Pleased to meet you* and *How do you do?* More casual greetings include *Hello, Howdy* (in the West), and *Aloha* (in Hawaii).
- Business cards are routinely exchanged in business settings, though not in social settings.

Conversation

- Americans enjoy talking about business, U.S. travel, current trends, and world events. Going to movies and restaurants are popular leisure activities.

*A person of Hispanic origin can be of any race. Therefore, these groups will total more than 100%.

- Baseball, football (American), basketball, golf, tennis, and bowling are among the many popular spectator and participant sports. Hunting and fishing are popular in rural parts of the country. Soccer has become popular in recent years among children but has yet to catch on as a major national sport.
- Expect for people to ask you in social gatherings, "What do you do?" (i.e., "What kind of work do you do?") and "Where do you work?" ("For what organization do you work?").
- Americans like their physical space and usually stand about 3 feet from each other during conversation.
- Good eye contact is usually considered to be direct eye contact for perhaps five to seven seconds, with breaks of two or three seconds. This sustained eye contact is perceived as a sign of interest, sincerity, and truthfulness.

Sensitivities

- Americans like discussing politics. Do more listening than talking.
- Don't criticize the United States. Even though Americans may be self-critical about their environment, they are usually patriotic and don't appreciate negative opinions from others.

Key Negotiating Pointers

- Make prior appointments and be punctual. Though Americans are very time-conscious, business meetings sometimes start ten to fifteen minutes after the appointed time.
- Be cordial but get to the point of your discussions after a limited amount of small talk. Americans sometimes suggest that "we dispense with the formalities and get down to business." Expect negotiations to move quickly.
- Be polite, but be direct and candid in your comments. U.S. negotiators expect you to "tell it like it is," which means to be open in your communication. Indirect answers may be mistaken for lack of confidence, insincerity, or even dishonesty.
- Don't expect large U.S. negotiating teams. Unless the negotiation is very complex, a typical American negotiation team probably consists of one to five persons.
- Make proposals and presentations detailed, factual, and formal. Be sure to have copies for all those present.

- Leave yourself some room to negotiate. U.S. negotiators often have very ambitious initial demands.
- A common tactic is for U.S. sellers to tell buyers to "take it or leave it."
- Expect U.S. negotiators to concede grudgingly, saving concessions until the end of the negotiation.
- Use patience to your advantage. U.S. negotiators sometimes make concessions in order to conclude the negotiation and get on to other business.
- Respect deadlines. Americans are extremely time-conscious.
- Expect contracts to be very detailed and lengthy.

Day-to-Day Pointers

Business Entertainment Guidelines

- Business entertaining is usually done in restaurants.
- Dinner is the main meal of the day, but business breakfasts, lunches, and dinners are common. Dinners start about 7:00 P.M. to 9:00 P.M. and continue for one-and-a-half to two hours.
- You may discuss business during a meal.
- In restaurants, tips are not usually included in the bill. A 15 percent tip is typical.

Table Manners and Food

- Napkins are usually placed in the lap. The left hand often rests in the lap during the meal.
- Americans usually eat with the fork in the right hand. The fork is switched to the left hand and the knife is held in the right for cutting.
- It is generally considered poor manners to rest one's elbows on the table, but many Americans are casual about this.
- There is a rich variety of foods, reflecting diverse cultural backgrounds. Beef, pork, and chicken are popular meats, though many Americans are eating a higher portion of vegetables and fruits for health reasons.
- The large number of fast-food restaurants reflects the busy U.S. lifestyle as well as food preferences.

Gender Issues

- Compared to other countries, U.S. women occupy more key professional and managerial positions.

- Businesspeople can expect to do business with women as well as men in every region of the country in many different product lines and services, though an Old Boy Network still remains in some business sectors.
- Women are projected to be about half of the work force by the year 2000.
- Both parents often work outside the home. Only 7 percent of the U.S. population lives in a "traditional American family": father at work, with mother and children at home.

Also Remember This . . .

- The United States has the world's largest economy, though not the highest per capita income. It is the financial capital of the world.
- Economic growth has slowed in recent years, largely the result of a huge budget deficit and a negative trade balance.
- The United States is an extremely diverse country, with a wide variety of ethnic, racial, and other backgrounds in the workplace.

Chapter 12

Negotiating in the Middle East

The Business Environment of the Middle East

The Middle East is a very diverse area, covering countries such as Saudi Arabia, Israel, Egypt, the United Arab Emirates, Syria, Iran, Iraq, Jordan, Lebanon, and Oman. The Arabs are relatively small in number, mainly centered in Saudi Arabia, Jordan, Iraq, and the Gulf states (e.g., the United Arab Emirates and Oman).

Negotiating, or bargaining, is part of the everyday life of Middle Easterners, particularly the Arab population. By bargaining, Arabs are able to make their own decisions, to mix socially with people at work, and to earn a living for their families. Just as the average North American would not think of bargaining even if he or she ended up with more profit, the average Arab would not think of doing without it even if he would end up with more profit.

Religion plays a large part in both the history and present-day business environment of the Middle East. Throughout much of the area, there is no separation between church and state as is the case in the United States. Political and religious differences predominate in the area, affecting any attempts to do business among countries in the region. For example, one cannot travel or do business between Israel and any Arab country except Egypt, where there have been diplomatic relations between the two countries since the 1978 Camp David accords. Anything close to a Middle Eastern Economic Community doesn't seem likely in the near future.

Be aware that *Hebrew* is the Semitic racial term for people from the twelve tribes, whose founder is Abraham. A *Jew* is one who believes in the tenets of Judaism. An *Iranian* is a native of Iran, speaks the Farsi or Persian language, and is not an Arab. Though the Farsi language is written in Arabic characters, Farsi is not Semitic-based. Judaism is the predominant religion for the Jews, and Islam is the predominant religion for the Arabs and Iranians. A Muslim, one who practices Islam, is not necessarily an Arab or an Iranian. (The most populous Muslim nation is Indonesia.)

The Islamic culture is based on the teachings of Mohammed. Muslims pray five times a day, bowing to the ground, facing Mecca. Each summer, during *Ramadan,* twenty-nine days are devoted to fasting during daylight hours. Normal working routines are sharply curtailed during this time.

Cultural Factors That Affect Negotiating in the Middle East

Use of Time

"Time" in the Middle East, as in most parts of the world, is not as precise as it is in North America. That is, Middle Easterners will often arrive half an hour late for a meeting, but this is *on time* for this person. Nor are appointments held in the esteem that they are in North America. The fact that your negotiating partner does not show up at all should not necessarily be taken personally.

Middle Easterners don't believe that schedules should rule their lives. Hurrying a Middle Easterner through a negotiation is an insult. Similarly, it is believed to be unlucky or unwise to plan too far ahead. There is some feeling of awe about the future, that if you plan in detail you take on too much upon yourself and invite disaster.

Individualism vs. Collectivism

There is a strong "we" orientation in Middle Eastern cultures, particularly when dealing with government or quasi-government Arab organizations, such as oil companies. The exception is the

Arab family merchant/businessman who prides himself on his ability to make his own far-reaching decisions. Success is defined more in terms of group memberships or group accomplishments than in individual accomplishments.

Do not try to save time in your negotiations by ruling out the discussion of any ideas that are not useful to the group as a whole. There is a great deference to those in positions of status and power. Such a tactic would be considered rude by their spokesperson and cause confusion and uncertainty among the underlings.

Role Orderliness and Conformity

There is a relatively high need for role orderliness and conformity in most Middle Eastern countries. Solid personal relationships are vital to the success of negotiations. Before the content of the negotiation is addressed, the parties spend a good amount of time chatting about things that have nothing to do with specific business issues.

Middle Eastern negotiations, particularly those in Arab countries, often seem chaotic to most U.S. negotiators: people coming in and out of the room when you are meeting, many telephone interruptions, or your counterpart stopping to talk about other matters when you are addressing a key point. You should expect such interruptions to take place.

For the Arab, it is masculine to read poetry, use intuition, and be sensitive. It's feminine to be cool and practical. Therefore, when you are negotiating, it sometimes helps to be a little emotional, or your sincerity may be doubted.

Patterns of Communication

Verbal Communication

Verbal communication in Israel is generally quite direct and open. Verbal communication in Arab countries, on the other hand, is quite indirect, vague, and expressive by North American standards. In such high-context cultures, the speaker does not feel obligated to be specific as long as the receiver of the message can infer the message. For example, Arabs will seldom give you a direct "no," even if they disagree with your idea, plan, or suggestion. If you ask whether something is a good choice and the person hesitates, then agrees, the hesitation is a strong clue that he or she might actually disagree were it not for the courtesies involved. So a white lie in the name of good manners and someone's feelings is considered better, just as it is to a lesser extent in the United States.

Americans are very quick to say, "I don't know, but I'll find out." This is not a good idea in most Arab countries of the Middle East. A person of status is not expected to hesitate over an answer. If you don't know, try to stall. Then quickly and privately find the answer or risk losing respect and power.

Don't be alarmed if Arabic to English translations sound very exaggerated. The Arab language is conducive to exaggeration. For example, there are common endings of words that are meant to be emphasized, along with numerous rhetorical devices to achieve even more exaggeration. Fantastic metaphors are common, and many adjectives are often used to modify the same word.

Arabs generally have a strong feeling that information is critical, and they are therefore masters at incremental disclosures— slow at letting you know what is really on their minds. The "truth" is considered something that can be cruel, dangerous, and rude, as well as a matter of negotiation.

Nonverbal Communication

Gestures are quite expressive in Middle Eastern countries, and negotiators generally maintain direct eye contact with their U.S. counterparts and have closer physical distance than in the United States. These combined behaviors are sometimes viewed as "coming on too strong" by some American negotiators. Arab men tend to touch each other (but not Arab women, except among themselves). Embracing upon meeting and holding hands in public is typical in Arab countries. This touching is not sexual, but a display of friendship.

If an Arab makes a short jerk upward with his head, he means no. Often it's accompanied by a "tsk" sound. If he tilts his head sideways, it means yes (*yes, I heard you*, not necessarily *yes, I agree*).

HOW NEGOTIATIONS WORK IN THE MIDDLE EAST

Negotiating Factors

1. Pace of Negotiations   Moderate

2. Negotiating Strategies
    Opening Offers vis-à-vis
      Settlement   High initial demands
    Presentation of Issues   One at a time
    Presentations   Informal
    Dealing With Differences   Usually passionate
    Concessions   Slow

**3. Emphasis on Personal
Relationships**   High

4. Emotional Aspects
    Sensitivity   Valued
    Degree of Emotions   Passionate

5. Decision Making
    Overall Method   Group consensus
    Emphasize   Concepts
    Emphasis on Group/Team   Low: Decisions from top person
    Emphasis on Face-Saving   Extreme
    Influence of Special
      Interests on Decision
      Maker(s)   Expected, condoned

**6. Contractual and
Administrative Factors**
    Need for an Agent   High
    Degree of Contract
      Specificity   Low
    Degree of Paperwork/
      Bureaucracy   Moderate
    Need for an Agenda   Low

EGYPT

(ARAB REPUBLIC OF EGYPT)

Fast Facts

Population:	52.1 million
GNP:	$31.4 billion
Per Capita Income:	$600
Monetary Unit:	Egyptian pound
Major Industries:	textiles, food processing, tourism, chemicals, cement, petroleum
Main Trading Partners:	
Exports/Imports:	U.S., EC, Japan, Eastern Europe
Key Exports:	raw cotton, crude and refined petroelum, cotton yarn, textiles
Key Imports:	food, machinery and equipment, fertilizers, wood products, consumer durables
Major Cities:	Cairo (cap.) (6.1 million), Giza (3.7 million), Mansoura (3.5 million), Alexandria (2.9 million)
Ethnic Groups:	descendants of native Egyptians and Muslim Arabs (90%), Greek, Italian, and Syro-Lebanese (10%)
Main Religions:	Muslim (mostly Sunni) (94%), Coptic Christian and other (6%)
Language(s):	Arabic; English and French are widely understood by the educated classes

---

Reducing Communication Noise

Greetings

- Shake hands with everyone present upon meeting and leaving. Men should wait for women to extend their hands first. Greetings tend to be expressive and elaborate, with the host welcoming the visitor many times.

- Titles are important. Address people by a title (such as *Mr., Mrs. or Miss*) with the first name, or with the last name if the person is of a high level or is a governmental official.
- Use business cards printed in both Arabic and English.

Conversation

- Egyptians enjoy talking about their culture's past and present achievements. Egyptian cinema and television programming is known throughout the Middle East.
- Soccer is the national sport. Tennis, swimming, and horseback riding are available in sports clubs.
- Egyptians tend to be expressive and emotional in their conversation. A favorite term is *ma'alesh*, generally meaning *don't worry* or *never mind* about concerns that are not serious or that you can do nothing about.
- Physical space among those of the same sex is closer in Egypt than in the United States. It is much further apart for members of the opposite sex.

Sensitivities

- Avoid discussing religion.
- Many Egyptians like discussing politics. Do more listening than talking.

Key Negotiating Pointers

- Egyptians are used to bartering in their everyday lives, normally in outdoor *souks* (markets) where businesses sell their goods.
- Egyptians are quite Westernized and are used to doing business with Americans and Europeans.
- Be punctual even though your counterpart may not be. Don't be shocked if meetings are delayed, postponed, or occasionally ignored.
- Allow plenty of time to get where you are going in Cairo. Traffic is among the heaviest in the world.
- Building a good relationship is vital. Take time to socialize before you get to the content of your discussions. Trust must be established before business can proceed.
- The pace of the negotiation is slower than in the United States, Western Europe, or Israel, but faster than in the rest of the Middle East.
- Do not be put off by frequent telephone calls, visitors, or many cups of tea during your negotiating meeting.

- Reliance on God influences negotiations. Various commitments are kept *Insha'allah* (if God wills).
- Be prepared to get a written contract and to renegotiate it later. A contract is more valued by Egyptians than by most others in the Middle East, but it remains a list of general guidelines rather than a specific, firm commitment.
- Get an agent who can make the right connections for you. After you have gotten to know your counterpart, however, you will probably want to deal directly with that person.

Day-to-Day Pointers

Business Entertainment Guidelines

- Lunch is the main meal of the day and usually extends from about 2 P.M. to 4 P.M. Dinner may not be served until 10:30 P.M. or later.
- If your client is male, invite him and a few of his associates and their wives to a European-style restaurant.
- Business may be discussed over meals, but let your host bring up the subject.

Table Manners and Food

- Wash your hands before and after the meal.
- It is usually considered inappropriate to eat everything on your plate. Leftover food is seen as a compliment to the host for providing so well, or, in a restaurant, as a sign of your wealth (you can afford to leave food on the plate).
- Since this is a Muslim country, do not use your left hand to eat, touch others, point, or give or receive objects.
- When Western eating utensils are used, the continental style is used, with the fork in the left hand and knife in the right.
- Do not eat, drink, or smoke in front of a Muslim in the daytime during *Ramadan*.
- Rice, bread, fish, lamb, chicken, turkey, and stuffed vegetables are common foods. Beef is very expensive but is available in the large hotels. Bread is eaten with every meal.
- Nonalcoholic beverages are generally served, although alcohol consumption is becoming more widely accepted.

Gender Issues

- For an Arab country, Egypt is a relatively good place for U.S. women to do business. Egyptians are liberal by Arab standards, with less segregation of the sexes.
- Women are part of social and business life in Egypt more than in most other parts of the Middle East.

Also Remember This . . .

- Along with playing a role in industrial pursuits, the Suez Canal is an important source of income for Egypt.
- There are separate Egyptian laws governing different types of organizations, e.g., government, public sector (owned by government), joint ventures, and free zone private companies.
- High inflation and a large foreign debt hinder economic progress.

ISRAEL

Fast Facts

Population:	4.6 million
GNP:	$50.9 billion
Per Capita Income:	$10,970
Monetary Unit:	new shekel
Major Industries:	food processing, diamond cutting and polishing, textiles and clothing
Main Trading Partners:	
Exports:	U.S., U.K., Germany, France, Belgium
Imports:	U.S., Germany, U.K., Switzerland, Italy

Key Exports:	polished diamonds, citrus and other fruits, textiles and clothing, processed foods, chemical products
Key Imports:	military equipment, rough diamonds, oil, chemicals, machinery
Major Cities:	Jerusalem (cap.) (429,000), Tel Aviv–Jaffa (328,000), Haifa (236,000)
Ethnic Groups:	Jews (83%), non-Jews (mostly Arab) (17%)
Main Religions:	Jewish (83%), Muslim (mostly Sunni) (13%), Christian (2%)
Language(s):	Hebrew; Arabic is official language of the Arabic minority; English is spoken by most people

---

Reducing Communication Noise

Greetings

- Shake hands upon meeting and leaving. Good friends may pat each other on the back or shoulders.
- First names are generally used. Israel is very informal, and titles are even less important than in the United States; for example, first names or nicknames are used even in the military.
- *Shalom* (meaning peace) is used for *Hello* and *Good-bye.*

Conversation

- Israelis enjoy lively, candid discussions. There is much to talk about. Israel is a study in contrasts—old versus new, tradition versus change.
- Most Israelis enjoy talking about their families. Visiting with family, friends, and neighbors is the most popular leisure-time activity. Many Israelis also attend music concerts.
- Soccer and basketball are the favorite sports.

Sensitivities

- Israelis love discussing politics. Be careful here, however. If you engage in a political discussion, be aware of the diversity of opinion that exists in

Israel, and do more listening than talking. Don't criticize the government, even if your counterpart seems antigovernment.
- Don't drive or smoke on the Sabbath in religious areas.

Key Negotiating Pointers

- Israelis are comfortable doing business with Americans.
- Make prior appointments and be punctual even though Israelis are sometimes casual about time.
- Be friendly, but firm.
- Expect the negotiating pace to be brisk and the style to be aggressive. Be tough and bargain hard. Soft sells may not get heard.
- Be patient. Conserve concessions.
- Don't be put off by expressive, strongly stated positions by your counterpart.
- Get local legal and accounting help. Religious laws strongly influence business transactions.

Day-to-Day Pointers

Business Entertainment Guidelines

- Lunch is more common than dinner for business entertaining.
- If you are invited to a private home, bring a book, candy, or flowers.

Table Manners and Food

- The host or oldest person begins eating first.
- Religious restrictions for pork, ham, and shellfish are common.
- The diverse backgrounds of immigrant Jews have resulted in a diverse cuisine. Popular dishes include *kabobs* (meat and vegetables on a skewer), Russian *borscht* (beet soup), and chicken soup. Vegetable salad is a staple eaten almost every day. *Falafel* (pita bread filled with fried chick-peas) is a national food.

Gender Issues

- Though *macho* attitudes prevail, U.S. women can successfully do business in Israel.

- The father has traditionally exercised great authority in the home, but women have gained more influence both inside and outside the home in recent years. Women serve in combat positions in the military, for example.
- The female clothing restrictions of more conservative Middle Eastern countries do not apply in Israel. Women can wear whatever they want.

Also Remember This . . .

- Israel has a fast-growing technological base that offers opportunities for investment, licensing, and franchising agreements and joint ventures.
- Although Israel is surrounded by Arab neighbors, business and social customs for the most part are different.
- Most Israeli workers belong to a labor union. Israeli unions are strong influences in the workplace.

SAUDI ARABIA

Fast Facts

Population:	14.9 million
GNP:	$86.9* billion
Per Capita Income:	$6,020*
Monetary Unit:	riyal
Major Industries:	crude oil, basic petrochemical refining
Main Trading Partners:	
Exports:	Japan (26%), U.S. (26%), France (6%), Bahrain (6%)
Imports:	U.S. (20%), Japan (18%), U.K. (16%), Italy (11%)

*Based on 1989 data.

Key Exports:	petroleum and petroleum products
Key Imports:	manufactured goods, transportation equipment, construction materials, processed foods
Major Cities:	Riyadh (cap.) (1.3 million), Jeddah (900,000), Mecca (400,000), Ta'If (203,000)
Ethnic Groups:	Arab (90%), Afro-Asian (10%)
Main Religions:	Muslim (100%)
Language(s):	Arabic

Reducing Communication Noise

Greetings

- Shake hands with everyone present with a light, brief grip upon meeting and leaving. There is a great deal of handshaking in Saudi. Greetings are elaborate.
- Saudi women are seldom present for business dealings. If a Saudi woman is there, however, men should not expect to shake hands or even be introduced.
- Saudi men often embrace each other and kiss both cheeks. This is not expected of Westerners.
- Address people by a title—such as *Mr., Sheik, Excellency* (for ministers), or *Your Highness* (for members of the royal family)—with the first name. For example, Sheik Mohammed Abdul Waheb is addressed as Sheik Mohammed; Prince Abdullah Ibn Feisal is Your Highness Prince Abdullah.
- Customary greetings are *Salahm alaykum* (Hello) upon meeting, then *Kaif halak?* (How are you?) as you are shaking hands. Other common phrases are *Sabaah al-khayr* (Good morning), *Massa' al-kayr* (Good evening), and *Shukran* (Thank you).
- Use business cards printed in both Arabic and English.

Conversation

- Saudis usually enjoy talking about their country's history, their city, or their taste in art. Try talking about the rapid growth of technology and the excellence of the coffee or tea.
- Though most Saudi businessmen understand basic English, speak plainly and slowly. Avoid jargon.

- Don't be surprised by the loud voices, animated facial expressions, and wide arm gestures exhibited by two Arabs talking. What might seem like an argument is probably a discussion about business or everyday affairs.
- You should maintain eye contact and use open hand and arm gestures.
- Don't praise an object too much. Your Saudi host will probably insist on giving it to you.
- Try to get comfortable with the closer physical space in Saudi Arabia than in the United States. Expect Saudis to sit and stand very close to you, rest a hand on your shoulder, tap your forearm with a finger, or exhibit touching in everyday conversation. Hand-holding among men walking down the street is a common sight. Backslapping by Westerners is not appreciated.
- A man who has made several trips to Saudi shouldn't be shocked if his counterpart takes his hand while walking. This is a sign of friendship and has no sexual overtones.

Sensitivities

- Avoid discussing religion, Middle Eastern politics, or the role of women. Remember that religion and politics are intertwined in most of the Middle East.
- Don't tell off-color jokes or use profanity in any way.
- Don't ask about the women or female children in a Saudi man's family. It is okay, however, to inquire about the family or his children in general.
- The bottom of one's foot should never face another person.

Key Negotiating Pointers

- Saudi negotiators have a reputation for being shrewd and knowledgeable about money-making.
- Make prior appointments and be punctual even though your counterpart probably will not be. Don't be surprised if your meeting is delayed, rescheduled, or ignored.
- Be prepared for social banter for several hours—or sometimes even several meetings—before you get down to business. Let your host take the lead in this.
- Build a level of confidence and trust. Price should be discussed as if it is a matter between friends. Maintain mutual respect at all times. Saudi negotiators see themselves as doing business with "the man" rather than "the company" or "contract."

- It may require frequent visits to build the relationship. It is probably futile to conduct business via telephone or written correspondence.
- Be patient. Don't press for an immediate yes or no during negotiations. This would be viewed as too aggressive. Allow time for deliberation.
- Bargaining usually starts with inflated proposals and proceeds with a series of ritualistic concessions. Hard sells do not work very well.
- There may be more than one meeting going on in your meeting place at the same time. It is typical for there to be several interruptions during your meeting, with a steady stream of people coming in.
- Expect deadlines often to be ignored.
- The meeting normally concludes with an offer of coffee or tea, and this is usually the time when future meetings are arranged.
- Reliance on God influences negotiations, whether it be an adherence to a meeting schedule or compliance with a contract. Meetings are kept *In-sha'allah* (if God wills).
- Be prepared to get a written contract and to renegotiate it later. You will probably run into resistance getting a detailed written contract. Try, however, to get the details in writing as soon as possible after agreement on the broad concepts. The contract is written in Arabic as well as English. A contract written in English is legal in Saudi Arabia.
- Get your proposal translated into Arabic. Even if your counterpart speaks excellent English, some of his associates may not.
- Get an agent when first doing business in Saudi. Connections are critical, and your agent can introduce you to the right people and save you a lot of time. After you have gotten to know your counterpart, however, you will probably want to deal directly with that person.

Day-to-Day Pointers

Business Entertainment Guidelines

- Business entertaining usually takes place over lunch at a hotel or a restaurant. There are no nightclubs or movie theaters and few restaurants.
- Lunch usually takes place between 1:00 P.M. and 5:00 P.M.
- Try the local foods. Many Westerners like them, and your host will be delighted to explain the different dishes.
- Gift giving is not considered appropriate by government officials, but it is common among business associates in the private sector. Reciprocate if you receive a gift, but check with your home office legal staff if it is other than a modest token of your appreciation.

Table Manners and Food

- Since this is a Muslim country, do not use your left hand to eat, touch others, point, or give or receive objects.
- Try to drink the coffee and tea.
- Do not eat, drink, or smoke in front of a Muslim in the daytime during the holy month of *Ramadan*.
- Saudi food comprises mainly rice with mildly spiced lamb or chicken. Lamb is the most prestigious meat. Muslims do not eat pork, and pork is not available in Saudi Arabia.
- No alcohol is served in Saudi Arabia, though nonalcoholic beer is occasionally available.

Gender Issues

- Saudi Arabia is a male-dominated society and is one of the most difficult places in the world for women to do business. It may even be difficult for a woman to get a visa to enter the country at all. It is, however, possible for Western women to conduct business effectively in Saudi Arabia. This should be done only after consulting someone who knows the individual Saudi negotiators. Women should also develop any resources available, such as expatriate spouses and local support networks.
- Local women are virtually nonexistent in professional or managerial jobs.
- Both Arab and Western women must cover their arms and legs (wearing a long skirt and a loose-fitting, long-sleeved blouse) and dress not to attract attention to their bodies. Western women need not wear a veil under any circumstances, though they are encouraged to wear the *abaya* (a black silk, cape-like cover) in public. Women are not allowed to drive.
- Arab wives are seldom seen during any business transaction, even in a Saudi home. However, Arab wives sometimes accompany their husbands on business trips abroad and should generally be treated as other guests in the United States.

Also Remember This . . .

- Saudi Arabia has a strong, growing economy, based almost exclusively on oil and oil products. There is little or no unemployment or inflation.
- Expatriate workers form the bulk of the labor force.
- Saudi Aramco Oil Company is the world's largest oil company. Most oil company activity is based in the Dharan-al Khobar area in the eastern province.

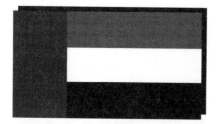

UNITED ARAB EMIRATES

Fast Facts

Population:	1.6 million
GNP:	$31.6 billion
Per Capita Income:	$19,860
Monetary Unit:	U.A.E. dirham
Major Industries:	crude oil, fishing, petrochemicals
Main Trading Partners	
Exports:	U.S., EC, Japan
Imports:	EC, Japan, U.S.
Key Exports:	crude oil, natural gas, reexports of dried fish and dates
Key Imports:	foods, consumer and capital goods
Major Cities:	Abu Dhabi (cap.) (243,000), Dubai (265,700), Sharja (125,100), Ras al Khaimah (42,000)
Ethnic Groups:	Southeast Asian (50%), Arab (23%), Emirian (19%)
Main Religions:	Muslim (96%), Christian, Hindu, and other (4%)
Language(s):	Arabic; English is spoken by many business-people

Reducing Communication Noise

Greetings

- Shake hands with everyone present with a light, brief grip upon meeting and leaving. There is a great deal of handshaking in the U.A.E. Greetings are elaborate.
- Local women are virtually never present for business dealings. If a local

woman is there, however, men should not expect to shake hands or even be introduced.
- Local men often embrace each other and kiss both cheeks. This is not expected of Westerners.
- Address people by a title—such as *Mr.*, *Sheik*, *Excellency* (for ministers), or *Your Highness* (for members of the royal family)—with the first name. For example, Sheik Rashid Abdul Mohammed is addressed as Sheik Rashid; Prince Mohammed Abdullah is Your Highness Prince Mohammed.
- Customary greetings are *Salahm alaykum* (Hello) upon meeting, then *Kaif halak?* (How are you?) as you are shaking hands. Other common phrases are *Sabaah al-khayr* (Good morning), *Massa' al-kayr* (Good evening), and *Shukran* (Thank you).
- Use business cards printed in both Arabic and English.

Conversation

- Emirians usually enjoy talking about their country's history, the rapid growth of technology, the excellence of the coffee or tea, and the gold *souk* (shopping area), Persian carpets, and other shopping concerns.
- Sizable crowds turn out to watch the local nobility race their prized camels.
- Though most Emirian businessmen understand basic English, speak plainly and slowly. Avoid jargon.
- Don't be surprised by the loud voices, animated facial expressions, and wide arm gestures exhibited by two Arabs talking. What might seem like an argument is probably a discussion about business or everyday affairs.
- Don't praise an object too much. Your negotiating counterpart will probably feel obligated to give it to you.
- Try to get comfortable with the closer physical space in the U.A.E. than in the United States. Expect Emirians to sit and stand very close to you, rest a hand on your shoulder, tap your forearm with a finger, or exhibit touching in everyday conversation. Hand-holding among men walking down the street is a common sight. Backslapping by Westerners is not appreciated.
- A man who has made several trips to the U.A.E. shouldn't be shocked if his counterpart takes his hand while walking. This is a sign of friendship and has no sexual overtones.

Sensitivities

- Avoid discussing religion, Middle Eastern politics, or the role of women. Remember that religion and politics are intertwined in most of the Middle East.

- Don't tell off-color jokes or use profanity in any way.
- Don't ask about the women or female children in an Emirian man's family. It is okay, however, to inquire about the family or his children in general.
- The body of water which the U.A.E. borders to the East is referred to in the U.A.E. as the Arabian Gulf, not the Persian Gulf.
- The bottom of one's foot should never face another person.

Key Negotiating Pointers

- U.A.E. negotiators have a reputation for being shrewd and knowledgeable about money-making.
- Remember that you may be dealing not only with Emirians but with those from other Arab countries and non-Arab countries. Emirians account for only 19 percent of the U.A.E. population.
- Get an agent when doing business in the U.A.E. Connections are critical, and your agent can introduce you to the right people and save you a lot of time. After you have gotten to know your counterpart, you will probably want to deal directly with that person.
- Make prior appointments. Be punctual, though this probably will not be reciprocated. Don't take it personally if your meeting is delayed, rescheduled, or ignored.
- It may require frequent visits to build the relationship. It is probably futile to conduct business via telephone or the mail. In-person visits are preferable.
- There may be more than one meeting going on in your meeting place at the same time. It is typical for there to be several interruptions during your meeting, with a steady stream of people coming in.
- Be prepared for social banter for several hours—or sometimes even several meetings—before you get down to business. Let your host decide when it's time to talk business.
- Be patient. Don't press for an immediate "yes" or "no" during negotiations. This will be viewed as too aggressive. Allow time for deliberation.
- Bargaining usually starts with inflated proposals and proceeds with a series of ritualistic concessions. A hardsell approach will not work very well.
- You must build a level of confidence and trust. Price should be discussed as if it is a matter between friends. Maintain mutual respect at all times. Emirian negotiators see themselves as doing business with "the man" rather than with "the company."
- Eye contact should be maintained, and hand and arm gestures should be open. Expect personal space to be very close, even in a formal negotiation.

- Expect deadlines to often be ignored, and in some cases, resented.
- The meeting normally concludes with an offer of coffee or tea, and is usually the time when future meetings are arranged.
- Reliance on God influences negotiations, from adhering to a meeting schedule to complying with a contract. These meetings will be kept *In-sha'allah* (if God wills).
- Expect to be reminded of the competition.
- Get your proposal translated into Arabic. Even if your counterpart speaks excellent English, some of his associates may not.
- Be sure to get a written contact, and be prepared to renegotiate it later. Recognize that you will probably run into resistance on getting a detailed written contract. The contract will be written in Arabic as well as English.

Day-to-Day Pointers

Business Entertainment Guidelines

- Business entertaining usually takes place over lunch at one of the U.A.E.'s fine restaurants, usually located in luxury hotels. Pubs, clubs, and discos are also available, though they are frequented mainly by Western businesspeople and tourists.
- Lunch usually takes place between 1:00 P.M. and 5:00 P.M.
- Try the local foods. Many Westerners like them, and your host will be delighted to explain the different dishes.
- Gift giving is not considered appropriate by government officials, but it is common among business associates in the private sector. Reciprocate if you receive a gift, but check with your home office legal staff if it is other than a modest token of your appreciation.

Table Manners and Food

- Since this is a Muslim country, do not use your left hand to eat, touch others, point, or give or receive objects.
- Try to drink the coffee and tea.
- Do not eat, drink, or smoke in front of a Muslim in the daytime during *Ramadan*.
- Emirian food comprises mainly rice with mildly spiced lamb or chicken. Lamb is the most prestigious meat. Muslims do not eat pork.
- Though alcohol is available to Westerners at special stores and in hotels and restaurants, do not drink alcohol with your Emirian counterpart.

Gender Issues

- Though still restrictive, the U.A.E. is much less conservative toward Western women doing business than Saudi Arabia.
- The U.A.E. is a male-dominated society and local women are virtually nonexistent in business organizations. However, expatriate women from Western countries work in a few professional and managerial positions.
- Women must cover their arms and legs (wearing a long skirt and a loose-fitting, long-sleeved blouse) and dress not to attract attention to their bodies. Western women need not wear a veil under any circumstances. Western women are allowed to drive in the U.A.E.
- Arab wives are seldom seen during any business transaction, even in a U.A.E. home. However, Arab wives sometimes accompany their husbands on business trips abroad and should generally be treated as other guests in the United States.

Also Remember This . . .

- The U.A.E. is considerably less conservative than its close ally, Saudi Arabia. Although it is a Muslim country, many of the restrictions found in Saudi Arabia are not enforced in everyday life.
- The U.A.E. was formed in 1971 and consists of seven emirates (or states): Abu Dhabi, Dubai, Sharja, Ras al Khaimah, Ajman, Fujaira, and Umm al Qaiwain.
- The ruling families of the U.A.E. are only a couple of generations from a bedouin lifestyle—nomadic tribes that roamed the desert.

Chapter 13

Negotiating in the Pacific Rim

The Business Environment of the Pacific Rim

Whether you are buying or selling, Pacific Rim countries should be a critical part of almost any company's global strategy. The vast potential of the Pacific Rim is characterized by the fact that it makes up a large portion of all U.S. trade. (One-third of all U.S. exports are to the Pacific Rim, and over 40 percent of imports are from there.) Japan's economy is second only to that of the United States. The business climate among Pacific Rim countries can be characterized as creative, aggressive cooperation, where there are alliances between government and industry and between banks and manufacturers. There are also strong, interlocked groups of companies such as the *keiretsu* of Japan and the *chaebol* of South Korea.

The only requirement for starting operations [in Hong Kong] is simply registering your business. You can set up a company in the morning, get registered, rent the premises by noon, and start making a profit in the afternoon if you're lucky.

Jack So, Executive Director, Hong Kong Trade Development Council[1]

Characteristic of the area's economic power are the so-called Four Tigers: South Korea, Taiwan, Singapore, and Hong Kong. South Korea, the first Tiger, has one of the world's fastest growing economies, moving from primarily an agricultural market to a low-cost producer of consumer goods for U.S. and Japanese markets. South Korea now seeks to focus on a medium-tech economy rather than the high-volume, low-tech manufacturing that is currently its mainstay. Korean firms have moved some of their manufacturing to the lesser developed Pac Rim nations such as Thailand, the Philippines, and Malaysia, where labor is less expensive. If you are looking to invest in South Korea, then consider electronics, general machinery, precision machinery, and chemicals. Though Korean labor costs are rising, they remain much cheaper than in the United States, and the work ethic rivals or surpasses that of Japan. South Korea's biggest challenge probably comes from other Pac Rim countries seeking to become significant low-cost producing players, such as Thailand, Malaysia, and China.[2]

Taiwan, another of the Four Tigers, is economically second only to Japan in Asia, and it has long had strong economic links with the United States. Taiwan's foreign reserves are $70 billion, the world's highest. About 80 percent of these are held in U.S. Treasury bonds. The country specializes in high technology and, with a relatively well-off middle class, is an excellent market for consumer goods. While trade is vital to Taiwan's economic health, direct investment is increasing by 20 percent a year. U.S. companies usually have the inside track on huge government contracts,

such as electrical and petrochemical plants and military hardware. Various infrastructure projects, such as those involving telecommunications and transportation, also offer excellent opportunities. Taiwan is currently focusing on improving its image as a quality producer of goods. Though the country is not under any immediate threat of sovereignty from China, be aware of China's official Taiwan policy of "one China, one government."[3]

Singapore, the third Tiger, is challenging the financial and technological supremacy of the other Tigers. Singapore built its reputation by attracting U.S. and Japanese manufacturers with its inexpensive skilled labor, political stability, and government-supported factories. The emphasis is now on high-tech, high-capital R&D, and banking and finance. Singapore is turning to the United States to gain access to high-tech research methods, something the Japanese are not usually willing to do. Singaporeans seek a wide assortment of consumer goods, some of which are made by Singapore-based American companies such as Apple Computer Inc., and Hewlett-Packard. Having had a reputation as a pirate of intellectual property, Singapore has provided tougher copyright protection laws in recent years.[4]

Hong Kong, the last of the Four Tigers, has long been a key example of free enterprise in the Pacific Rim, with a vigorous manufacturing and financial center. The big question involving Hong Kong is its economic and political viability after reversion to Chinese rule in 1997. Speculation varies widely as to the ultimate effect on business, but most experts agree that Hong Kong will continue to be a key Pacific Rim player. The optimism is largely based on the fact that Hong Kong has traditionally depended on China for its natural resources, and this need helped create the free enterprise, market-driven system that has generated its success. Nevertheless, Hong Kong currently faces a brain drain: an exodus of educated professionals concerned about the colony's future. Still, with a trendy, relatively well-off population, Hong Kong represents a key market for retailers.

China, with its enormous human and other resources, is always a key factor in the region's economics and politics. Negotiating in China can be tough, however. Foreign trade is a state-run monopoly. You are almost always dealing with the Chinese government and its Communist policies, whether it be for a joint venture or a bank, and the bureaucracy is extremely cumbersome. For example, arranging shipments into China can be complex whether under Chinese tariffs or duty-free. It may take months before a shipment actually takes place. Few things happen quickly, so it is important to have the cash to sustain both the negotiation and the project through its development stages.

Cultural Factors That Affect Negotiating in the Pacific Rim

The Pacific Rim countries have in common ancient histories characterized by sophisticated cultural achievements, dynastic rule, and social stratification. For example, China, the world's oldest living civilization, was ruled by a series of dynasties from about 2000 B.C. until the twentieth century. Hong Kong belonged to China until it was ceded to Great Britain in 1842, and the Taiwanese are descendents of Chinese immigrants who began settling the islands in the seventh century. Japan was founded some 2,000 years ago, and Japan's line of emperors continues to the present. Korea traces its origins back 4,300 years, with a history of kings and dynastic rule. Singapore was under British rule from 1824 until it became an independent nation in 1965.

Use of Time

You can expect extreme patience from your Pacific Rim counterpart. Every stage of the negotiation process is likely to be slower than in North America. This protracted process is due to three main reasons: (1) emphasis is put more on the long-term relationship than on the task of negotiating the deal; (2) the custom is to have several people on each negotiating team; and (3) the decisions tend to be made by the entire group.[5] Negotiations in Singapore and Hong Kong are likely to move more rapidly than in other parts of the Pacific Rim.

Individualism vs. Collectivism

Pacific Rim cultures are as "we" conscious as Americans are "I" conscious. This characteristic has many implications for the business setting. For example, helping one's counterpart to "save face" and recognizing the importance of group consensus are important aids in negotiating.

Decision making is likely to be slow, with approval of the group made at almost every level. However, once made, decisions can usually be implemented quickly.

Super Nobodies?

We have some mainframe computers that have to be up all the time. What we thought would be a simple negotiation to get our equipment left on at night wasn't exactly straightforward. You would think that the director of the Computer Center could arrange that, but he had to go all the way to the chairman of the bank because no one was willing to make a commitment on something that was different and because the person might be scrutinized for it later—"what if the equipment caught on fire" or "what if the building burned down" and several other "what ifs." One must deal with a lot of people who cannot make decisions, but ultimately, if you circumvent them, could make your life miserable. In China, you deal from the bottom-up and meet a lot of "super nobodies" when it comes to making decisions.

> Manager of contracts administration for a global payment services franchise

---

Role Orderliness and Conformity

The need for role orderliness and conformity helps explain why it is so important for those in the Pacific Rim cultures to build a relationship with their negotiating counterpart. Getting to know one's negotiating counterpart is a way to bring orderliness and certainty to one's world.

Social stratification over the centuries and the influence of the Confucian ethic make proper social relationships extremely important. These relationships form the basis for such social traditions as rituals of courtesy, formality in behavior, excessive politeness, loyalty to and identification with the group, deference to the elderly, avoidance of direct conflicts, and extreme modesty when speaking of one's status, accomplishments, and family.

Patterns of Communication

Verbal Communication

There are strong elements of Confucianism, Buddhism, and Taoism in Pacific Rim cultures, creating such communication values as humility, silence, modesty, and mistrust of words. Verbal communication in Pacific Rim cultures is generally quite indirect. In high-context cultures such as Japan or China, people expect the person to whom they are talking to know what is on their mind. They give the other person all the necessary information except the crucial piece. This can be illustrated in the way negotiators say "no." Instead of saying it directly, as would be the case with most American negotiators, this message may be conveyed by saying, "We will study the matter" or "We want to get more opinions on your idea." This communication pattern makes it imperative that you listen carefully.

Nonverbal Communication

Body language is generally more reserved than in North America. Expressive gestures are seldom seen, and eye contact is almost always brief. Personal space is a little closer than in the United States, but touching in business settings is generally restrained. Brief handshakes or bows, rather than hugs and other forms of touching, are typical.

Notes

1. Yue-Sai-Kan, *Doing Business in Hong Kong* (Boulder, Colo.: Avery Press, 1990): p. 3.
2. Karen Matthes, "Korea Capitalizes on Growth," *Management Review* (February 1991): 12–13.

3. Marlene C. Piturro, "The Taipans of Taiwan," *Management Review* (February 1991): 28–29.
4. Karen Matthes, "Laissez-Faire Paradise," *Management Review* (February 1991): 36–37.
5. Frank L. Acuff, "Negotiating in the Pacific Rim," *The International Executive* (May–June 1990): 20–21.

HOW NEGOTIATIONS WORK IN THE PACIFIC RIM

Negotiating Factors

1. Pace of Negotiations   Slow

2. Negotiating Strategies
Opening Offers vis-à-vis
  Settlement   Moderate to high initial demands
Presentation of Issues   Group of issues may be presented
Presentations   Fairly formal
Dealing With Differences   Polite; quiet when right
Concessions   Slow

3. Emphasis on Personal Relationships   High

4. Emotional Aspects
Sensitivity   Valued
Degree of Emotions   Usually not visible

5. Decision Making
Overall Method   Group consensus
Emphasize   Logic
Emphasis on Group/Team   High: Decisions from middle and
                                                   lower level groups
Emphasis on Face-Saving   Extreme
Influence of Special
  Interests on Decision
  Maker(s)   Openly influenced

6. Contractual and Administrative Factors
Need for an Agent   Average
Degree of Contract
  Specificity   Moderate
Degree of Paperwork/
  Bureaucracy   Moderate
Need for an Agenda   Moderate

CHINA

(PEOPLE'S REPUBLIC OF CHINA)

Fast Facts

Population:	1.1 billion
GNP:	$415.9 billion
Per Capita Income:	$370
Monetary Unit:	yuan
Major Industries:	iron, steel, coal
Main Trading Partners:	
Exports:	Hong Kong, Japan, U.S., Russia, Singapore
Imports:	Hong Kong, Japan, U.S., Germany, Russia
Key Exports:	manufactured goods, agricultural products, grains, oil, minerals
Key Imports:	grains, chemical fertilizers, steel, industrial raw materials, machinery
Major Cities:	Beijing (cap.) (6.7 million), Shanghai (7.2 mil.), Tientsin (5.5 million), Shernuang (4.4 million)
Ethnic Groups:	Han Chinese (93%), Zhuang, Uygur, Hui, Yi, and numerous other nationalities (7%)
Main Religions:	officially atheist, but religions such as Confucianism, Taoism, and Buddhism exist
Languages:	Standard Chinese (*Putongahua*), based on the Mandarin dialect; other dialects include Wu (in Shanghai), Min, and Yue

Reducing Communication Noise

Greetings

- Westerners are normally given a brief handshake upon meeting in business situations. Not everyone uses that gesture, however, so wait for your

Chinese counterpart to extend a hand first. The most common form of greeting is a nod or slight bow from the shoulders (not from the waist).
- The Chinese are quite formal and use titles and last names. First names are used only among close friends.
- The family name always comes first in Chinese, so that Chang Paio is Mr. Chang.
- A common greeting is *Ni hao?* (How are you?).
- Bring plenty of business cards, translated into standard Chinese on one side.

Conversation

- Try talking about the weather, the sights, Chinese culture, shopping, the excellent food, life in Western countries, your family, and your personal hobbies.
- The Chinese like to share with Westerners the progress that China has made over the past several years.
- The country should be referred to as the People's Republic of China, or simply China.
- Personal distance is generally greater among business associates than in the West, unless the relationship is well established. The Chinese are not a "touchy" society in a business environment and do not like to be touched or patted on the back or shoulders.

Sensitivities

- Avoid discussing and joking about sex, government, politics, and Taiwan.
- Avoid excessive use of the word *I,* a reference that is perceived as self-centered. Keep your comments group-oriented.
- Don't use a map showing British Hong Kong or an independent Taiwan.

Key Negotiating Pointers

- Make prior appointments and be punctual.
- Give your counterparts advance notice as to what you would like to accomplish in China. This is a courtesy they appreciate and reduces any concerns they may have about being surprised by your intentions.
- Demonstrate respect and build a solid relationship. Politeness, rank, and protocol are essential. A good deal of small talk is important before getting to the content of the negotiations. Trust and mutual connections are important.

- Never do or say anything that might embarass your counterpart. Be subtle and sensitive in your disagreements. Try not to ask direct questions. Your Chinese counterpart is proud to deal with you as an overseas client even though he probably can't make key decisions alone.
- Focus on long-term benefits.
- Expect slow decision making that must work its way through a cumbersome bureaucracy. Remember that while your negotiating counterpart may not be able to make a decision to go forward on a project, he may be able to veto it or hinder your progress in the bureaucracy.
- The highest-ranking person on your negotiating team should lead the group when entering a business meeting. The highest-ranking person should be the spokesperson.
- Be reserved and dignified in your personal style. Loud, overly expressive behavior is perceived as very offensive.
- Presentations should be detailed, technical, and factual. Speak often of trust and cooperation between you and your counterpart. Keep your presentations brief if a large group is involved.
- Chinese negotiators are characterized by a soft sell and hard buy. Give yourself plenty of room to negotiate. Extreme initial offers are the norm. The Chinese will be offended if there are not sizable concessions.
- Expect long periods when there is no movement in the Chinese negotiating position. Realize that there may be people not present during your discussions who will strongly influence the Chinese negotiating team.
- There is another reason to give yourself a lot of negotiating room. A common Chinese tactic is to pressure you into lowering your price by holding out the promise of their huge market. Keep in mind that China is still more of a potential market than an actual one.
- Be patient and persistent. Several trips to China will probably be necessary before you reach a business agreement. Keep your return plans flexible.
- Don't go it alone in China. The Chinese prefer to deal with a group than a single negotiator. Be sure to have technically competent engineers and other experts with you.
- Emphasize that you "specialize" in China, if you feel you can justify it.
- Beware of the Chinese "shaming" tactic, whereby your counterpart suggests that you have broken the bond of friendship if you do not agree to the final contract proposals they have made.
- Be patient in agreeing to a contract. Entering into a formal agreement can take months, with many translations and lengthy reviews. English rather than Chinese versions are usually signed. For all the fuss, don't be surprised if the Chinese do not feel that strict compliance to a contractual document is mandatory.
- Consider using your own interpreter. Chinese negotiators often prefer this

even if they speak excellent English. The Chinese prefer to negotiate through an intermediary so as not to lose face. Use an intermediary if you sense conflict.

- Use a Chinese agent as trade consultant to make initial contacts.

Day-to-Day Pointers

Business Entertainment Guidelines

- An invitation to a Chinese home is unusual, since the government must normally give prior approval.
- You are likely to be treated very graciously when visiting China, and this will include an evening dinner party (banquet) at a hotel or restaurant. Try to reciprocate as soon as you can, preferably on the same trip. Always allow your Chinese hosts to issue the first invitation.
- Include everybody with whom you have dealt in making the invitation list for your banquet. Who has the ultimate authority on the Chinese team is often ambiguous, so this will avoid the risk of excluding the most important person. Include Chinese and Western spouses.
- Business is not usually discussed during meals.
- *Gambei* (bottoms up) is the usual toast. Raise your glass in a toast, even if you fill your glass with water instead of alcohol. Toast the deal you are making and the friendship of your company with the other side.
- Consider only modest gifts, such as a logo gift. Expensive gifts may be an embarrassment to your counterpart.

Table Manners and Food

- Expect to eat at a round table with dishes in the center and to take food from serving plates to individual bowls. Don't pass serving dishes around. Use chopsticks to reach for food.
- Try to sample every dish.
- Hold the bowl close to your mouth when eating rice.
- Never leave rice on your plate.
- If you don't want more tea, leave some in your cup.
- The serving of fruit signals the end of the meal.

Gender Issues

- China is a tough place for any Western person to do business. Western women find acceptance, though hardly with open arms. It has been only a few years since Chinese women's feet were unbound.

- Women make up over half the Chinese labor force, and equality between the sexes is a key Communist tenet. Still, few women reach key government positions.
- When Chinese women hold key positions, however, they are treated with respect, even if this is not the case in their personal lives.

Also Remember This . . .

- China has a relatively high GNP, but with its large population, one of the lowest per capita incomes in the world.
- You must have an invitation to do business in China. This may take a year or so to obtain. Papers should be translated into Chinese to speed up the process.
- Foreign trade is a state-run monopoly. There is very little private sector in China, so business is done with the support of an official government body.

HONG KONG

Fast Facts

Population:	5.8 million
GNP:	$66.7 billion
Per Capita Income:	$11,540
Monetary Unit:	Hong Kong dollar
Major Industries:	textiles, clothing, tourism, electronics, plastics, toys, watches and clocks
Main Trading Partners:	
Exports:	U.S. (31%), China (14%), Germany (8%), U.K. (6%), Japan (5%)
Imports:	China (31%), Japan (20%), Taiwan (9%), U.S. (8%)

Key Exports:	clothing, plastic articles, textiles, electrical goods
Key Imports:	raw materials, transportation equipment, food
Major Cities:	Victoria (cap.) (1.1 million)
Ethnic Groups:	Chinese (98%)
Main Religions:	eclectic mixture of local religions (90%), Christian (10%)
Language(s):	Chinese (especially the Cantonese dialect); English is used to conduct business

Reducing Communication Noise

Greetings

- Shake hands lightly upon meeting and leaving. A nod or slight bow from the shoulders may accompany a handshake. Introductions are formal.
- Address people by title. The family name always comes first, so that Lee Chen is Mr. Lee, or Li Wong is Madame Li.
- The term for *thank you* is pronounced doe-jay, from the Cantonese dialect.

Conservation

- Acceptable topics of conversation include general inquiries about one's health, business conditions, the excellent cuisine, and Hong Kong shopping.

Sensitivities

- Avoid discussing the political situation in China.
- If the subject of reunification comes up, do more listening than talking.
- Avoid wearing blue and white, the Chinese colors for mourning.

Key Negotiating Pointers

- Make prior appointments since Hong Kong appointment calendars are usually quite full. Be punctual. Though a thirty-minute courtesy time is usually allowed, your counterpart will probably be punctual.

- Prepare a detailed agenda for negotiating sessions, and send this in advance of your trip.
- Don't plan a short visit. Hong Kong is a high-pressure business environment, though the pace of the negotiations remains slower than in the United States. While decisions are made crisply, it takes time to build trust and personal confidence.
- Expect the tone of the negotiation to be generally formal and reserved, with emphasis on politeness and mutual respect. Don't be shocked, however, if you encounter Hong Kong negotiators who are louder and more assertive than you may have thought. Hong Kong is a busy place, and a certain amount of aggressiveness does exist.
- Be gracious and respectful, but limit small talk. Expect your counterpart to get to the point after initial formalities.
- Avoid asking direct questions that might embarrass your counterpart. An open conflict could cost you the deal.
- A favorite tactic of Hong Kong negotiators is to remind you of the competition when they ask sellers to lower their price. Another favorite when asking buyers to pay more is to use facts and information as a basis for building a consultative relationship. This documented information helps the seller make the sale.
- Hong Kong negotiators tend to make concessions in an escalating pattern, beginning with a low amount and increasing it at subsequent sessions.
- Hong Kong Chinese tend to discuss all aspects of the deal, saving concessions (discounts) until the end.
- Personal trust will probably be placed above the fine legal points of the deal.
- Terminology in contracts is less problematic than in mainland China, as a result of Hong Kong's experience dealing with the West.
- Though negotiations are conducted in English, speak slowly and avoid slang. Politely check for understanding.
- Work through an agent or commissioned representative. Keep in mind that the right contacts keep changing with the new political realities of 1997.

Day-to-Day Pointers

Business Entertainment Guidelines

- A lunch or dinner banquet is a key part of the negotiating process. Breakfast meetings are not popular.
- Come hungry. Eight- to twelve-course meals are common.
- The most common toast is *yum sing*. Toasting is an important part of the

social etiquette. There will probably be a welcoming toast by your host, and it is customary for you to reciprocate by rising and thanking the host on everyone's behalf at the end of the meal.

- The Chinese retire early and usually leave immediately after a dinner banquet.
- Offer to pay the bill in a restaurant, though your offer will not be accepted. Never offer to split the bill; this would be considered loss of face.
- Gifts are routinely exchanged between business associates as well as friends during the Chinese New Year (usually around February).
- In restaurants, a 10 percent service charge is usually added to the bill, but it is customary to add another 5 percent. Where no service charge is added, 10 percent is acceptable.

Table Manners and Food

- Don't eat or drink before your host does.
- Hong Kong is world-famous for its cuisine. Chinese dishes are often prepared with pork, fish, chicken, and vegetables, with rice as the staple food.

Gender Issues

- Hong Kong is the best place in the Pacific Rim for Western women to do business.
- Women are on local negotiating teams, a factor that is influenced by the large amount of business done with the United States, Canada, and other Western countries, and the egalitarian principles of mainland China.

Also Remember This . . .

- Hong Kong is a good place for Americans to do business and is a center for banking and finance. It also has an essentially free port—no import restrictions and low export duties. Hong Kong does not have a large domestic market—only about 6 million people.
- Hong Kong is very cosmopolitan—a blend of Asian and European cultures—and has a highly educated and motivated work force.
- There is political risk. On July 1, 1997, Great Britain is scheduled to return Hong Kong to mainland Chinese rule. Some investors, such as the Japanese, have increased investments, while others, such as the British, have reduced investments. Officially, there will be "one country, two systems" after unification, with a continuation of capitalism in Hong Kong.

INDONESIA

Fast Facts

Population:	181.6 million
GNP:	$101.2 billion
Per Capita Income:	$560
Monetary Unit:	Indonesian rupiah
Major Industries:	petroleum, textiles, mining
Main Trading Partners:	
Exports:	Japan (42%), U.S. (16%), EC (11%), Singapore (9%)
Imports:	Japan (26%), EC (19%), U.S. (13%), Singapore (7%)
Key Exports:	petroleum and liquified natural gas, timber, textiles, rubber
Key Imports:	machinery, chemical products, manufactured goods
Major Cities:	Jakarta (cap.) (7.3 million), Surabaja (2.2 million), Medan (1.8 million), Bandung (1.6 million)
Ethnic Groups:	Javanese (45%), Sudanese (14%), Madurese (8%)
Main Religions:	Muslim (88%), Protestant (6%), Roman Catholic (3%)
Language(s):	Indonesian (a form of Malay), Javanese, Dutch; English is spoken by many businesspeople

Reducing Communication Noise

Greetings

- Men and women usually shake hands and nod their head when introduced for the first time. After that, it is unusual to shake hands in greeting; a nod or slight bow is appropriate.

- The social kiss takes place mainly in Jakarta: first on the right, then on the left cheek as one shakes hands.
- Exchange business cards after shaking hands or bowing.

Conversation

- Indonesians enjoy talking about their culture and traditions.
- Soccer, volleyball, tennis, and bicycling are popular sports. Indonesians are among the world's best badminton players.
- There tends to be a lot of touching in Indonesia compared with most other Pacific Rim countries.

Sensitivities

- Avoid discussing politics, the role of the Indonesian Chinese, or foreign aid.
- The bottom of one's foot should never face another person.

Key Negotiating Pointers

- Indonesians are used to bargaining in their everyday lives, as they barter for daily goods.
- Be punctual, even though your counterpart probably won't be.
- Negotiations may occur at several levels—between senior executives and between technical people at the operating level.
- Build a solid relationship. Loyalty is given more to family and friends than to personal concerns or organizations.
- Be patient. Indonesian negotiations are usually long, slow, and frustrating.
- Be restrained in your demeanor. Avoid conflict and embarrassing your counterpart publicly.
- Avoid fast concessions: You will be viewed as naive.
- Payments to obtain services are a routine part of Indonesian business life. Be sure to gain legal counsel from the home office in this regard.
- Be aware that mysticism is still sometimes influential and may be a reference point for your counterpart in making a decision.
- View the contract as a guideline rather than a precise statement of duties and responsibilities. Indonesians tend to deal with probabilities rather than facts.
- Get a local agent to help you weave through the complicated Indonesian government bureaucracy.

Day-to-Day Pointers

Business Entertainment Guidelines

- Graciously receive gifts. Be careful about opening them in public, however, so as not to embarrass the giver in front of others (as being too lavish or too miserly).
- At restaurants, tips are usually included in the bill.

Table Manners and Food

- Don't eat or drink until invited to do so by your host.
- Keep both hands above the table.
- There is a strong Muslim influence, so do not use your left hand to eat, touch others, point, or give or receive objects.
- Compliments about the food are appreciated.
- Finishing a drink implies you want more.
- Don't eat or drink in front of a Muslim in the daytime during *Ramadan*.
- Rice is the main food, served with vegetables, fish, and hot sauces. Fruits are often eaten as dessert. Beef and buffalo are common. Muslims do not eat pork or drink alcohol.

Gender Issues

- Indonesia is a challenging environment for U.S. women, but less so than many other Muslim countries.
- There are women in senior positions in Indonesian companies.
- Indonesian women have more rights than Muslim women elsewhere, with rights in property settlements, inheritances, and divorce. The women don't wear veils.

Also Remember This . . .

- Indonesia is very diverse, with many different cultures, languages, and business practices.
- Indonesia consists of 13,500 islands, 6,000 of which are inhabited by people.
- Indonesia is one of the most populated countries in the world. It is the most populous Muslim nation.

JAPAN

Fast Facts

Population:	123.5 million
GNP:	$3,140.9 billion
Per Capita Income:	$25,430
Monetary Unit:	yen
Major Industries:	metallurgical and engineering, electrical and electronic, textiles
Main Trading Partners:	
Exports:	U.S. (34%), Southeast Asia (22%), Western Europe (21%)
Imports:	Southeast Asia (23%), U.S. (23%), Western Europe (16%), Middle East (15%)
Key Exports:	manufactured goods, machinery, motor vehicles, consumer electronics
Key Imports:	manufactured goods, fossil fuels, machinery, nonfuel raw materials
Major Cities:	Toyko (cap.) (8.2 million); Yokohama (3.1 million), Osaka (2.5 million), Nagoya (2.1 million)
Ethnic Groups:	Japanese (99%)
Main Religions:	Shintoist and Buddhist
Language(s):	Japanese; English is often used in business

Reducing Communication Noise

Greetings

- Take your cue from the Japanese on whether to bow or shake hands. Though Japanese bow to each other, it is common for them to shake hands with Westerners.

- The depth and length of a bow indicates the amount of respect you want to show. In general, when bowing to a peer, bow as low and as long as your Japanese counterpart. The Japanese put a lot of emphasis on nonverbal communication. A proper bow (from the waist) is considered very important.
- Address people as *Mr., Miss, Mrs.,* or *Ms.* Use the Japanese suffix *san* added to the last name after you have gotten to know the person, as in Mr. Jones-san. Never use first names.

Conversation

- Try talking about Japanese food, the beauty of Japanese architecture, sports (especially baseball and golf), and other countries you have visited. Ask questions about Japan.
- Avoid constantly expressing your own opinion about things or appearing to have excessive pride about being an American or about yourself. The Japanese stress the group more than the individual.
- Write down your question if you are having trouble communicating. The Japanese often understand written English better than spoken English.

Sensitivities

- Avoid discussing World War II.
- If your Japanese host gives you a personal gift, don't open it in public. Your host might lose face if his associates view the gift as too lavish or too inexpensive.

Key Negotiating Pointers

- Be punctual. Allow considerably more time than you think you need to get where you are going in Tokyo, since traffic delays can be lengthy.
- Approach a Japanese company with an introduction from a third party—preferably someone who knows you, your background, your organization, and the Japanese organization with which you want to deal. The introduction could be with a letter or in person.
- The business relationship is very important. You must sell yourself before you can sell the product or service. The Japanese probably want to know your age, the university you attended, and about your family. Business comes later. Show the same interest in your counterparts.
- Don't go it alone. Expect a team of negotiators from your Japanese counterparts.

- Your proposals should be factual, technical, and detailed.
- Present written material, translated into Japanese, well in advance of discussing a subject. The Japanese don't like surprises. There should be copies for each member of the negotiating team; this will speed the decision-making process.
- Remember that the Japanese tend to focus on long-term viability and on property and physical plant, rather than on short-term profit or cash flow.
- Avoid abrupt, direct statements or questions that might embarrass your counterpart.
- Be patient. The group decision-making system, or *ringi,* is slow and involves all levels of the organization.
- Be patient for another reason. Progress may seem slow, but remember that Japanese negotiators consider a group of issues, rather than resolving issues one at a time as do Americans.
- Remember that a direct *no* to your proposal is considered rude. Surface harmony is very important. The Japanese may therefore say *hai* (yes), but this doesn't necessarily signify agreement. It may only mean, "Yes, I understand your point," or "Yes, it deserves further study."
- Accept that there will be less direct eye contact and more silence than you may be used to. The Japanese may frequently be silent during the negotiation. Be patient and allow them to speak first.
- Be aware that in Japan, suppliers don't just sell parts; they may also participate in product development.
- The contract must be approved at each level of the company. Implementation can be immediate after the decision is made, however.
- Be prepared to use an intermediary to help resolve a dispute.

Day-to-Day Pointers

Business Entertainment Guidelines

- Most business entertaining is done in restaurants. Let the Japanese issue the first invitation to a dinner; they do a great deal of this and occasionally want a break.
- Expect to be taken to a nightclub called a *karaoke* bar, where group singing takes place. The typical drink is called *mizuwari* (Scotch and water). You will usually be served this unless you specifically ask for something else.
- After being taken to a *karaoke* bar, reciprocate by inviting your Japanese counterpart to a restaurant.
- Few business deals are sealed without dinner in a restaurant or a drink at a bar.

- Go easy on the alcohol, since there are many toasts during the course of an evening. *Kanpai* (meaning Cheers) is a typical toast. Match your hosts toast for toast, but try to drink as little as possible. Filling your glass with water is acceptable.
- When you begin a business relationship with a Japanese company, you are usually given a gift. After receiving it, present a group gift, such as an item that represents your organization or region of the country, fine wine, rare Scotch, golf balls, books about your area of the country, or a subscription to a magazine. Thank your host profusely for any gift that you receive.

Table Manners and Food

- At meals, you receive a disposable set of chopsticks in a paper wrapper.
- When taking food from a communal serving bowl, turn your chopsticks and use the blunt ends so you won't contaminate the food.
- Hold the bowl close to your mouth when eating rice. Use chopsticks to bring food up to your mouth for other dishes.
- Don't finish your soup before eating other dishes. It should accompany the entire meal.
- Taste the various dishes, one at a time, alternating with rice.
- When you have finished your meal, leave the chopstick on the chopsticks rest. Do not leave them standing in a bowl of rice or other food.

Gender Issues

- U.S. women can be effective negotiators in Japan. However, Japanese men are still not comfortable with women in positions of power.
- You are unlikely to be negotiating with Japanese women. Though well educated, few Japanese women reach key professional or managerial positions. Japan is one of the most male-dominated cultures in the world, though younger Japanese businesswomen are starting to assert themselves. Women are in a few key government positions.
- Higher Japanese prices have made two-income families a more acceptable idea.
- Women make up about 40 percent of the Japanese work force.

Also Remember This . . .

- Japan has one of the world's most powerful economies.
- The United States is Japan's biggest trading partner.
- The economy is manufacturing-oriented. Over 95 percent of exports are from the manufacturing sector.

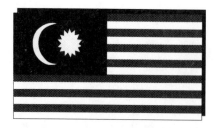

MALAYSIA

Fast Facts

Population:	17.8 million
GNP:	$41.5 billion
Per Capita Income:	$2,340
Monetary Unit:	ringgit
Major Industries:	Malaysian Peninsula—rubber and palm oil processing and manufacturing, light manufacturing; Sabah—logging, petroleum production; Sarawak—agriculture, processing, petroleum production and refining, logging
Main Trading Partners:	
Exports:	Japan, Singapore, U.S., Russia, Australia, EC
Imports:	Japan, EC, Singapore, Germany, U.K., Thailand, China
Key Exports:	natural rubber, palm oil, tin, timber, petroleum
Key Imports:	foods, crude oil, capital equipment, chemicals
Major Cities:	Kuala Lumpur (cap.) (920,000), Ipoh (293,000), George Town (248,000)
Ethnic Groups:	Malay and other indigenous groups (59%), Chinese (32%), Indian (9%)
Main Religions:	Islam is the official religion; ethnic Malays are usually Muslim, Chinese on the peninsula are mainly Buddhist, Indians are chiefly Hindu
Language(s):	Bahasa Malay; Chinese speak one of the Chinese dialects; Indians speak Tamil; English is widely spoken in business

Reducing Communication Noise

Greetings

- Shake hands with men upon meeting and parting. Men and women seldom shake hands with each other; rather a man should nod or bow slightly to a woman and offer verbal greetings.
- Address people by a title (such as *Mr., Mrs.,* or *Miss*) to show respect.
- Common greetings are *Salamat pagi* (Good morning) and *Salamat petant* (Good afternoon). *Halo* (Hello) is a casual greeting.
- Business cards are exchanged after greetings.

Conversation

- Malaysians enjoy talking about their country's economic successes, the beautiful scenery, sports, and food. They appreciate polite inquiries about the general state of their family.
- Soccer is Malaysia's most popular sport, along with badminton, field hockey, cricket, rugby, and table tennis. Kite flying is popular on the peninsula.

Sensitivities

- Avoid discussing religion. There has been a history of antagonism among the various groups.
- Avoid comparisons between the West and Malaysia.

Key Negotiating Pointers

- Malaysians generally practice a soft sell and hard buy.
- Make prior appointments and be punctual even though your counterpart may not be.
- Be prepared for lengthy small talk unrelated to business issues before business items are discussed.
- Build rapport and trust. The relationship forms the basis for the business aspects of the negotiation.
- Expect discussions to be long and detailed. Be prepared to provide a lot of information. Malays are quite detailed in their approach, and they formulate their position gradually and carefully.
- Expect Malay negotiators generally to be courteous. Etiquette is important.

- Respect the concept of face. Status is important. Avoid asking direct, probing questions that could be embarrassing.
- Be diplomatic in the rejection of your counterpart's proposal. A direct rejection of the position is sometimes considered to be a rejection of the person.
- Be prepared for much diplomacy from your Malaysian counterpart. Read between the lines to determine the real positions.
- Expect Malay negotiators to graciously but firmly keep the pressure on for you to make concessions and to remind you of the business potential in Malaysia.
- Malays tend to make concessions in an escalating pattern, beginning with a low amount and increasing it at each session.
- Get a written agreement, but remember that Malaysians view written contracts as less important than personal trust.
- Expect a request for an escape clause if things don't work out. Making and keeping contractual commitments is not usually a high priority for Malay negotiators.

Day-to-Day Pointers

Business Entertainment Guidelines

- Business entertaining, normally done in restaurants or hotels, is a key part of the negotiating process in Malaysia. Follow important meetings with lunch or dinner.
- Dinner is eaten about 7 P.M. or 8 P.M.
- If treated by your host, send a thank you note or flowers the next day.
- Gift giving among business associates is not expected or traditional, but it is acceptable. Give and receive gifts with both hands.

Table Manners and Food

- Do not use your left hand to eat, shake hands, touch others, point, or give or receive objects.
- Drinks are offered and received with both hands.
- A wide assortment of foods are eaten as a result of Malaysia's cultural diversity. Rice is Malaysia's staple food, and fish is very common. Food is generally spicy. Fruits such as durians (large, oval fruits with a prickly rind), bananas, pineapples, and papayas are plentiful.
- Muslims do not eat pork or drink alcoholic beverages, and Hindus and some Buddhists do not eat beef.

Gender Issues

- U.S. women may experience a few problems doing business in Malaysia, due mainly to the conservative Muslim influence.
- Although about 45 percent of the population is Muslim, the Chinese dominate the business community and will probably be your negotiating counterparts. They tend to be more egalitarian than the Muslims.

Also Remember This . . .

- Malaysia was granted independence from Britain in 1957.
- Malaysia consists of two different and distinct land regions and is very culturally diverse. Peninsular Malaysia, south of Thailand, is one region, and East Malaysia, on the island of Borneo, is the other. East Malaysia in turn consists of two states, Sabah and Sarawak.
- The Chinese generally live in urban areas. Ethnic Malays are mostly Muslim and live in rural areas.

PHILIPPINES

Fast Facts

Population:	66.4 million
GNP:	$43.9 billion
Per Capita Income:	$730
Monetary Unit:	Filipino peso
Major Industries:	textiles, pharmaceuticals, chemicals
Main Trading Partners:	
Exports:	U.S. (36%), EC (19%), Japan (18%), ESCAP* (9%)

*Economic and Social Commission for Asia and the Pacific.

Imports:	U.S. (25%), Japan (17%), ESCAP* (13%), EC (10%)
Key Exports:	electrical equipment, textiles, minerals and ores, farm products
Key Imports:	raw materials, capital goods, petroleum products
Major Cities:	Manila (cap.) (1.6 million), Quezon City (1.7 million), Davao City (610,400)
Ethnic Groups:	Christian Malay (92%), Muslim Malay (4%), Chinese (2%)
Main Religions:	Roman Catholic (83%), Protestant (9%), Muslim (5%), Buddhist and other (3%)
Languages:	English, Filipino (based on Tagalog); English is the main language of business, government, and education

---

Reducing Communication Noise

Greetings

- Shake hands with both men and women upon meeting and parting. Greetings are friendly and informal.
- First names are commonly used, but do not use them until you are invited to do so. The exception is for very senior people in rank or age, where a title (such as *Mr., Mrs.,* or *Miss*) and last name are used.

Conversation

- Filipinos like general discussion about their families and enjoy hearing about yours. Movies are also a popular subject. Many North American movies are available, and the Philippines is the fourth largest producer of movies in the world.
- Basketball is a popular national sport. Horse racing and cockfights have many fans.
- There tends to be a lot of touching in the Philippines compared with most other Pacific Rim countries.

*Economic and Social Commission for Asia and the Pacific.

Sensitivities

- Avoid discussing politics, religion, social conditions, and corruption.
- Be careful with the issue of U.S.–Filipino relations. Filipino politics are chaotic, and widely differing views are held on the U.S. presence and influence.

Key Negotiating Pointers

- Be punctual even though your counterpart may not be. Filipinos are casual about time, and meetings or appointments often start about ten to twenty minutes after the appointed time.
- Be sincere. Though Filipinos are fun-loving and casual, insincerity is easily detected.
- Be sensitive and avoid direct criticism. Honor is an important virtue to Filipinos, and the perception of open criticism could bring shame on the individual. Candor is sometimes viewed as a lack of culture.
- Keep proposals practical and conservative. Radical changes or innovation are not usually well accepted. Success is often attributed to fate more than to effort or ability.
- Be prepared for a "take it or leave it" tactic when Filipinos are the sellers asking for a lower price.
- When asking the buyer to pay more, Filipinos tend to play with the numbers, stressing percentage figures rather than absolute figures, costs per unit rather than total costs, or rounded figures rather than exact figures.
- Filipinos tend to make concessions in an escalating pattern, beginning with a low amount and increasing it at each session.
- Be aware of subtle bribery. Seek legal counsel from the home office if you have a question.

Day-to-Day Pointers

Business Entertainment Guidelines

- Business entertaining is normally done in restaurants or clubs.
- Don't discuss business over meals.
- Your host will probably invite you out for dinner. Try to reciprocate.
- In restaurants, tips are usually 10–15 percent.

Table Manners and Food

- Eating heartily is a compliment to your host.
- Leave a small portion on your plate to indicate that you have finished eating.
- Filipino cuisine is diverse, reflecting the influence of many cultures. Rice is the staple food. A typical meal consists of boiled rice, fried fish or pork, a vegetable, and fruit or dessert.
- A wide variety of food is available in restaurants. Local dishes include *adobo* (a stew of chicken and pork in garlic, soy sauce, and vinegar) and *kare-kare* (a stew of meats and vegetables served in a peanut sauce). Meals are often skewered.

Gender Issues

- The Philippines is a good place for U.S. women to do business. Filipino women generally enjoy equality with men and hold prominent positions in business and government.
- Filipino men often exhibit the Latin idea of *machismo*. For example, comments by men about women passing on the street are common (but should be ignored).
- Many Filipino women as well as men are educated in U.S. universities.

Also Remember This . . .

- Agriculture is the Filipino economy's backbone, employing almost half the labor force and providing about 30 percent of all export earnings.
- The Philippines is very diverse, having been influenced by the Chinese, Malaysian, Spanish, and U.S. cultures.
- Individual accomplishment tends to be less important than family considerations.

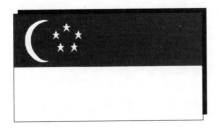

SINGAPORE

Fast Facts

Population:	2.7 million
GNP:	$33.5 billion
Per Capita Income:	$12,310
Monetary Unit:	Singapore dollar
Major Industries:	petroleum refining, electronics, oil-drilling equipment
Main Trading Partners:	
Exports:	U.S. (24%), Malaysia (13%), Japan (9%), Hong Kong (6%), Thailand (6%)
Imports:	Japan (22%), U.S. (16%), Malaysia (14%), EC (12%)
Key Exports:	petroleum products, rubber, electronics, manufactured goods
Key Imports:	capital equipment, petroleum, chemicals, manufactured goods
Major Cities:	Singapore (cap.) (2.7 million)
Ethnic Groups:	Chinese (77%), Malay (15%), Indian (6%)
Main Religions:	Buddhist (29%), Christian (19%), Muslim (16%), Taoist (13%)
Language(s):	Malay, Mandarin Chinese, Tamil, English; English is used to conduct business

Reducing Communication Noise

Greetings

- Shake hands upon meeting and leaving, with an additional slight bow for the Chinese and older people present.
- Address people as *Mr., Mrs.,* or *Miss* unless you are invited to do other-

wise. For the Chinese, the family name is first, the middle name is next, and the given name is last, so that Lee Tse Chen is Mr. Lee.
- Business cards are important.

Conversation

- Try talking about the wide variety of cultural arts, the progressive economy, Singapore's beauty, and the excellent shopping.
- Soccer, badminton, basketball, tennis, and golf are all popular sports.

Sensitivities

- Avoid discussing religion or politics.
- Avoid telling jokes unless you know your counterparts well. Singaporeans are friendly, but they are not great joke tellers or receivers. Humor is subdued.
- Finger gestures, such as the rounded *okay* sign or pointing, are considered rude.
- Don't touch people on the head.

Key Negotiating Pointers

- The Singaporean business culture is largely British, combined with the Chinese reputation for driving a hard bargain.
- Make prior appointments and be punctual. Being late is considered rude.
- Expect fast-paced negotiations. Singaporeans have a reputation as an entrepreneurial and industrious people.
- Singaporean negotiators are generally more direct and open than those in many other Pacific Rim countries.
- The concept of face is very important. Public embarrassment would seriously damage, if not end, a potential deal.
- Be direct on money matters. Prices and schedules are generally key issues.
- To help counter the price issue, stress your organization's ability to produce fast deliveries and other indications of customer responsiveness.
- Expect Singaporean negotiators to remind you of the competition and to keep the pressure on you to make concessions.
- Singaporeans tend to make concessions in an escalating pattern, beginning with a low amount and increasing it at each session.
- The new generation of Chinese have adopted many Westernized business practices, emphasizing facts, technical specifications, and detailed contracts. More traditional Chinese consummate a deal based on trust, with simple, general contracts.

- Avoid even the hint of any action that might constitute bribery. The Singaporean government has a reputation for being squeaky-clean in this regard.

Day-to-Day Pointers

Business Entertainment Guidelines

- Most business entertaining is done in restaurants.
- Singapore is one of the few non-Western countries where business can be discussed over a meal.
- If your counterpart is from the private sector, it is appropriate to invite him or her to dinner only after several meetings. Government officials are not allowed to accept invitations.
- Unlike the case in many Pacific Rim countries, gift giving is not a custom among businesspeople.
- Tips are not customary and are discouraged by the government. Modest tips for bellhops are the exception.

Table Manners and Food

- Don't use your left hand if with Malay Muslims.
- Try to use chopsticks.
- With its ethnic mix, Singapore offers a tremendous variety of superb cuisine. Every type of Chinese food (e.g., Cantonese, Mandarin, Szechuan) is available, and there are many Malay, Indian, and European restaurants.

Gender Issues

- Singapore is a good place for U.S. women to do business.
- Singaporean women are often highly educated and fill professional positions.

Also Remember This . . .

- This small island (about the size of Chicago) is considered an economic miracle by many and is often rated as economically and politically safe as Switzerland.
- Singapore has the highest standard of living in Asia, second only to Japan.
- Singapore is already effective at producing high-tech goods.

SOUTH KOREA

(REPUBLIC OF KOREA)

Fast Facts

Population:	42.8 million
GNP:	$231.1 billion
Per Capita Income:	$5,400
Monetary Unit:	won
Major Industries:	textiles and clothing, footwear, food process-ing, cement, automotive
Main Trading Partners:	
Exports:	U.S. (33%), Japan (21%)
Imports:	Japan (28%), U.S. (25%)
Key Exports:	textiles and clothing, electrical machinery, footwear, automobiles, steel
Key Imports:	machinery, oil, steel, transportation equip-ment, textiles
Major Cities:	Seoul (cap.) (9.6 million), Pusan (3.5 million), Taegu (2.0 million), Inchon (1.4 million)
Ethnic Groups:	ethnic Korean, except for small Chinese mi-nority
Main Religions:	Confucian (50%), Christian (30%), Buddhist (15%)
Language(s):	Korean; English and Japanese are spoken by many businesspeople

Reducing Communication Noise

Greetings

- Bow slightly and shake hands with men upon meeting. The left hand may support the right forearm during the handshake to show respect. Women shake hands less often than men.

- Present and accept business cards with both hands after a handshake. Hand everything with two hands or support your right hand with your left, under the elbow or forearm.
- The majority of the population shares only three family names: Kim, Park, and Lee. Address people by title and family name, which comes first, so that Kim Won-Song is Mr. Kim.
- A common greeting is *Annyong haseyo?* (Are you at peace?).

Conversation

- Try talking about Korean culture and the country's economic success. Koreans are proud of these accomplishments.
- Soccer, baseball, boxing, and basketball are very popular sports. The martial art tae kwon do comes from Korea and is very popular. Mountain climbing and hiking are favorite pastimes.
- Koreans are very modest. Compliments are graciously denied.
- A person may respond by laughing when embarrassed.
- It is not unusual to see younger Korean men holding hands or walking with their hands on each other's shoulders. This is an expression of friendship.

Sensitivities

- Avoid discussing politics.
- Don't give compliments. This could be very embarrassing to your Korean counterpart.
- Avoid comparisons between Korea and Japan. Koreans are fierce competitors with the Japanese.
- Don't place your feet on a desk or chair.

Key Negotiating Pointers

- Koreans are tough negotiators. Be firm, consistent, but not aggressive.
- Eating and drinking precede getting down to business.
- Build a strong relationship. This is vital to your success in Korea. Mutual trust and respect are highly valued.
- Be very diplomatic and gracious. Candor and bluntness could cost you the deal. Peace and harmony are important.
- Be patient. Results will be slow, but a proper investment in time can pay big dividends.

- Negotiations are likely to be repetitive. Be prepared to give detailed information.
- Don't be alarmed if you are asked questions that you may already have answered. The Koreans are trying to make sure they are correct in their decisions. A major mistake is cause for embarrassment, and the person might resign his job or be fired. Consistently repeated answers will help you more than fresh creative answers.
- Don't appear to be excessively proud of the accomplishments that you or your company have made.
- Listen carefully to your Korean counterpart. Koreans are seldom direct and open in their communication.
- Even though English is spoken, use an interpreter, particularly for big or sensitive deals.
- Get a government-approved agent. This is a tough market.
- Be aware that a written contract is subject to change and renegotiation.

Day-to-Day Pointers

Business Entertainment Guidelines

- Drinking large quantities of alcohol, usually *soju* (the traditional Korean rice wine), is common at business dinners.
- There are likely to several toasts. Raise your drink with your right hand and say *Gun-bei* (Raise cup).
- Wives are seldom included in business entertainment.
- Exchanging gifts is very common among businesspeople. Food or small mementos are appropriate. If you receive a gift, be sure to reciprocate. Open your gift in private.
- In restaurants, tipping is not expected. A service charge is usually included in the bill.

Table Manners and Food

- Use your left hand to support your right forearm or wrist when items are passed or drinks are poured.
- Chopsticks and spoons are the usual eating utensils.
- Korean food is generally spicy. Rice and *kimch'i* (spicy pickled cabbage) are popular. Lots of fish is also eaten. A favorite delicacy is *pulkogi,* strips of marinated and barbecued beef.

Gender Issues

- Although few South Korean women are in management, South Koreans are quite accepting of international businesswomen—more so, for example, than the Japanese.
- Women should try to use an elevated title.
- Touching members of the opposite sex is usually not appropriate.

Also Remember This . . .

- Japanese management practices prevail in South Korea.
- The "big four" South Korean companies are Daewoo, Hyundai, Samsung, and Gold Star.
- The *chaebol,* huge conglomerates that make up the bulk of Korean exports, are still run by their founding Korean families such as Samsung, Daewoo, Sungyong, and Sangyong Group. These families concentrate in electronics, shipbuilding, and construction and industrial equipment.

TAIWAN

(REPUBLIC OF CHINA)

Fast Facts

Population:	20.5 million
GNP:	$167.8 billion*
Per Capita Income:	$8,000*
Monetary Unit:	new Taiwan dollar
Major Industries:	textiles, clothing, electronics, chemicals

*Based on March 1991 data.

Main Trading Partners:
Exports: U.S. (36%), Japan (14%)
Imports: Japan (31%), U.S. (23%), Saudi Arabia (9%)
Key Exports: machinery and equipment, textiles, communi-
                        cations equipment, basic metals
Key Imports: machinery and equipment, chemicals and
                        chemical products, basic metals, crude oil
Major Cities: Taipei (cap.) (2.7 million), Kaohsiung (1.4 mil-
                        lion), Taichung (700,000)
Ethnic Groups: Taiwanese (84%), mainland Chinese (14%),
                        Aborigines (2%)
Main Religions: mixture of Buddhist, Confucian, and Taoist
                        (93%), Christian (5%)
Language(s):   Mandarin Chinese; Taiwanese (a variant of the
                        Fukien dialect) is commonly spoken; English
                        is spoken by many businesspeople

Reducing Communication Noise

Greetings

- A smile and nod of the head, accompanied by a slight bow, are appropri-
ate when meeting. Handshakes are usually reserved for acquaintances
and friends.
- Stand when a guest, elderly person, or superior enters the room.
- First names are rarely used alone. Address people by a title with the last
name.
- For Chinese names, the family name comes first. It is common to have
both an English and Chinese first name.
- Common greetings are *Ni hao ma?* (How are you?) and *Ching dzwo*
(Please sit).
- Bring plenty of business cards, printed in both Chinese and English. (There
are numerous printers in Taiwan who can fill such an order in two to three
days.)

Conversation

- Polite inquires about health are considered appropriate. Also, show an
appreciation for the significant economic gains that Taiwan has achieved.

- Movies, music, baseball, and hiking are popular pastimes. Taiwanese Little League champions consistently do well in the Little League World Series (they were the champs in 1991).
- Loud behavior is considered in poor taste.

Sensitivities

- Although it is a hot, open topic among Taiwanese, avoid discussing mainland China or reunification with mainland China.
- Don't print "simplified" Chinese characters (used in mainland China) on written documents.
- It is impolite to wink.
- Don't push a chair, door, or other objects with your feet (feet are considered dirty).

Key Negotiating Pointers

- Taiwanese negotiations are characterized by a soft sell and hard buy.
- Take part in polite chitchat prior to discussions on content, but expect Taiwanese negotiators to get to the point faster than is typical in most other parts of the Pacific Rim.
- Give respect to the group as a whole in your comments, but try to determine the key decision maker. This person may or may not be at the negotiating table.
- Though the Taiwanese are competitive negotiators, bargain in the spirit of harmony and respect. Maintain friendliness in a reserved way. Taiwanese negotiators are generally quiet, refined, and friendly.
- Cultivate the relationship, even though relationships are not as strong and close as they are in Japan.
- Taiwanese negotiators usually don't like to say no directly. Instead, they will give you a "soft no" or leave it unsaid.
- Avoid candor, abruptness, or criticism. Public embarrassment, or loss of face, can kill a negotiation.
- This is a very competitive market, and price is often a key sticking point. If the result is a slim profit margin, you may be able to make some of it up in this large potential market.
- Many Taiwanese have been socialized to be very respectful of others, and to a Westerner, this can be perceived as being unassertive. This is not necessarily true of many of your negotiating counterparts, however—particularly those who work for Citibank, Dow Corning, and many other U.S. or Western companies. These individuals can be quite hard bargainers

and not at all shy about occasionally interrupting you and forcefully making their point, especially during the final stages of negotiations.

- Be patient—don't rush the negotiation. You might find the negotiations moving along faster than you thought, but let your Taiwanese counterpart take the lead.
- Be well prepared and consistent in your presentations.
- Common Taiwanese negotiating tactics are saying "take it or leave it" to remind you of your competition, and, if you are the buyer, reminding you of their superior capabilities.
- Taiwanese tend to make concessions in a "deescalating" pattern: generous at first, then tapering off.
- Detailed contracts are typical. Allow ample time for review by TOS, however.
- Many of your negotiating counterparts probably speak some degree of English, though as a rule, it is important to speak simply and slowly. Don't be surprised if many of your counterparts have worked or been educated in the United States or other Western countries.

Day-to-Day Pointers

Business Entertainment Guidelines

- The banquet is an important part of the negotiation. Taiwanese negotiators—particularly the men—like to entertain during the evening in restaurants. You are not expected to reciprocate.
- Business is not usually discussed during meals. If it is, let your host bring up the subject. Conversation during meals often centers on the meal itself—the ingredients and how the meal was prepared.
- Dinner usually begins about 6:00 P.M. to 7:00 P.M., and can easily continue for two or more hours as your host orders several courses of Chinese fare.
- Your Taiwanese hosts may drink a toast to you and then pass you the empty glass. It will then be filled by one of the hosts. You are expected to toast your hosts and drink the whiskey or wine. The drinking sessions can carry on for many hours. Pace yourself.
- Bring a small gift to your counterpart.
- In most cases, tipping is not necessary. A 10 percent service charge is usally added to restaurant bills. It is appropriate, however, if you want to leave change when you pay the bill.

Table Manners and Food

- Food is placed in the center of the table. For a formal banquet, you normally serve yourself. For a family-type (or home) banquet, each person is given a personal bowl of rice in addition to the food in the center. The bowl is held near the mouth and chopsticks are used to eat the food.
- Eat sparingly; there are many courses. Leave a small amount of rice at the bottom of the bowl when you are finished eating so that your bowl won't be refilled.
- Rice is eaten with nearly every meal. Soup, seafood, pork, chicken, vegetables, and fruit are commonly eaten. Many foods are stir-fried. Local Taiwanese cuisine and Peking, Cantonese, Szechwan, and other cuisines are available.

Gender Issues

- Taiwan is generally a good place for U.S. women to do business.
- Although they are not common in local businesses, Taiwanese women occupy professional positions in Western-owned or managed businesses.

Also Remember This . . .

- Taiwan is a fast-growing, aggressive economy.
- Taiwan is an excellent market for high-tech and infrastructure companies (e.g., telecommunications and transportation) and for petrochemicals, plastics, and chemicals. The country's well-educated and well-off middle class is also a rising market for consumer goods. The key competition is from Japan.
- The Taiwanese generally like Americans, and Taiwan is Westernizing quickly.

THAILAND

Fast Facts

Population:	55.8 million
GNP:	$79.0 billion
Per Capita Income:	$1,420
Monetary Unit:	baht
Major Industries:	textiles and clothing, agricultural processing, beverages
Main Trading Partners:	
Exports:	U.S. (18%), Japan (14%), Singapore (9%)
Imports:	Japan (26%), U.S. (14%), Singapore (7%)
Key Exports:	textiles, fishery products, rice
Key Imports:	machinery and parts, petroleum products, tapioca, chemicals
Major Cities:	Bangkok (cap.) (5.5 million), Songkla (172,600), Chon Buri (115,400)
Ethnic Groups:	Thai (75%), Chinese (14%)
Main Religions:	Buddhist (96%), Muslim (4%)
Language(s):	Thai; English is often spoken by those with advanced education

Reducing Communication Noise

Greetings

- Westerners are greeted with handshakes. The most common greeting among Thais is a *wai*—placing the palms of your hands together, with fingers extended at chest level, and bowing slightly. The *wai* can mean Hello, Thank you, and I'm sorry.
- Address people as *Mr.*, *Mrs.*, or *Miss*, with the last name. Thais them-

selves use first names in everyday discussions, preceded by *kuhn*; they use surnames for formal occasions.

Conversation

- Thais love talking about their cultural heritage.
- Soccer, table tennis, badminton, and volleyball are the most popular sports.
- Thai is a tonal language that is very difficult for most Westerners to speak. Try to learn a few basic phrases, however.
- Avoid telling your negotiating counterpart that you admire a particular object. Your counterpart may feel obligated to give it to you.
- There tends to be a lot of touching in Thailand compared with most other Pacific Rim countries. However, while good friends of the same sex may hold hands, men and women generally do not touch each other or show affection in public.

Sensitivities

- Avoid discussing drug trafficking or regional politics.
- Avoid any negative reference to the King or Queen of Thailand. They are very respected by most Thais.
- It is considered offensive to cross your legs when sitting. Avoid stamping your feet and using them to move or point at objects, or pointing your feet at others. The bottoms of your feet are considered the least sacred part of your body.
- Avoid stepping on a doorsill of a private home or temple (*wat*). Thai tradition says a soul resides in the doorsill.
- Women should not touch or offer to shake hands with a Buddhist monk.

Key Negotiating Pointers

- Make prior appointments and be punctual. Punctuality is important.
- Be reserved, though a sense of humor and laughter are highly regarded.
- Bargaining is expected, but it should be done in the spirit of cooperation and friendship. Being loud or showing anger can cost you respect.
- Avoid comparisons to the "U.S. approach." Thais do not see development as a need to Westernize.
- Thais tend to make concessions in a deescalating pattern: generous at first, then tapering off.
- Contracts must be written in the local language as well as English.

Day-to-Day Pointers

Business Entertainment Guidelines

- If you are invited to a private home, it is not necessary to bring a gift unless your stay is an extended one.
- In restaurants, tips are not usually necessary, though a 10 percent tip for extremely good service is appreciated.
- Let your host bring up the subject of business during a meal.

Table Manners and Food

- Various dishes are placed at the center of the table, from which you choose foods to eat with rice.
- Thais use forks and spoons, except for chopsticks in Chinese homes and restaurants.
- Rice is the staple food of Thailand. It is usually served with very spicy dishes that consist of meat, vegetables, fish, eggs, and fruits. Curries and pepper sauces are popular.

Gender Issues

- Thailand is generally a good place for U.S. women to do business.
- There are women in senior positions in many private Thai companies.

Also Remember This . . .

- Thais are proud of the fact that their country has avoided foreign rule (except for Japanese occupation during World War II).
- Buddhism deeply affects Thais' daily lives.
- Tourism is the largest source of foreign exchange.

Chapter 14

Negotiating in Other Important Countries

There are five other important countries with which you may be doing business, but they are not geographically, culturally, or politically part of the other six regions of the world that we have examined.

Here are Negotiating Primers for Australia, India, New Zealand, Nigeria, and Pakistan. Each of these countries is either a major trading partner of the United States or a large potential market.

AUSTRALIA

Fast Facts

Population:	17.0 million
GNP:	$290.5 billion
Per Capita Income:	$17,080
Monetary Unit:	Australian dollar
Major Industries:	mining, machinery, motor vehicles
Main Trading Partners:	
Exports:	Japan (26%), U.S. (11%), New Zealand (6%), South Korea (4%), Singapore (4%)
Imports:	U.S. (22%), Japan (22%), U.K. (7%), Germany (6%), New Zealand (4%)
Key Exports:	wheat, barley, beef, lamb, dairy products
Key Imports:	manufactured raw materials, capital equipment, consumer goods
Major Cities:	Canberra (cap.) (270,000), Sydney (3.4 million), Melbourne (3.0 million), Brisbane (1.2 million)
Ethnic Groups:	Caucasian (95%), Asian (4%), Aboriginal and other (1%)
Main Religions:	Anglican (26%), Roman Catholic (24%), and other Christian faiths (24%)
Language(s):	English

Reducing Communication Noise

Greetings

- Shake hands upon meeting and leaving. Australians are informal and shake hands warmly. This may be accompanied by a casual *Good day* (pronounced guday), particularly by men.

- First names are widely used, but do not use them until you are invited to do so.

Conversation

- Try talking about physical fitness and recreation. There is a great sporting awareness of Australian football, soccer, rugby, cricket, basketball, tennis, golf, bicycling, and swimming. Many Australians follow the America's Cup yachting event.
- Avoid American slang. Try to learn how English is used in Australia. There are a number of terms that Americans use that are offensive in Australia (and vice versa).
- Many expressions are different from English usage in the United States— for example, *no worries* (no problem), *rubber* (eraser), and *bird* (young woman). Men normally refer to their friends as *mate*.
- Australians often use nicknames for common terms such as *uni* (university), *tele* (television), or *barbie* (barbecue).
- Humor is almost always appreciated.

Sensitivities

- Avoid comparisons between Australia and the United States or the United Kingdom.

Key Negotiating Pointers

- Make prior appointments and be punctual. Australians are easygoing, but they are sticklers about time.
- Be informal, but courteous. Americans tend to feel very comfortable dealing with Australians, who regard extreme formality as insincere and artificial. Efforts to impress usually are hurtful.
- Try to get connections and introductions at senior executive levels.
- Expect Australian negotiators to be as direct and open in their negotiating style as Americans.
- Don't be afraid to use humor.
- Make presentations detailed and factual, and be prepared to respond evenly to pointed questions.
- Negotiations move crisply. Make brief preliminary comments and then get quickly down to business.
- Keep your administrative requirements to a minimum. Australians don't like being told what to do and operate with few rigid lines of authority.

- Stress the practical over the conceptual. Australian negotiators are pragmatic and profit-oriented.
- Make the opening offer fairly close to your "really asking" position, but leave yourself some room for movement. Australians don't tend to be "blue-sky" bargainers (i.e., haggling for long periods from very high initial offers).
- Expect Australian negotiators to remind you of the competition and to keep the pressure on to make concessions. Patience is another often-used Australian tactic, as they hope to wait it out for you to concede.
- Australians tend to make concessions in a deescalating pattern: generous at first, then tapering off.
- Contracts are written, specific, and firm.
- Get representation within Australia because of the great distances among locations.

Day-to-Day Pointers

Business Entertainment Guidelines

- Don't discuss business during meals or at social occasions.
- Dinner is the main meal of the day, eaten in the evening. The noon meal is called *lunch; supper* is a snack before bed. On Sundays, however, there is often a large noon meal called *dinner,* and a lighter meal *(tea)* in the evening.
- In restaurants, tipping is not traditional, though it is becoming more popular.

Table Manners and Food

- If you are visiting someone's home, you receive a plate already served, rather than helping yourself to the various dishes.
- When yawning, cover your mouth and excuse yourself. It is considered a sign of boredom.
- All varieties of meat and fish are available. Popular meals are fish and chips and pastries (turnovers filled with meat).

Gender Issues

- U.S. women can readily do business in Australia, but there is a strong Old Boy Network.

- Women should not plan on having a drink with their Australian male counterparts after dinner. Australian men often prefer to do this with their male mates.

Also Remember This . . .

- Australia is technologically progressive and sophisticated.
- Australian labor unions are a strong workplace influence.
- If you engage in golf, tennis, or another competitive sport, sportsmanship will be applauded. Your Australian counterpart commonly says *Bad luck* when you miss a tennis or golf shot.

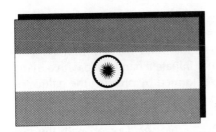

INDIA

Fast Facts

Population:	849.5 million
GNP:	$294.8 billion
Per Capita Income:	$350
Monetary Unit	rupee
Major Industries:	textiles, food processing, steel
Main Trading Partners:	
Exports:	EC (25%), U.S. (19%), USSR (former) (17%), Eastern Europe (17%), Japan (10%)
Imports:	EC (33%), Middle East (19%), Japan (10%), U.S. (9%), USSR (former) (8%)
Key Exports:	tea, coffee, iron ore, fishery products
Key Imports:	petroleum, edible oils, textiles, clothing
Major Cities:	New Delhi (cap.) (273,000), Bombay (8.2 million), Delhi (4.9 million), Calcutta (3.3 million)

Ethnic Groups:	Indo-Aryan, (72%), Dravidian (natives) (25%), Mongoloid and other (3%)
Main Religions:	Hindu (83%), Muslim (11%), Christian (2%), Sikh (2%)
Language(s):	24 languages with a million or more speakers each; English is the language of business and national connection

---

Reducing Communication Noise

Greetings

- Shake hands lightly upon meeting and leaving. Men do not usually shake hands with Indian women in business situations, though educated Indian women usually shake hands with both men and women from Western countries. A Western woman should not initiate a handshake with a man.
- The traditional greeting is the *namaste*, formed by pressing the palms together, fingers up, below the chin. A slight bow may be added to show respect.
- Address people by a title (such as *Mr.*, *Professor*, *Doctor*) with the last name to show respect.

Conversation

- Indians enjoy talking about their rich artistic and architectural heritage and life in other countries. Also, ask about India's thriving motion picture industry; movies are a popular Indian pastime.
- Soccer, cricket, and hockey are popular sports.

Sensitivities

- Avoid personal questions. Polite inquiries about the general state of one's family are appropriate.
- Avoid discussing India's poverty, politics, and religion. Political and religious upheaval is commonplace in India. Discussion of India-Pakistan relations is a sore subject.
- Don't dwell on the weather. Indian weather is often hot and humid.

Key Negotiating Pointers

- Deal with the highest-level person possible. Decisions are made at the top.
- Be reserved and controlled in your overall style and presentations.
- There are few routine courtesies.
- Be patient. Indian bureaucracy is extremely cumbersome. Several visits will probably be necessary to get into serious business items. Expect many meetings as you weave your way through the multilayered levels of management. You may see this as inefficient, but don't tell this to your counterpart.
- Don't expect a direct *no* if your Indian counterpart disagrees with you. An emphasis on social harmony influences the negotiating process.
- Indian managers generally have high security needs and work in very autocratic organizations. This means that middle-level managers with whom you negotiate check and recheck decisions with various layers of management.
- Contracts must be written in the local language as well as English.
- Get an Indian agent. Knowing the right families is important, and an agent can be helpful.

Day-to-Day Pointers

Business Entertainment Guidelines

- Business entertainment usually takes place in prestigious hotels; restaurants are not usually popular trade meeting places.
- Husbands should be invited to bring their wives along to social functions. The exception is Muslims, whose wives are kept from public view.
- Business can be discussed during meals, but let your host initiate the discussion.
- Business meals usually take place in the evening. The traffic and humidity limit luncheon meetings.
- The typical tip for meals is ten percent of the bill.

Table Manners and Food

- Hindus do not let anyone outside their caste or religion touch their food.
- Use the *namaste* gesture to signify that you have finished your meal.
- Vegetarian diets are common, mainly for religious reasons. Hindus, who consider cows sacred, do not eat beef (or use leather). Muslims do not eat

pork, and strict Muslims do not drink alcohol. Orthodox Sikhs do not eat beef or smoke.
- Foods vary widely in India according to culture. For example, *roti* (wheat bread) is the staple in the North, and rice is the staple in the South. Curry—eggs, fish, meat, or vegetables in a spicy sauce—is a basic food.

Gender Issues

- India is a tough place for anyone to negotiate in, but particularly women. India is a male-dominated society where women are often not involved in social functions or conversation, much less business. U.S. women may be accepted, however, if there is a perception that the woman's position and title warrant it. The use of an agent can be helpful in this regard.
- Indian women usually wear a *sari*, a long, colorful dress. Both single and married women may wear a *bindi*, or dot, on their foreheads.

Also Remember This . . .

- India has the world's second largest population (after China) and is a large potential market. India has been a democracy since 1947 despite its great cultural diversity.
- India remains primarily an agricultural nation in spite of rapid industrial growth. It has slowly moved toward a market economy since the early 1980s. There are efforts to loosen up the degree of state control, eliminating government-set limits on industrial production and permitting foreign investors to own larger shares of individual Indian companies.
- Indians are generally religious and family-oriented. Simple material comforts are emphasized. Physical and spiritual purity are highly valued, and humility and self-denial are respected.

NEW ZEALAND

Fast Facts

Population:	3.4 million
GNP:	$43.2 billion
Per Capita Income:	$12,680
Monetary Unit:	New Zealand dollar
Major Industries:	food processing, wood and paper products, textiles
Main Trading Partners:	
Exports:	EC (18%), Japan (18%), Australia (18%), U.S. (14%), China (4%)
Imports:	Australia (20%), Japan (17%), EC (17%), U.S. (15%), Taiwan (3%)
Key Exports:	wool, lamb, mutton, beef, fruits, fish
Key Imports:	petroleum, consumer goods, motor vehicles, industrial equipment
Major Cities:	Wellington (cap.) (325,200), Auckland (841,700); Christchurch (300,700)
Ethnic Groups:	European (88%), Maori (9%), Pacific Islander (3%)
Main Religions:	Christian (81%), Hindu or Confucian (1%)
Language(s):	English, Maori (used mainly for Maori ceremonies)

Reducing Communication Noise

Greetings

- Shake hands upon meeting and leaving. Men should wait for women to extend their hands first.
- First names are usually used after initial introductions.
- Typical greetings are *Good day* (pronounced gidday) or a simple *Hello*.

Conversation

- The weather is a good conversation opener in New Zealand, since it is often so pleasant. New Zealanders also appreciate sincere compliments on their gardens and homes.
- Try talking about recreational activities. New Zealanders are very sports-minded. Rugby and soccer are popular winter sports, and cricket and tennis are popular during the summer. Mountaineering, hiking (tramping), fishing, and hunting (on a restricted basis) are also popular.
- *Kiwi* is a Maori word meaning New Zealander.

Sensitivities

- Avoid discussing religion or racial issues.
- New Zealanders like discussing national and international politics. Do more listening than talking.
- Avoid comparisons with Australia. New Zealanders are proud of their autonomy.

Key Negotiating Pointers

- Make prior appointments and be punctual or early for meetings. Your counterparts will routinely be five minutes early.
- Be informal in your style, yet courteous.
- Expect negotiations to move crisply.
- Be practical in your approach; deemphasize concepts. Make presentations detailed and factual.
- Leave yourself some bargaining room, but keep the opening offer close to your "really asking" position. New Zealanders are not likely to have highly inflated initial positions.
- New Zealanders tend to make concessions in a deescalating pattern: generous at first, then tapering off.
- Expect New Zealander negotiators to remind you of the competition and to be extremely patient in getting what they want from you.
- Contracts are specific and firm.

Day-to-Day Pointers

Business Entertainment Guidelines

- It is customary that you, as the visitor, invite your counterpart to lunch at a hotel or restaurant. Otherwise, you meet in your counterpart's office.

- Dinner is the main meal of the day, usually eaten in restaurants about 7:00 P.M. to 8:00 P.M. A light supper is sometimes eaten late in the day.
- Tipping is not common and is often refused.

Table Manners and Food

- Keep you hands (but not elbows) above the table.
- Place your utensils parallel on the plate to signify that you are finished eating.
- There is a British influence in the diet, with mutton, beef, and pork the key meats. Fish is also a key part of the diet. Potatoes, vegetables, and pudding (dessert) are common.
- Coffee is often served at the end of the meal.

Gender Issues

- U.S. women can readily do business in New Zealand.

Also Remember This . . .

- New Zealand has a modern industrial economy, though agriculture is important in international trade.
- New Zealand is the world's largest exporter of wool.
- Prices and wages were deregulated in 1985.

NIGERIA

Fast Facts

Population:	117.5 million
GNP:	$31.3 billion
Per Capita Income:	$270

Monetary Unit:	naira
Major Industries:	crude oil, food processing, vehicle assembly, textiles
Main Trading Partners:	
Exports:	EC (51%), U.S. (32%)
Imports:	EC (n.a.), U.S. (n.a.)
Key Exports:	oil, cocoa, palm products, rubber
Key Imports:	consumer goods, capital equipment, chemicals, raw materials
Major Cities:	Lagos (cap.), (5.5 million), Ibadan (2.0 million), Kano (1.0 million), Enugu (500,000)
Ethnic Groups:	more than 250 tribal groups, of which 65% are the Hausa and Fulani in the North, the Yoruba in the Southwest, and the Ibo in the Southeast
Main Religions:	Muslim (50%), Christian (40%), indigenous beliefs (10%)
Language(s):	English; each ethnic group has its own language

Reducing Communication Noise

Greetings

- Shake hands lightly upon meeting and leaving. Handshakes are becoming more common in business.
- Address people by a title (such as *Mr., Mrs., Miss, Chief, Doctor,* or) with the last name. *Sir* and *Ma'am* are used if the individual's name is omitted.
- There is a wide variety of ethnic groups in Nigeria, and for that reason, English is widely spoken. Common greetings are *Hello, Good morning, Good afternoon,* and *Good evening.* Be cheerful and courteous when greeting.

Conversation

- Nigerians enjoy talking about the cultural heritage of their particular ethnic group, as well as Nigeria's industrial achievements and plans for future development.
- Nigerians may want to discuss a recent movie they've seen. Many English-speaking movies play in Nigerian theaters.

- Soccer, wrestling, polo, cricket, and swimming are popular sports.
- Though English is widely spoken, avoid the use of jargon or colloquialisms.
- Try to get comfortable with the closer physical distance in Nigeria than in the United States.

Sensitivities

- Avoid discussing religion and ethnic distinctions. There is a history of conflict among the different ethnic groups.
- Generally avoid discussing politics, though some Nigerians enjoy discussing the country's contributions to the OAU (Organization of African Unity) and ECOWAS (Economic Community of West African States).
- Avoid such words as *native, jungle,* or *witchcraft* that imply Nigeria is still a backward country with half-dressed, spear-throwing people. Refer to a home (not hut) and clothes (not costume).

Key Negotiating Pointers

- Make prior appointments, particularly with government officials. Be punctual even though you may be kept waiting. Allow plenty of time to reach your destination, since most modes of transportation are not timely.
- Start at the state government level rather than the federal government level. State officials generally want your business, are receptive, and can help you with their unique rules and regulations.
- Conduct business in person. Telephone or mail communication renders the matter trivial.
- Consider sending older individuals to do the negotiating or to be the chief spokesperson. Nigerians are very respectful of age and connect wisdom with years of experience.
- Be patient. Nigerians are casual about time, and Nigerian bureaucracy is among the most cumbersome in the world.
- Be formal and respectful. Project a refined, confident image. Expect your Nigerian counterpart to be extroverted, friendly, and talkative. Be aware, however, that Nigerians are tough negotiators. Occasional open criticism is not unusual.
- Form a solid relationship in order to get and keep business. The concept of friendship is important in business dealings.
- Make good on delivery times, specifications, and quality. Failure to do so is particularly harmful. Fulfillment of such promises helps maintain mutual trust.

- Try to drink some of the tea, coffee, or soft drink that is sure to be offered to you. Refusal may be taken as an offense.
- Be sure to seek home office legal advice regarding gifts and payments for various services. The government officially discourages "dash" (payments) that resembles bribery, such as those for obtaining visas, clearing customs, and other government responsibilities. The practice remains widespread, however, and can enter into your business relationship if you are not careful.
- Get a Nigerian partner: This is a legal requirement to do business in Nigeria. Be sure to check the person's reputation carefully. One source is the U.S. Embassy's commercial officer.

Day-to-Day Pointers

Business Entertainment Guidelines

- You may be invited to the home of your counterpart. If so, be sure to accept the invitation.
- In first-class restaurants, a service charge is normally included in the bill. Tips are given for many other services.

Table Manners and Food

- There is a large Muslim influence, so do not pass objects with your left hand.
- Nigerians usually eat hot, spicy food. Yams, cassava (a starchy root), and rice are traditional foods.
- Many Nigerians now eat continental meals as well.

Gender Issues

- U.S. women doing business in Nigeria get a hearing if not total acceptance.
- Although there is a strong Muslim influence in Nigeria, local women have relatively more freedom in both the family and the marketplace than their Muslim counterparts in many other parts of the world. Women are quite independent, running their own businesses in trading commodities within Nigeria.
- Many Nigerian businessmen are educated in the United States or have experience with Western companies, and they therefore have a heightened awareness of women's professional role in U.S. business.

Also Remember This . . .

- Nigeria's economy is one of the strongest in Africa.
- A large national debt hinders progress.
- Nigeria is a multicultural nation. Muslims predominate in the North, Christians in the South. Among tribal groups, the Hausa are practicing Muslims who are slow decision makers. The Yoruba tend to be outgoing and have an "eat, drink, and be merry" philosophy of life. The Ibo are excellent businesspeople, hardworking and conscientious, and they expect Westerners to conduct themselves similarly.

PAKISTAN

Fast Facts

Population:	113.7 million
GNP:	$42.6 billion
Per Capita Income:	$380
Monetary Unit:	rupee
Major Industries:	cotton, textiles, food processing
Main Trading Partners:	
Exports:	EC (31%), U.S. (11%), Japan (11%)
Imports:	EC (26%), Japan (15%), U.S. (11%)
Key Exports:	rice, cotton, textiles
Key Imports:	petroleum and petroleum products, machinery, transportation equipment, edible oils
Major Cities:	Islamabad (cap.) (204,400), Karachi (5.2 million), Lahore (3.0 million), Faisalabad (1.1 million)
Ethnic Groups:	Punjabi (65%), Sindhi (12%), Baluchi (9%), Pashtun (8%)
Main Religions:	Sunni Muslim (77%), Shia Muslim (20%)

Language(s):   many languages are spoken, with Urdu en-
                                couraged as the unifying language; English
                                is used by the government and educated
                                elite

Reducing Communication Noise

Greetings

- Shake hands lightly with men upon meeting and leaving. It is considered inappropriate for men to shake hands with women or touch them in public.
- Address people by a title (such as *Mr., Mrs., Miss,* or *Doctor*) with the last name.

Conversation

- Pakistanis enjoy talking about their own ethnic group and the general progress that Pakistan has made.
- Field hockey, cricket, squash, soccer, and tennis are popular sports. Pakistanis are world-class competitors in field hockey and squash.
- Ask about *ghazal,* a form of Urdu poem. It is enjoyed by all levels of Pakistani society.

Sensitivities

- Avoid discussing politics, religion, or the standard of living.
- Avoid comparisons with India. There is a history of acrimony between the two countries. The territory of Kashmir, in northern India, is under dispute between India and Pakistan.
- Don't expose the bottom of your foot or shoe to another person.
- Don't be offended if you notice that someone is staring at you. Staring is a common practice in Pakistani culture.

Key Negotiating Pointers

- Be punctual. Pakistanis are somewhat casual about time, but they are familiar with Western views about time and expect you to be on time.

- Take time to socialize and build rapport before the business content is discussed. A solid relationship is important.
- Expect to be offered several cups of tea or coffee. Try to graciously accept these offers and pace yourself.
- Don't ask direct, probing questions that could be embarrassing.
- Be patient. Pakistani bureaucracy is extremely cumbersome. Several visits will probably be necessary to get to serious business items. Expect many meetings as you weave your way through multilayered levels of government. You may see this as inefficient, but don't relate this to your Pakistani counterpart.
- Expect decisions to be checked and rechecked.
- Don't be put off if your counterpart takes an extreme position on an issue.
- Expect concessions to be made slowly.
- Contracts must be written in the local language as well as English.

Day-to-Day Pointers

Business Entertainment Guidelines

- The business meal is an important part of the overall negotiating process, where your host is expressing hospitality and getting to know you better. It is appropriate to reciprocate and invite your counterpart to lunch or dinner.
- Do not discuss business during a meal.
- Expect to socialize for a time before the meal, then to leave soon after the meal is over.
- Pakistani businessmen generally don't bring along their wives for business entertainment.
- A typical tip for a meal is ten percent of the bill.

Table Manners and Food

- Western eating utensils are used, although many of the traditional foods are eaten by hand. There is a heavy Muslim influence, so do not use your left hand to eat, point, or give or receive objects.
- Muslims do not eat pork and avoid alcohol. As a Westerner, you can buy alcohol at your hotel, but don't drink it in public.
- *Chapati* or *roti*, an unleavened bread similar to a Mexican tortilla, is the mainstay of the Pakistani diet. Pakistani food is usually hot and spicy, with curry a common spice. Lamb, beef, chicken, and fish are common in hotels and restaurants. *Kabobs*, strips or chunks of meat barbecued on a skewer, are popular.

Gender Issues

- Pakistan is one of the toughest places in the world for U.S. women to do business.
- Pakistani women have few legal rights, and only a small minority have achieved success in business. Illiteracy is particularly high among women.

Also Remember This . . .

- Parkistan is primarily an agricultural economy, though the industrial sector is growing. Natural resources, such as natural gas, are largely underdeveloped.
- Karachi, the largest city, is the primary business center.
- Pakistan is composed of many diverse ethnic groups, and politics are generally turbulent. The Muslim religion is a unifying force, and most Pakistanis are devout Muslims, believing that the will of God (Allah) is evident in all things.

References

Axtel, Roger E., ed. *Dos and Taboos Around the World*, 2nd ed. New York: Wiley, 1990.

Axtel, Roger E. *Gestures*. New York: Wiley, 1991.

Adler, Nancy J. *International Dimensions of Organizational Behavior*, 2nd ed. Boston: Kent Publishing, 1990.

Copeland, Lennie, and Lewis Griggs. *Going International*. New York: Random House, 1985.

Gudykunst, William B., and Young Yun Kim. *Communicating With Strangers: An Approach to Intercultural Communication*. New York: Random House, 1984.

Hall, Lynne. *Latecomer's Guide to the New Europe: Doing Business in Central Europe*. New York: American Management Association, 1992.

Harris, Philip R., and Robert T. Moran. *Managing Cultural Differences*, 2nd ed. Houston: Gulf Publishing, 1987.

Hendon, Donald W., and Rebecca Angeles Hendon. *World-Class Negotiating: Dealmaking in the Global Marketplace*. New York: Wiley, 1990.

Kremenyuk, Victor A., ed. *International Negotiation*. San Francisco: Jossey-Bass, 1991.

Moran, Robert T., and William G. Stripp. *Successful International Business Negotiations*. Houston: Gulf Publishing, 1991.

Rossman, Marlene L. *International Business of the 90s: A Guide to Success in the Global Market*. New York: Praeger, 1990.

Skabelund, Grant P., ed. *Culturegrams for the '90s*. Provo, Utah: David M. Kennedy Center for International Studies, Brigham Young University, 1991 ed.

Wright, John W., ed. *The Universal Almanac 1992*. Kansas City, Mo.: Andrews & McMeel, 1991.

The World Bank Atlas 1991. Washington, D.C.: World Bank, 1991.

Index

[Numbers in *italics* refer to exhibits.]

Africa, *see* Nigeria
agendas, 91
agents and local representatives, 89
American negotiators, 41–64
  foreign perceptions of, 39, 41–43
  integrity in, 55
  key traits of, 43–49
  myths cherished by ineffective, 51–53
  report card on, 53, *54*, 55
  seven sins of, 55–63
  task orientation of, 50–51
  see also problems of negotiators
Argentina, 94–95, 207–210
Asia, *see* India; Japan; Pacific Rim; Pakistan
aspirations, maintaining high, 100–104
Australia, 304–307

banking, global, 5, *8*
Belgium, 148–150
Belize, 59
body language, 74–77, 107
Brazil, 210–213
  communication patterns in, vs. U.S. and
    Japan, *76*
bribery, 127–130
bureaucracy, 90–91
business environment
  in Eastern Europe, 183–185
  in Latin America, 201
  in Middle East, 238–239
  in North America, 224–225
  in Western Europe, 143–144

Canada, 224, 227, 230–233
China, 90, *117*, 261–262, *263*, 267–271
collectivism, *see* individualism vs. collectivism

Colombia, 214–216
communication, 72–77
  directness in, 44–45, 73
  in Eastern Europe, 186–187
  in Latin America, 204–205
  in Middle East, 240–241
  noise in, 72–73
  nonverbal, 74–77, 107
  in North America, 228
  noticing barriers in, 60
  in Pacific Rim, 264
  verbal, 73–74
  in Western Europe, 146
concessions, 80–81, 114–115
  select cultures' views of, *117*
contractual and administrative factors, 88–
  91
cultural factors in negotiations, 67–91,
  139–142
  communication patterns, 72–77
  contractual and administrative factors,
    88–91
  decision making, 86–88, 91
  in Eastern Europe, 185–187
  emotional aspects, 85–86, 91
  gender and, 92–95
  individualism vs. collectivism, 69–71
  in Latin America, 201–205
  negotiation strategies, 78–84
  pace, 77–79, 91
  in Pacific Rim, 262–264
  personal relationships, 84–85, 91
  problem of ignoring, 56–58
  quick quiz on, 15–18
  role orderliness and conformity, 71
  time, 68–69
  in Western Europe, 145–146

cultural literacy
  as negotiating strategy, 116–119
  relative lack of, among Americans, 14,
    15, 47
culture shock, 121–123
Czechoslovakia, 189–191

deals, closing, 36–37
decision making, 27, 86–88, 91
  cultural differences in, *87*
directness in communications, 44–45, 73

Eastern Europe, 13–14, 183–200
  business environment in, 183–185
  countries of, 189–200
  cultural factors in, 185–187
  negotiation factors in, 188
Egypt, 79–80, 243–246
emotional aspects of negotiations, 85–86
English language
  Arabic language translations into, 241
  slang and sports analogies in, 61–63
  using simple, 104, *105*
Europe, *see* Eastern Europe; Western Europe
European Community (EC), 143–144

financial arrangements, 13
Foreign Corrupt Practices Act, 127, 129
foreign investment in United States, 8–10,
  11
foreign languages, training of American
  executives in, *15*
Four Tigers, 260–261
France, 150–154

games, negotiating, 81, *82–83*, 84
gender issues, 92–95
General Electric, 13–14
Germany, 154–158
  quiz on negotiating savvy in, 16–17
global economy, emergency of, 4–8
Great Britain, *see* United Kingdom
Greece, 158–161

handshakes, 74
home office as negotiator's problem, 124–
  125
Hong Kong, 259, 261, 271–274
Hungary, 13, 191–194

India, 90–91, 307–310
individualism vs. collectivism, 69–71
  in American negotiators, 45–46, 226–227
  in Eastern Europe, 186
  in Latin America, 202–203

  in Middle East, 239–240
  in North America, 226–227
  in Pacific Rim, 262–263
  in Western Europe, 145
Indonesia, 275–277
  quiz on negotiating savvy in, 17
information, 25–26, 90
integrity, 55, 112–114
international business arrangements, 11–
  14
international outlook, relative lack of, in
  United States, 14, *15*
investment strategies in Eastern Europe,
  183, *184*
Israel, 246–249
Italy, 161–164

Japan, 278–281
  business environment, 259
  communication patterns in, *76*
  decision making in, 88
  keiretsu in, 47, 259
  negotiating style in, 24–25, 48, 61, 70–71
  perceptions of Americans in, 42, 46
  quiz on negotiating savvy in, 15–16
joint ventures, 11, 130–133, *134–135*

keiretsu, Japanese, 47, 259

languages
  American executives' training in foreign,
    15
  Arabic to English translations of, 241
  common negotiating, 73–74
  using simple, 104, *105*
  see also English language
Latin America, 61, 68, 201–233
  business environment, 201
  countries of, 201–223
  cultural factors in, 201–205
  negotiating factors in, 206
law, different systems of, 89
legalisms in American negotiations, 48–49
licensing agreements, 12
listening skills, 60, 104–108
location of negotiations, 133–137
loyalty, 85–86

machismo, 202, 203
Malaysia, 282–285
management contracts, 12–13
Mexico, 61, 217–220
Middle East, 57, 68–69, 238–258
  business environment in, 238–239
  countries of, 243–258

cultural factors in, 239–241
negotiating factors in, 242
multinational corporations (MNCs), 4–5
ranking of nations and, 6–7

negotiating skills, 3–19
as critical to success, 14–19
emergence of global economy and need
for, 4–8
foreign investment in U.S. and need for,
8–10
increase in international business arrangements and need for, 11–14
negotiations, 20–37, 67–95
closing deals and, 36–37
cultural factors affecting, *see* cultural factors in negotiations
defining process of, 21–22
gender issues in, 92–95
planning, 29–36, 97–99
stages of, 25–28, 29–30
strategies for, *see* strategies, negotiating
subject of, 22
win-win, 22–25
negotiators, *see* American negotiators;
problems of negotiators
Netherlands, 165–168
New Zealand, 311–313
Nigeria, 313–317
North America, 224–237
business environment of, 223–225
countries of, 230–237
cultural factors in, 226–228
negotiating factors in, 229
see also United States

opening offer, 78–79
opponents in negotiations, *see* TOS (the
other side)
orientation and fact-finding, 25–26, 90

pace of negotiations, 77–78, 79, 91
Pacific Rim, 259–302
business environment of, 259–262
countries of, 167–302
cultural factors in, 262–264
negotiating factors in, 266
Pakistan, 317–320
patience as negotiating strategy, 115
payoffs, questionable, 127–130
personal relationships in negotiations, 84–
85, 91
deemphasized by Americans, 48
failure to take into account, 60–61
as negotiating strategy, 108–112
Philippines, 127–128, 285–288

physical space between people, 75
planning negotiations, 29–36
developing strategies and tactics, 30–31
establishing settlement range, 30
identifying issues, 29–30
prioritizing issues, 30
Poland, 194–197
problems of negotiators, 120–137
boss and staff at home as, 124–125
bribery as, 127–130
joint ventures as, 130–133, *134–135*
location of negotiations as, 133–137
negotiating teams as, 125–126
overcoming culture shock, 121–123
profit concept in Eastern Europe, 184, 185
punctuality, *see* time issues

questioning skills, 104–108

resistance stage of negotiations, 26–27
role orderliness and conformity, 71
in Eastern Europe, 186
in Latin America, 203–204
in Middle East, 240
in North America, 227
in Pacific Rim, 263–264
in Western Europe, 145–146
Russia, 92, 117, 197–200
quiz on negotiating savvy in, 16

Saudi Arabia, 249–253
quiz on negotiating savvy in, 17–18
settlement range, 30
preparation of, 33
reasons for movement within, 33–36
zone of "doability" within, 31–33
short-term perspective in negotiations, 46–
47
Singapore, 24–25, 261, 289–291
South Korea, 259, 260, 292–295
Spain, 168–171
strategies, negotiating, 78–84, 91, 96–119
concessions as, 80–81, 114–115
cultural literacy, as, 116–119
developing, 30–31
high aspirations as, 100–104
language usage as, 104
opening offer, 78–79
patience as, 115–116
personal integrity as, 112–114
personal relationships as, 108–112
planning as, 97–99
questioning and listening skills as, 104–
108
reformulation of, 27
win-win approach as, 99–100

subcontracts, 12
Sweden, 92–93, 172–175
Switzerland, 175–179

tactics, developing, 30–31
Taiwan, 85, 260–261, 295–299
teams, negotiating, as problem, 125–126
Thailand, 300–302
time issues, 68–69
    American negotiators' time frame, 79
    in Eastern Europe, 185
    excessive haste and impatience in nego-
        tiating, 45, 58–60
    in Latin America, 201–202
    in Middle East, 239
    in North America, 226
    pace, 77–78, 91
    in Pacific Rim nations, 262
    quick quiz on punctuality, 18
    in Western Europe, 145
TOS (the other side), 22
    information about, 98
    meeting needs of, 24, 58
    typical games of, 81, 82–83
turnkey projects, 12

United Arab Emirates, 57, 69, 254–258
United Kingdom, 73, 85, 179–182, 227
United States, 233–237
    banking in, 5
    business environment in, 224–225
    communication patterns, 76
    cultural factors affecting negotiating in,
        226–228
    foreign investment in, 8–10, 11
    in global economy, 5–7
    negotiators from, see American negotia-
        tors
    trading partners of, 5, 9, 10

Venezuela, 220–223

Western Europe, 143–182
    business environment, 143–144
    countries of, 148–182
    cultural factors in, 145–146
    negotiation factors in, 147
WIIFT (What's In It For Them), 24, 99
win-lose negotiations, 23, 56
win-win negotiations, 22–25, 99–100
women, see gender issues